A GUIDE TO COLLEGE WRITING ASSESSMENT

A GUIDE TO COLLEGE WRITING ASSESSMENT

PEGGY O'NEILL
CINDY MOORE
BRIAN HUOT

UTAH STATE UNIVERSITY PRESS
Logan, Utah
2009

Utah State University Press
Logan, Utah 84322-7800
© 2009 Utah State University Press
All rights reserved

Manufactured in the United States of America

ISBN: 978-0-87421-732-2 (paper)
ISBN: 978-0-87421-733-9 (e-book)

Cover design by Barbara Yale-Read

Library of Congress Cataloging-in-Publication Data

O'Neill, Peggy.
  A guide to college writing assessment / Peggy O'Neill, Cindy Moore, Brian Huot.
     p. cm.
  Includes bibliographical references and index.
  ISBN 978-0-87421-732-2 (pbk. : alk. paper) – ISBN 978-0-87421-733-9 (e-book)
  1. English language–Rhetoric–Study and teaching (Higher)–Evaluation. 2. English language–Composition and exercises–Study and teaching–Evaluation. 3. College prose–Evaluation. I. Moore, Cindy. II. Huot, Brian A. III. Title.
  PE1404.O43 2009
  808'.042076–dc22
                                2008054892

CONTENTS

ACKNOWLEDGMENTS

We would like to thank the folks who have supported us over the last several years, as this book went from an offhand suggestion to a textual reality. We want to begin by thanking our families, who helped provide us with the time and space to think and write, who listened to our ideas and musings, and who continue to remind us daily about what is truly important. We would also like to acknowledge the reviewers for Utah State University Press, who pushed and prodded us to do more, and participants at various conference workshops and presentations, who were the initial audiences for several parts of the manuscript, providing valuable feedback as we worked through ideas and drafts. A special thanks to the many colleagues, both near and far, who read drafts of different parts of the manuscript, provided feedback, and listened to our ramblings, especially Norbert Elliott, Linda Adler-Kassner, Michael Williamson, and Bill Smith. Finally, thanks to Michael Spooner and others at USU Press, who continued to encourage and support us through the various stages of publishing.

A GUIDE TO COLLEGE WRITING ASSESSMENT

1

INTRODUCTION
Embracing the Power of Assessment

> Can we have not simply writing-across-the-curriculum but also writing-assessment-across-the-curriculum? If the Department of Writing could model this for the rest of us, that would be great.

This question, asked in an e-mail from a dean at a liberal arts college to the composition director, illustrates just how central writing and writing assessment have become to discussions about institutional assessment goals and practices that are occurring at colleges and universities across the country (and around the globe). When considered within a historical context, the contemporary embrace of writing as a means for evaluating learning outside of the composition classroom is not surprising. Writing, after all, has been linked to large-scale assessment ever since college entrance examinations evolved from oral tests of literacy abilities to written ones (Brereton 1995; Elliot 2005; Trachsel 1992) and is still a component of entrance evaluations at most institutions of higher education. Writing frequently plays a role in campus-wide assessments of individual student achievement as well, through rising-junior exams, graduation tests, and other competency certifications (Haswell 2001a; Murphy, Carlson, and Rooney 1993).

That a composition director would be included in discussions about institutional assessment is not surprising either, given that more and more program-level administrators are being asked to provide information for campus-wide self-studies and accreditation reviews. Colleges and universities are under such pressure these days to demonstrate the quality of their programs that it is rare for any administrator to be excluded from calls for assessment data of one kind or another. This is especially true for writing program administrators, who typically participate in cross-curricular general education initiatives by way of coordinating introductory composition courses and supporting the instructors who teach them.

What is, perhaps, most compelling about the e-mail query is the implicit message, conveyed by the second sentence, about the potential role of the composition director in the broad-based assessment this dean is beginning to imagine. The dean seems not to be ordering or cajoling the writing program administrator (WPA) to fall in line with an assessment regimen that has already been envisioned (as higher-ed administrative lore might encourage us to expect) but rather inviting the WPA to take an active part in designing and facilitating what promises to become a significant campus-wide initiative.

The proposition embedded within this e-mail is an important one indeed. As research shows, writing assessments do much more than simply allow administrators to demonstrate that their institutions, departments, and programs are successful; they have the power to influence curriculum and pedagogy, to categorize teachers and writers, and, ultimately, to define "good writing" (e.g., Hillocks 2002; O'Neill, Murphy, Huot, and Williamson 2005). In fact, specific writing assessments, especially those perceived to have high stakes for students and teachers, function as what Deborah Brandt (1998) calls "literacy sponsors" because they encourage and support the development of certain types of writing and writing abilities over others. In short, a department-level administrator who embraces assessment—especially the kind of assessment that extends beyond the boundaries of her specific program—is in a position not only to help set the agenda for campus-wide assessment initiatives, but to affect, even "transform," teaching and learning across the university community (Bean, Carrithers, and Earenfight 2005).

Unfortunately, while the particular WPA in this real-life scenario understood the positive aspects of involvement and was willing to help her dean think through how a college-wide writing initiative might be used, simultaneously, to evaluate learning across campus, many writing program administrators are not inclined to assume an active role in assessment—even when department chairs or deans show confidence in their doing so. A key reason for the reluctance is that while the negative aspects of program-level assessment are well known (and well publicized through listservs, conference presentations, and articles), the positive potential remains, to a large degree, unrealized—both by individual writing specialists and by composition and rhetoric, at large.

This guide is intended to help address what we see as both a serious problem and an overlooked opportunity: just as writing program administrators (and writing faculty, in general) are being asked to assume more responsibility for large-scale assessment, many are uninspired—or unprepared—to do so. Some resist the very idea of assessment efforts that seem externally motivated and, thus, ultimately unconcerned with improving student learning. Others struggle to justify the time and effort needed for an activity that often appears extraneous to the work they were hired to do (e.g., coordinate courses, supervise instructors, teach, conduct research, advise students, and so on). Still others understand the potential importance and relevance of large-scale assessments but have trouble making them work for their programs, faculty, and students.

We seek to meet the needs of a wide range of colleagues—those who direct (or help direct) writing programs and those who teach within them, those who are resistant to assessment generally and those whose prior experience with poorly conceived or inappropriate assessments has made them suspicious or cynical, and those who want to participate in—or even lead—large-scale assessment efforts but don't possess the knowledge to do so confidently or well. Our aim is not to minimize the challenges associated with assessment (there are many) but to help readers confront and contextualize these challenges so they will feel able to design and facilitate assessments that support the educational goals of their institutions and, in the process, enhance teaching and learning within their departments and programs. Because assessment is central to teaching and learning in general (Johnston 1989; Moss 1992; Shepard 2000) and to writing in particular (Huot 2002; White 1994), and because the stakes are so high for faculty and students, WPAs and their composition and rhetoric colleagues must find ways to help promote meaningful assessments and participate in the powerful acts of analyzing and using results. This guide's key contention is that creating the conditions that support meaningful assessment hinges on appreciating not only the range of available assessment practices but understanding the history and theories informing those practices as well as the critical components of our particular teaching contexts.

CONFRONTING THE CHALLENGES

As writing program administrators and faculty understand, far too often assessment initiatives are imposed from the top-down, rather than invited or encouraged. When assessment is imposed (or perceived to be imposed), its relevance may not be apparent. This is especially the case when people outside of a program (a dean, provost, or institutional effectiveness director) dictate the parameters of the assessment (e.g., the purpose(s), guiding question(s), and methods for data collection, analysis, reporting, and eventual use). An assessment that is not framed by questions important to the program administrators and faculty gathering the data and whose results, therefore, may not seem meaningful likely will be viewed as pointless busywork, completed simply to help others fill in the blanks of reports that, if they are read at all by decision-makers, will never be acted upon. Worse yet, if the purposes, audiences, and implications of externally initiated assessments are not made clear, program administrators and faculty may assume that results will be used in undesirable ways, for example, to exclude students, monitor faculty, and control curriculum, as has too often been the case at higher-ed institutions (e.g., Greenberg 1998; Gleason 2000; Agnew and McLaughlin 2001).

Negative feelings about assessment can be further exacerbated when program administrators are unfamiliar with possibilities for approaching large-scale assessment, as well as the key concepts, documented history, and recorded beliefs associated with various approaches. This unfamiliarity is reflected in multiple ways—through urgent postings on disciplinary list-servs asking for the "best way" to assess student work for course placement or curricular review, through assessment workshops in which program directors clamor for practical advice on how to confront administrative assessment mandates, and through the now-ubiquitous short articles in the *Chronicle of Higher Education* and elsewhere about tensions between various constituencies (e.g., faculty, university administrators, legislators) over the presumed "validity" and/or "reliability" of particular assessment methods.

Unfortunately, even the most informed responses to public pleas for assistance or reassurance do not magically solve the crises because, as assessment scholars know, good assessments are those that are designed locally, for the needs of specific institutions, faculty, and students. As a result, well-intentioned pleas often lead to poor assessments, which, in a circular way, can reinforce bad feelings about assessment generally. As Ed White (1994) and others have suggested, when writing program administrators are not knowledgeable or confident enough about assessment, they become vulnerable to individuals and agencies whose beliefs, goals, and agendas may not support writing curricula, pedagogy, and faculty, and may in fact conflict with what we define as best practices. Core disciplinary activities and values can be undermined by writing assessments that are at odds with what our scholarship supports. In short, when policymakers, university administrators, and testing companies—instead of knowledgeable WPAs and faculty members—make decisions about writing assessment, we risk losing the ability to define our own field as well as make decisions about our programs and students.

Unfamiliarity with approaches to large-scale writing assessment is understandable, given that many people charged with administering writing programs and facilitating program assessments do not have degrees in composition and rhetoric. A survey of composition placement practices conducted in the early 1990s indicated that while 97 percent of writing programs are administered by full-time faculty, only 14 percent of these administrators had a degree in composition and rhetoric or were pursuing scholarship in writing assessment (Huot 1994, 57–58). Similarly, research conducted later in the decade on employment prospects for composition and rhetoric specialists, indicated that there were more jobs in the field than specialists available to fill them (Stygall 2000). Given the relative stability of composition requirements over the past ten years and the concurrent reduction of tenure-track professorial lines nationwide, it is reasonable to expect that the number of non-specialists directing writing programs has increased (and will account for a large portion of the readership for this guide).

Yet, even a degree in composition and rhetoric does not guarantee familiarity with key aspects of writing program assessment. Though many writing administrators and faculty matriculated through composition and rhetoric programs that grounded them in composition theory and pedagogy, most are not familiar with the literature on large-scale assessment, nor did they take part in this type of assessment during graduate school. Sometimes the opportunities simply do not exist for gaining expertise and experience. Graduate courses that focus on assessment are relatively rare, for instance, and while teaching assistants may take part in large-scale assessments by reading placement portfolios or submitting sample first-year composition papers to the WPA, they aren't often asked to help design such assessments. When opportunities to learn about or participate more fully in assessment *are* provided, students do not always take advantage of them; despite evidence to the contrary, students do not believe they will ever need to know more than the assessment "basics" to succeed in their future academic roles.

As most experienced composition and rhetoric professionals know, however, many (if not most) positions in the field—whether tenure-line or not—include an administrative component, either on a permanent or rotating basis. In addition to highlighting general employment trends in the field, Gail Stygall (2000) notes that 33 percent of the composition and rhetoric positions advertised in 1998 included some form of administration—nearly a 10 percent increase since 1994 (386). Our more recent analysis of job ads suggests that the current percentage of positions requiring administration is more than 50 percent. Given that writing program administration of any kind necessarily involves assessment of curricula, student achievement, and/or faculty performance, it is reasonable to assume that a majority of composition and rhetoric specialists will not only end up administering programs but assessing them, whether or not they are sufficiently prepared to do so.

Without a background in large-scale assessment, WPAs and their composition and rhetoric colleagues may find concepts typically associated with such assessment strange and intimidating. Having developed their professional identities within the humanities, for the most part, they may cringe at references to "measuring" or "validating," which reflect a traditional social-science perspective. Though scholarship on writing assessment offers ways of negotiating liberal-arts values with those from the sciences, and though publication of such scholarship has increased significantly over recent years, it often goes unread. Until recently, much of the most useful literature was difficult to find, appearing in a seemingly scattered way in essay collections and journals focused on topics other than large-scale assessment. The more accessible literature, though not irrelevant, has often been of the "tool-box" type, focusing on methods used by a particular department or program with scant discussion of supporting research and theory. As a result, many writing specialists are confronted with terms, definitions, and interpretations imported from other disciplines with little knowledge about how they should be applied to situations that require evaluation of writing abilities, development, and instruction. Thus, many are left feeling unprepared to argue for the kinds of assessments that make sense on an intuitive level or, more likely, argue against those that appear inappropriate.

AN ILLUSTRATION

Cindy's early-career narrative provides a good illustration of how frustrating it can be to possess a basic understanding of current writing assessment practice, without having a real familiarity with assessment history and theory. Like many composition and rhetoric specialists, Cindy was hired right out of graduate school to direct a substantial writing program at a mid-sized university. The three years of practical administrative experience she obtained as a PhD student, along with the courses she took in composition theory and pedagogy, prepared her well to take on many of the challenges of her first position, including hiring, course scheduling, and faculty development. Unfortunately—and largely due to her own decisions (e.g., electing not to take her program's course in assessment)—her graduate-school apprenticeship did not fully equip her for what became one of the most important aspects of her position: designing, arguing for, and facilitating meaningful large-scale assessments.

During her first semester (fall 1998), Cindy was confronted with several assessment issues that needed to be addressed. Among these was a writing-course placement process that relied on a computerized multiple-choice exam taken by students during summer orientation. Many faculty and students complained about the exam, which seemed inappropriate in many ways. Among other problems, the exam rested on the assumption that students' ability to write well in college courses correlated with their ability to correctly answer questions about grammar and usage. However, because student placement was a university issue, affecting faculty, staff, and administrators outside of the English Department, Cindy and her colleagues could not just make changes unilaterally. In addition to speaking to other faculty within their department, they would need to consult staff in the testing office, the VP of student affairs, and other departments, such as mathematics, that relied on a similar placement test. They would need to convince others that the test was problematic and that there were viable alternatives.

Having participated in a program assessment as a graduate student and taken pedagogy courses that addressed classroom assessment practices, Cindy understood that direct methods for assessing student writing (i.e., methods that require students to actually write) are preferred in the composition and rhetoric community to indirect methods like multiple-choice exams. This preference seemed consistent with classroom assessment methods promoted by prominent scholars at the time—methods such as portfolio evaluation and holistic scoring. The problem was that others outside her department—those who were familiar with standardized testing but not with writing assessment—pointed to validity and reliability data offered by the exam manufacturers as reason enough to keep the test as it was.

Though she was suspicious of data provided by the very agency that profited from her school's use of the exam and uncomfortable with the company's context-deficient definitions of *validity* and *reliability*, Cindy could not, with any confidence, argue against the data. Because she was unfamiliar with the history of writing assessment, she did not know that tests are most often chosen not for their "ability to describe the promise and limitations of a writer working within a particular rhetorical and linguistic context" (Huot 2002, 107), but because they are a cheap, efficient means of sorting people into convenient categories. Further, because she did not know that there were alternative, context-oriented definitions of *validity* and that reliability statistics alone say nothing about a test's appropriateness, she could not confidently question the test manufacturer's use of these terms or her university's belief in their persuasive power. Though she was, in the end, able to convince the testing office to add some background questions to the test—questions aimed at gathering information about students' actual writing experience—the test itself remained (and ten years later still remains) essentially unchanged.

Fortunately, as Cindy was struggling with these issues, Brian and Peggy were working steadily to help administrators like her become more aware of the options available for assessment as well as the historical and theoretical assumptions informing them. Through Conference on College Composition and Communication workshops, edited collections, and articles, they and other scholars were developing a disciplinary literature that would allow administrators to both make informed assessment decisions and discuss their merits and drawbacks with others. The fact that Cindy was able to achieve some success with the placement process and to facilitate other important assessment initiatives during her first years as a WPA, was due to her willingness to read some of the more accessible assessment scholarship being published (such as Brian's 1996 *CCC* article "Toward a New Theory of Writing Assessment") and ask Peggy for details about the many panels and workshops that she and Brian were organizing to help

WPAs understand connections among assessment practice, research, and theory. Still, it was not until very recently (during the summer of 2006) that Cindy took the time to sit down and read the assessment literature, both within composition and rhetoric and in other, ancillary, fields and begin to fully appreciate how much better her assessment practice could have been over the years if she had truly understood the assumptions informing it.

What has bewildered all of us—and inspired this current volume—is that Cindy's experience is both all-too-typical and, in terms of her efforts to educate herself about history and theory, problematically atypical. We have discovered that even those faculty and administrators who *do* recognize the importance of assessment, are willing to do it, and know the basics of large-scale assessment often have trouble translating their understanding and knowledge into assessments that work. As is true with classroom teaching, it is one thing to possess a general sense of the assumptions supporting particular methods; it is another thing to be able to enact beliefs and values in consistently productive ways and convince others of their success (or the potential for it).

CONTEXTUALIZING THE CHALLENGES

As we've thought over the last few years about what kind of resource would be most useful to writing administrators and faculty who are poised to design and conduct large-scale assessments, we have often returned to our own experiences and to the assessment stories that appear throughout the composition and rhetoric literature (many of which inform later chapters). What we've determined is that while assessment is never simple, it can be quite meaningful and very gratifying—if the faculty designing and conducting the assessment are able to contextualize it in a variety of ways. Those who are successful with assessment are able to perceive it as integral to their work as teachers and scholars (and to help others see it this way), understand it within a larger historical and theoretical framework, and negotiate various aspects of the local institutional, departmental, or programmatic situation.

The Professional Context

Writing administrators and faculty who experience success with large-scale assessment are not only able to see the relevance of the assessment to their department or program but to their own professional lives. One way to achieve this feeling of connectedness is to resist the temptation to perceive assessment as something separate from teaching, research, and/or writing and view it as an important vehicle for purposeful, sustained inquiry that will help reveal the value and impact of more traditional academic work. Scholars like Duane Roen, who highlight the links between administration, in general, and other professional activities, have helped lay the foundation for such a view. As Roen (1997) argues, writing program administration almost always requires teaching, or the ongoing support of teaching, through various TA- and faculty-development initiatives. Further, in order to succeed at "the teaching of other teachers," WPAs must keep up with the scholarship in their own field as well as the fields of colleagues outside of writing or English who are participating in cross-disciplinary writing initiatives (44).

Drawing upon Ernest Boyer's "reconsideration" of the traditional distinctions between teaching, scholarship, and service, Roen goes on to explain that while administrative activities may not result in refereed publications, they often require just as much, or even more, original research and writing (in the form of "hundreds of reports, memos, and letters" written each year), synthesis of others' published ideas, and applicability to the "'consequential problems'" of teaching and learning (44, 52–53). Our contention, in this guide and elsewhere (see, for example, Huot and Schendel 2002), is that within the general framework of administration, large-scale assessment presents one of the best arguments for appreciating the intersections among various professional activities in the ways that Roen, Boyer, and many others suggest. Because in order to be valid, assessments must generate data that are ultimately used to improve learning, they necessarily inform teaching. Additionally, because sound assessment practice involves articulating hypotheses or guiding questions, choosing methods appropriate for answering the questions, systematically analyzing results, and sharing findings in a manner that will allow others to use them, it is similar to any other scholarly endeavor. In fact, while administration, on the whole, may seem to fit best within Boyer's "scholarship of application" (Roen 1997, 53), we hope to show in subsequent chapters that the most meaningful—and far-reaching—assessment efforts can be considered within any of his scholarly categories, whether they highlight original "discovery," "integration" of published research and theory, "application" to community problems, or classroom teaching.

The Disciplinary Context

While writing specialists take for granted the importance of understanding the values and beliefs that inform classroom instruction, many neglect to consider theory-practice connections when designing or overseeing large-scale assessments. In fact, if professional listservs like WPA-L are any indication, many writing program administrators and faculty are unaware that, as with teaching, every approach, every methodological choice, is necessarily imbued with decades of discussions about adequacy, appropriateness, and implications—the conversations that comprise the history and theory not only of educational assessment but of our discipline and other, related disciplines. As suggested earlier in this chapter, it is not uncommon to see posts to professional listservs that ask for the "best way" to place first-year students or evaluate programs without any recognition that what is "best" depends not only on the particular purpose of the assessment but on the specific context (e.g., institutional mission, students, faculty) and the potential impact on teaching and learning. In fact, these general tenants form the basis of current writing assessment theory. Beyond being "accessible," or transparent to everyone involved, meaningful assessment design requires that the assessment be site-based, locally controlled, context-sensitive, and rhetorically based (Huot 2002, 105). It also should be consistent with current research and theories on language learning and literacy.

Though sometimes difficult to translate into effective assessment practice, knowledge of theory (and the history behind it) is essential for success. As with teaching, theory is what allows us to make informed choices, to adapt methods to different situations and to convince others, such as faculty peers, upper-level administrators, and students, of the appropriateness of our decisions. History helps us appreciate why, at a given time or place, some strategies are preferred or promoted over others. As chapter 2 suggests, for example, it can be very useful to understand, and be able to explain, that writing and large-scale assessment of learning have been linked since 1874, when Harvard instituted the first written English composition entrance exams and, as a result of these exams, the first required composition courses. In fact, as a field, composition studies was, in essence, created in response to large-scale assessment (O'Neill 1998). Further, it is helpful to know that contemporary approaches to assessment have not evolved in a neat, linear way since the late 1800s, from those that were inappropriate to those that are more meaningful. On the contrary, far from being a series of "waves" with different focuses or emphases that can be discretely identified, the history of writing assessment is much more web-like, with trends cycling in and back as a result of ongoing negotiations among various groups including educators, researchers, test designers, and legislators whose views reflect, to a large degree, broader social and political pressures.

In addition to understanding history well enough to contextualize current methods, WPAs benefit greatly from understanding the theoretical trends that reflect that history. Cindy's story offers compelling examples of how the quality of an assessment can be compromised when underlying assumptions are not clear or conflict with what we know about literacy and learning. If she had understood the points made in chapter 3 about the complexity of validity, for example, or the insufficiency of reliability, she would have been able to more confidently argue against the data provided by the computerized placement test manufacturers. At the very least, she may have been able to convince upper-level administrators to consider the data within context—as a partial representation of a particular student's abilities to perform isolated tasks that bear little resemblance to the content of any course the school was offering.

The Rhetorical Context

While assessment-related texts, such as prompts, criteria, and responses, are subject to rhetorical analysis, the assessment itself also needs to be considered within a rhetorical framework (Huot 2002). Those who experience success with assessment understand it as a rhetorical act, involving consideration of exigency, purpose, and audience. From a rhetorical standpoint, it becomes important to ask questions such as "What is motivating assessment at a particular moment?" and "What is the ultimate purpose or purposes in terms of teaching and learning?" For example, there may be a pressing assessment need, such as accreditation review. Or there may be less formal reasons for assessment, such as curiosity on the department's part to discover the effect of first-year composition on students' attitudes toward writing or a practical desire to determine if the extra resources devoted to the basic writing courses are a worthwhile use of the department's limited resources. In these situations, the ultimate goal is to improve teaching and learning, but the specifics of each require different ways of defining what improved learning means, which requires attention to the local culture—the values, beliefs, and perceptions that characterize a particular institution, department, or program.

To understand the local culture, those charged with conducting assessment need to gather demographic as well as attitudinal information. As chapter 4 demonstrates, the best assessments are not only informed by history and theory but designed with particular programs, courses, faculty, and students in mind. It is quite common for WPAs and faculty charged with large-scale assessment to look toward other schools and programs for model approaches and methods. While considering what others have done can be a good starting place, models must be carefully adapted for the local context. An exit exam used successfully at a small liberal arts college may not generate any useful information about students at a large comprehensive university if it is simply transplanted without thoughtful modification. First, the curricula and instruction supporting, or leading up to, the exam would likely differ between the two schools. Further, the backgrounds and attitudes (e.g., toward school and testing) of students might differ considerably, which would not only influence the results themselves but the meaning of those results.

When designing an assessment, then, it is necessary to ask questions about the general purpose of the assessment but also about curriculum—and its relationship to the assessment (e.g., "How will our data inform our courses?"), about faculty (e.g., "How will instructors participate in assessment and make use of assessment results?"), and about students (e.g., "Who are our students?" "What writing experiences and abilities do they have, and how do we know?"). Also, because upper-level administrators may need to be convinced of the value of a particular assessment and/or the relevance of the data, WPAs and faculty benefit from asking questions about this particular audience—questions about their disciplinary backgrounds, for example, their beliefs about teaching and learning, and their perceptions of assessment. Even understanding administrative preferences for how data should be analyzed and reported can be essential in ensuring the ultimate success of an assessment.

In these ways, the work conducted to design a meaningful, theory-grounded assessment is much like ethnographic research pursued to understand writers, writing, and writing cultures. Though such inquiry need not be as labor-intensive as a formalized research study, it should be systematic and thorough enough to generate useful results.

Practice in Context

Many readers have probably noticed by now that, unlike other books on teaching, research, administration, and, especially, assessment, this guide provides information about the ever-evolving assumptions informing good practice *before* it discusses specific approaches and methods. As should be clear by now, our organizational scheme reflects our concern that while those charged with assessment may know—or have easy access to—the range of available practices, they are not typically familiar with the assumptions that inform these practices and, as a result, are often unable to apply them in meaningful, useful ways. Also, though we have devoted half of this guide to various assessment practices, we are careful in our more practical chapters to regularly connect back to the history, theory, and contextual factors described in the first part. We hope that this strategy reinforces our belief that, in order to work well, practices should not—cannot—be considered outside historical, theoretical, and situational scenes.

While readers will see that we do favor some assessment methods over others—because of our understanding of history and theory—we also recognize that the most theoretically informed practices do not always work and that sometimes "the ideal" must be compromised in order to get anything done at all. In terms of placement and exit assessments, for example, institutional constraints may affect the kind of approach that can be used. Though it might be ideal to place students into first-year composition courses based on multiple samples of writing (as is the case with portfolio-based placement), it may not be realistic for programs situated at very large universities, where first-year classes comprise several thousands of students, or at any institution that is unwilling to support such an assessment by, for example, paying faculty readers or requiring portfolio-submission fees. Readers will see that, throughout the guide, we demonstrate an awareness of what individual WPAs and faculty members can reasonably be expected to do and what particular contexts can support or "tolerate." That said, the guide also shows, through both examples and analysis, that there is often more room for negotiating toward ideal assessments than a WPA may initially assume.

Because there are numerous resources available to assist faculty in assessing the writing of individual students in particular classrooms, we have chosen to focus on approaches to the kinds of assessment that typically happen outside of individual classrooms: placement evaluation, exit examination, programmatic assessment, and faculty evaluation. Our means for categorizing the content of the second part of the guide should not imply that the assessment approaches we discuss are separate from classroom assessment (in fact, for assessment to work at all it should be able to inform the teaching and learning that goes on in specific classrooms); and certainly these approaches are not separate from one another. Obviously, information gathered through placement assessments should inform curricula and faculty development, just as observations about instruction should inform analyses of exit-testing results. Still, each type of assessment will be guided by an overriding purpose, with methods chosen and results used primarily in accordance with that purpose.

To supplement practice-oriented chapters, we also provide appendices, which include sample materials that can be modified for particular assessments, short readings that can inform assessment design and help support arguments for meaningful assessments, an annotated bibliography for further study, and a glossary of assessment terms. Taken as a whole, we hope that readers will see this book as both practical and theoretical, as a source to help you address a particular writing assessment need as well as a guide to help you continue to learn about writing assessment as a field of study. After all, writing assessment—as with educational assessment in general— has become an increasingly significant activity in higher education, and writing faculty and administrators need to be informed assessment practitioners to maintain and develop effective writing programs.

2
HISTORICIZING WRITING ASSESSMENT

Although many writing administrators and teachers are resistant to it, assessment is a powerful force—whether positive or negative—in the classroom and beyond it. Because assessment can have deleterious effects on curriculum, teacher agency, and student learning, it is important for writing teachers and WPAs not only to be well informed about the nuts and bolts of writing assessment practices but also to understand the social, technical, and historical forces that shape current writing assessment theory and practice.

Understanding writing assessment and harnessing its power to improve teaching and learning requires understanding its history. The notion of writing assessment history that we present here is both complicated and generative, and it is necessarily partial. Although one might argue that all histories are partial and situated, these facts are not always acknowledged. Our reasons, however, for choosing specific incidents, historical figures, and topics are rhetorical and political in that their selection helps us tell a specific history of writing assessment, one that will be useful for writing teachers and program administrators. The events we choose to cover and the accounts we select to tell of this history favor certain theories of and positions about assessment. Our theoretical trajectories privilege the ways language and literacy function and the ways they are learned as well as their connections to the educational measurement community at large. For us, writing assessment should always be about improving writing instruction— a strongly supported tenant of current validity theory. Although much of our account focuses on measurement history, we are mindful of the perspective of writing faculty and administrators, not only because they are our audience but also because we are, after all, WPAs and writing teachers ourselves. The more we learn about writing assessment, the more we realize that those closest to the teaching of writing are able to make the most valuable assessment decisions (Broad 2003; Huot 2002; O'Neill 2003; Pula and Huot 1993; Smith 1993). However, this local and disciplinary expertise cannot exist in a vacuum. Understanding the historical contexts for the development of writing assessment as a field and the roles of technical assessment concepts such as reliability and validity are crucial because assessment now, as well as in the past, is involved with assigning value and making decisions about access, opportunity, and resources.

FROM THE BEGINNING

What is the beginning of writing assessment? The Chinese administered written examinations hundreds of years ago. In 1840, Horace Mann called for written tests to replace oral examinations in the Boston schools. We could argue, though, that these were written exams but not really tests of writing per se. For that, we probably need to go to Harvard's instantiation of written exams in English composition for admissions in 1874. After these exams, Harvard's English A (an early form of first-year composition) was established, and Wendell Barrett and his colleagues became some of the first compositionists. This relationship between writing assessment and required writing courses supports Peggy O'Neill's (1998) contention that writing assessment exerted a strong influence on the creation and development of composition as a field of work and study.[1] Harvard's practice was soon taken up by the majority of colleges in the northeast and by the turn of the twentieth century, the College Entrance Examination Board (CEEB) was established, and writing assessment as a funded, researched, and professional field and industry was born.[2] No longer were colleges creating their own exams. Writing assessment had been outsourced, and the CEEB's long association with writing assessment began; it continues with the recent SAT that includes a scored writing sample being marketed for placement.

The development of CEEB, then, is part of the history of writing assessment. However, accounts on how it developed vary, illustrating themes in assessment that still play out today. An early account of the establishment of the College Board (formerly the CEEB) written a decade or so ago by Paul Diederich (1996), an important historical figure in the development of writing assessment at the Educational Testing Service (ETS) for nearly four decades, focuses on the practical problem of individual, competing exams' given independently by a range of colleges: "At that time each college set its own requirements and entrance examinations so that a student who wanted to go to Harvard had to go to Cambridge to take its examination, while one who wanted to enter Yale had to go to New Haven" (352). Diederich recalls the many problems with such a system, including complaints from parents who were told that a specific high school could only prepare students for a specific college's entrance exam. According to Diederich, then, these complaints and problems led the presidents of Harvard and Columbia to propose the establishment of what eventually became the CEEB.

---

1.   Along with Peggy O'Neill's dissertation, we also recommend Mary Trachsel's book *Institutionalizing Literacy* for readers wanting to know more about writing assessments and their influence at postsecondary schools during the first part of the twentieth century.

2.   While the CEEB, like ETS, is a nonprofit corporation, it is nonetheless a corporation employing extensive marketing and management strategies to generate revenue.

Norbert Elliot (2005) tells quite a different story about the establishment of the CEEB. The impetus for the CEEB, according to Elliot, came not from the colleges themselves but from the secondary schools that were preparing students to pass the individual exams to enter college. In fact, a high school English teacher was one of the primary authors and supporters of the plan to create an organization that would centralize, supervise, and implement college admissions testing. As Elliot explains, in 1895, Wilson Farrand, headmaster of Newark Academy, was elected president of the Schoolmasters' Association of New York and Vicinity. In his inaugural address, Farrand outlined the rationale and structure of an organization based upon five guidelines that would eventually become the CEEB. The first of Farrand's guidelines included a certificate from the secondary institution documenting a student's progress and achievements, which would guide the content and extent of the examination necessary for each student; the other four guidelines focused on the examination itself. In 1899, under the direction of Nicholas Murray Butler, a dean from Columbia, the Association of Colleges and Preparatory Schools of the Middle States and Maryland proposed the establishment of the CEEB, and Farrand was named the first secretary. All but one of Farrand's guidelines were incorporated in the structure of the CEEB. The missing guideline was the certificate from the secondary school that provided contextual information about the academic achievement of each student.

These competing accounts of the establishment of the CEEB are interesting for several reasons. For Diederich (1996), the establishment of the CEEB was about solving the problem of how to examine incoming college students and make admissions decisions. Naturally, the problem would be solved by the colleges' upper administrators, which diminished the role of teachers. Diederich's account also emphasizes a need for the practical and efficient examination of students, since the impetus for the exam is the ability to have one examination given in many localities for a variety of colleges to make admissions decisions. In this first version of how the CEEB came to be, teachers share no role, nor is teaching really an issue except in terms of preparing students to take specific exams, a problem the CEEB solved. In this respect, Diederich celebrates the creation of a separate organization for testing.

In addition to attributing the founding of the CEEB to Farrand, Elliot's version is important for another reason: it includes what was omitted from Ferrand's original proposal by the college-level participants. In his proposed plan, a student's high school would participate in the process of her college admission by certifying what she had learned in order to document academic achievement and direct the kinds of admissions testing necessary. This was the only part of his proposal not adopted. This kind of omission seems fairly important to our purpose in this history because it signals that over one hundred years ago, teacher judgments about student preparation were found suspect. A test was assumed to be better at helping university admissions personnel make important, consequential decisions about students than judgments of secondary teachers. From the beginning (if the establishment of the CEEB can be called the beginning of writing assessment), teachers would have to struggle to be a part of important decisions made on the basis of the assessment of student writing. In addition to the unequal power relationships and the unfounded faith in examinations, this omission of a student's performance in high school is bad practice at the very least, since high school performance has, over the years, remained the best single predictor of success in college. In summarizing the research on the ability of SAT scores and grades to predict college success, Peter Sacks notes, "Indeed, it is almost always the case in studies of the SAT effectiveness that high school grades are more powerful than any test score" (1999, 271). Nonetheless, faith in so-called objective measures of writing assessment persists. For at least one hundred years, then, reliable and valid writing assessment outside of a school context has been envisioned as a better source of evaluative information about students than teachers. Throughout the history of writing assessment, its integrity and value for educational reform and efficacy is usually examined in terms of its ability to be reliable and valid in a technical sense. Educational measurement in general has defined itself and its history in terms of reliability and validity, as indicated in the Standards for Educational and Psychological Testing. The rest of our history is organized around reliability and validity and their influences on writing assessment, writing teachers, WPAs, and the teaching and learning of writing.

RELIABILITY

The two most important terms in educational measurement in general and writing assessment in particular have remained *reliability* and *validity*. Educational measurement as a field is about as old as writing assessment itself. As writing assessment began in the late nineteenth century and culminated with the establishment of the CEEB at the turn of the century, educational measurement began in the late nineteenth century with studies on human physical and mental properties exemplified by Wundt's perceptual laboratory in Leipzig which produced physical data related to human behavior, such as how long it took a person to react to physical stimuli or how the eye moved when reading. At the turn of the century, laws were passed that mandated that all children attend school for a period of time. One of the results of these laws for mandatory universal education was a flurry of activity in mental testing supported by the, then, recent laws requiring all children to attend some type of school for a minimum period of time. Existing schools were stretched with a population of students they did not know how to teach:

> One consequence of the new laws in the United States was to bring into the schools for the first time large numbers of children whose parents did not have an education or were not native English speakers. . . . The new waves of pupils were exposed to curricula and academic standards that had been developed for a more select group of students, so the rate of failure rose dramatically, sometimes reaching 50 percent. (Thorndike 1997, 4)

In addition to mandatory universal education, the entry of the United States into World War I less than two decades later created a need to sort the millions of men necessary to fight the war, and standardized testing was used to meet this need. The combination of the interest of a great many researchers in the, then, fledgling field of psychology and the need for an effective form of classification in the schools and military created a great deal of energy and activity that resulted in the creation of the field of intelligence testing and the test development industry. As we all understand in the year 2009, the standardized test has become the tool not only for intelligence testing but for a wide range of achievement and aptitude assessments used to make high-stakes decisions about students and others. At times, testing seems like some grand illusion in the face of evidence that scores on writing tests can be predicted by how much students write (Perlman). We believe testing has never been able to muster enough evidence to warrant its use in making important decisions about students, programs, and institutions.

From the beginnings of both educational and psychological measurement in general and writing assessment in particular, reliability—or consistency—has been seen as a key issue. In the late 1890s, Charles Spearman devised the mathematical formula for correlations. This formula was important because it allowed test developers to draft various forms of the same test and to make sure the results were mathematically similar. As well, the statistical formula for correlations helped researchers and test developers know what measures produced similar results. In writing assessment, this formula was important because it helped to document in early studies, such as that reported by Daniel Starch and Edward Elliot (1912), that teachers could not agree on grades for the same papers.

Because of the need for independent judges to read and judge writing, reliability has remained one of the most crucial aspects for writing assessment: "*Reliability* refers to how consistently a test measures whatever it measures" (Cherry and Meyer 1993, 110). This definition assumes a difference between instrument reliability—the consistency of the overall scores, usually measured by what scores the same test-takers received in multiple uses of the same test—from interrater reliability, which is the consistency of independent scorers who read and score student writing or other performances. Although reliability is regularly expressed in numerical coefficients, this was not always the case. It was not until after World War I that reliability appeared in statistical and mathematical expressions and formulas. During World War I, Carl Brigham, Robert Yerkes, Louis Terman, and others worked on testing and classifying millions of soldiers for the US Armed Forces (Elliot 2005). The development of the Army Alpha test, along with its database of millions of test scores, spawned the publication of thirteen other examinations in the 1920s and '30s, including the SAT (Wasserman and Tulsky 2005). Testers became more adept at understanding and applying the technologies that test the greatest numbers in the shortest time for as little expense as possible (Madaus 1994).

In a very real sense, writing assessment history can be seen as a reliability-driven march to more consistent (reliable) scoring—this is the way early reviews, like the one in Gottschalk, Swineford, and Coffman (1966, 1–5) from the middle 1960s, described writing assessment. In other words, the problem for writing assessment (Huot and Neal 2006, 1) was *"framed"* (Schön 1982, 40) as what could be done to make independent readers agree on the same scores for the same papers. This is not an easy or inconsequential task. Without consistency in scoring, students' scores on their writing would depend upon who read the papers rather than who wrote them. Without consistency in scoring, it would be impossible to argue for the validity of decisions based upon such scores. As Cherry and Meyer reiterate, *"Reliability is a necessary but not a sufficient condition for validity"* (emphasis in original, 1993, 110). To this day, scoring reliability and instrument reliability are important aspects of validity inquiry into the decisions made on behalf of writing assessments.

While scoring reliability in writing assessment is undeniably important, it has been equally difficult to deliver. Up until the early 1930s, the CEEB consisted of essay exams in specific areas. In 1937, the CEEB began to experiment with administering in April the Scholastic Aptitude[3] Test (SAT) for students who were applying for scholarships, since their admission information was needed more quickly than that of the regular population of students who sat for CEEB exams for an entire week in June and whose results were not available until late July. In 1939, the SAT option was made available to all students. By the beginning of the 1940s, the CEEB was con-

3.   In the 1930s, the test was called Scholastic Aptitude, but this was revised to read Scholastic Achievement in the 1970s after it became apparent that coaching would help students produce higher scores, since presumably aptitude could not be altered by test preparation.

vinced that the SAT exam provided useful information (better statistical correlations) for admissions with much less labor and expense and without the problems associated with consistency in scoring. When Pearl Harbor was attacked on December 7, 1941, the CEEB determined that this was the right opportunity to terminate the use of essay exams and implement the SAT for all students (Fuess 1967). Because of the current crisis and war, the CEEB argued that the new exams would provide a quicker turnaround for students who were being required to enter the military (Fuess 1967; Palmer 1960). By the end of December 1941, the CEEB announced that all CEEB examinations for the coming year would take place in April with the administration of the SAT. Because of outside pressure from writing teachers unhappy with the termination of all essay exams for college admission, the CEEB agreed to offer the English Comprehensive Examination (ECT) in June to over two hundred institutions who requested it. The one-hour English test elicited a 500-word essay with:

> No literary interpretation. No question involving reading background. No choice of topics. Only a theme. . . (Since the schools not only had to administer the test but read it, some of the English teachers may have lived to regret their vociferous outcries). (Palmer 1960, 12)

The official response to English teachers' resistance to dismantling the essay exams of the CEEB comes from John Stalnaker, who was the board's associate secretary in 1943 when he penned these words:

> The type of test so highly valued by teachers of English, which requires the candidate to write a theme or essay, is not a worthwhile testing device. Whether or not the writing of essays as a means of teaching writing deserves the place it has in the secondary school curriculum may be equally questioned. Eventually, it is hoped, sufficient evidence may be accumulated to outlaw forever the "write-a-theme-on" . . . type of examination. (Fuess 1967, 158)

The sarcasm and rancor, not to mention the apparent support for a curriculum without writing, is a bit startling to read. It's also probably important to note that Stalnaker's call for a greater influence of multiple-choice testing in English classes seems prophetic given Arthur Applebee's findings in the late 1970s that writing had all but disappeared from the secondary curriculum (1981). Of course, we will not argue that Stalnaker or the SAT was the cause for the diminishing role of writing in high school English classes, but the status of writing assessment and the teaching of writing in the 1940s is probably a little different from what we are used to seeing in more current contexts, considering that the SAT, ACT, GRE, LSAT, and even the MCAT for medical school admission now all include a writing portion. It might also be argued that the implementation of state-mandated writing tests and No Child Left Behind (NCLB) have influenced high schools to spend more time teaching writing and preparing students to take writing tests. In addition to the acrimonious tone toward those who would insist upon looking at student writing for college admission, it's important to note that the movement from essay testing to multiple choice was predicated upon the crisis brought on by the Unites States' entry into World War II. As with the universal requirement for education at the turn of the century or the need to classify recruits for the world wars or subsequent crises in literate behavior, the answer seems to be more and better assessment. In this way, the use of tests to solve real or perceived crises in writing and writing instruction limits the role of teachers or characterizes them as conservative, recalcitrant obstructers of progress:

> Not even the *obiter dicta* of professional researchers could suppress the widespread conviction that the writing of an essay offered valuable evidence as to a pupil's ability to use and understand his own language. The defenders of this belief virtually forced the Board to add in 1943 a one-hour test in English composition to the group of achievement tests. (Fuess 1967, 159)

In 1947, the Educational Testing Service was founded, and the search for reliable ways to score student writing, especially for the English Composition Test (ECT), intensified:

> A sincere attempt was made to give these teachers and critics the type of evaluation instrument they wished . . . in 1951, 1952, and 1953, and . . . in 1954, 1955 and 1956. Unfortunately, and perhaps inevitably, this ambitious attempt at a reliable essay foundered and sank on the reef of low reader reliability. (Palmer 1960, 14)

Palmer's obituary for reliable (and therefore valid[4]) writing assessment comes in 1960 after several years during the 1950s when CEEB and ETS researchers struggled in vain to produce reliable writing assessment (see Elliot 2005, 136–52). At this point, ETS and CEEB were no longer administering writing tests that had students actually writing. Multiple-choice tests of grammar usage and mechanics that correlated well enough with essay scores were used instead. These tests were euphemistically called indirect measures of writing.

This "demise" of writing assessment, however, was short lived. Two blockbuster studies from ETS changed the face of writing assessment permanently. In 1961, Paul Diederich, John French, and Sydell Carlton had fifty-three judges, representing six professional fields (English, social science, natural science, law, writing and editing, and business), score 300 papers

---

4.   More in the next section on validity about how reliability was often used interchangeably for validity.

on a 9-point scale. At first glance, this study would seem to be an odd choice to cite as a saving grace for writing assessment, since 94 percent of the papers received at least seven different scores, and no paper received less than five scores. The interrater reliability was .31, which is considered unacceptably low (a score of 1 would indicate perfect agreement and 0 would indicate no agreement at all). In addition to the scores, however, the researchers collected and analyzed 11,018 comments made by the judges. Using factor analysis, a complicated statistical procedure, the researchers were able to isolate five main types of responses from the readers: ideas, form, flavor (style), mechanics, wording. These five categories were used by Diederich to develop a generic scoring rubric that became the basis of analytic scoring, one of the three main kinds of writing assessment along with holistic and primary trait scoring that became available in the 1970s. The Diederich, French, and Carlton study reaffirmed what was considered a "fact" by many—that is, readers cannot agree on the same scores for the same papers. (Of course this hardly seems surprising to us today, because the readers represented very different disciplines and received no preparation or contextual information from which to score the writing.) However, this study signaled the beginning of looking beyond reader disagreement and asking questions about what criteria readers used to make decisions about writing. As we will discuss in the next section on validity, this move from looking only at interrater reliability to considering other aspects of writing assessment, rater scores, and reader judgment would be the beginning of a new research base for writing assessment, one that would eventually spawn an entirely new set of writing assessment practices.

If the Diederich, French, and Carlton study heralded a new research path for writing assessment, the study published by Godshalk, Swineford, and Coffman (1966) established the possibility that readers could achieve acceptable rates of scoring reliability by following a specific protocol that involved training readers to agree on a scoring guideline and then monitoring their progress throughout the scoring session. Although the study did suggest that the best writing scores for students should include performance on multiple-choice tests, it opened up the floodgates for direct writing assessment. By the end of the 1970s, holistic scoring was being used on a widespread basis for a range of assessment purposes (Cooper 1977; Elliot 2005; White 1994; Yancey 1999). During the 1990s, as holistic scoring became more and more a part of the assessment landscape, work on automated scoring, started in the 1960s by Ellis Page (1966), began to produce even more reliable scores than could human judges. Programs like Accuplacer and E-Rater, available from testing companies, could boast higher rates of agreement with local judges on student writing than could conventional holistic scoring. With the current availability of automated scoring, the search for reliable essay scoring appears to have been achieved once and for all (although it in no way ensures that the scores are valid). This is no small feat for the generations of researchers, primarily from CEEB and ETS, who worked on the problem off and on for the better part of an entire century. Beginning with the fact that those scoring writing could not agree on the same scores for the same papers at a rate of consistency that would elevate the meaning of these scores beyond the whimsy of an individual reader, we progressed beyond just being able to conduct scoring sessions in which raters agree at statistically acceptable rates to the use of computer software that can duplicate better than human judges scores given by specific readers. We now turn our attention to validity—which is considered the critical concept in contemporary measurement theory—and its role in the development of writing assessment.

VALIDITY

Unlike reliability, the term *validity* does not appear in early measurement scholarship at the turn of the century when intelligence testing was fermenting into what would become the field of measurement and the testing industry. As far as we can tell, the word *validity* does not appear at all until the 1920s (Mayrhauser, 2005). It was not studied, nor was there much written about it, though in theory it was considered an essential component for effective testing. At first, validity was seen as something that the test maker guaranteed by the fact that he or she had made such a test (Angoff 1988; Ittenbach, Esters, and Wainer 1997; Mayrhauser 2005). As Ittenbach, Esters, and Wainer explain, "who better to judge the utility of Binet and Simon's early scale with children experiencing learning problems in 1904 than the architects of the instruments themselves . . . authors and publishers of the instruments were considered experts on the validity of their instruments" (22). By the mid-1930s, Carl Brigham (author of the SAT) "defined validity in purely operational terms, as simply the correlation of scores on a test with 'some other objective measure of that which the test is used to measure' (Brigham 1937, 214)" (Angoff 1988, 20). This practice of testing score correlations with another valued measure evolved into the concept of criterion validity. In 1946, J. P. Guilford published what was considered at the time the definitive statement on test validity: "In a very general sense, a test is valid for anything with which it correlates" (429). This lack of a real scholarly base about what is supposed to be the most important concept for testing has not gone unnoticed.

> Validity has always been regarded as most fundamental and important in psychometrics. It is therefore curious that serious work in clarifying the concept did not begin in earnest until the profession was fifty years old. (Angoff 1988, 19)

Of course, there are many possible reasons why validity was not developed more thoroughly by the measurement community for five or so decades. One possibility comes from the literature about writing assessment. In 1980, Anne Gere (1980), who wrote one of the first articles on writing assessment theory, reasoned that the field of writing assessment was too busy trying to get itself established and paying attention to developing and practicing needed writing assessments to work on theory. Five years later in their germinal book on writing assessment, Lester Faigley, Roger Cherry, David Jolliffe, and Anna Skinner (1985) offered a similar explanation. This position, however, assumes that the same people who develop and implement the assessments would—or should—be writing the theory. Carl Brigham had opposed the establishment of ETS because he was wary of a single organization that would develop, administer, market, and validate the use of tests (Lemann 1999). In writing assessment, the lack of attention to validity was compounded by the composition community's reliance on an outmoded notion of validity as the degree to which a test measures what it purports to measure (Huot 2002; White 1994; Yancey 1999), a definition that comes from the 1930s (Angoff 1988, 19) and ignores the revolutionary changes in assessment since the 1950s. This reliance by composition scholars on a sixty-plus-year-old definition of validity is part of the disconnect between college writing assessment and the educational measurement community (Huot 2002; Moss 1998).

Huot's call for an appreciation of more current theories for validity in writing assessment piggybacks on composition scholars' (White 1984; Yancey 1999; and others) overall emphasis on validity instead of reliability, which had dominated writing assessment scholarship as we discussed above. This historical emphasis on reliability was undoubtedly influenced not only by the problem with reliable scoring but also by educational measurement's lack of interest and research into validity in its early years. For example, Charles Spearman, considered one of the founders of psychometrics who first worked out the statistical and theoretical principles of the correlation, "used the term validity to mean reliability and believed the predictiveness [i.e., validity—even predictive validity] would follow on experimental consistency" (Mayrhauser 2005, 313). In truth, the first fifty years of validity as an "evolving"[5] concept focused the majority of testers' efforts on providing reliable measurement since "reliability" could more easily be measured. This emphasis on reliability, as we discussed earlier, was especially true for writing assessment in which interrater reliability was

---

5.   Almost all of the authors we have consulted in looking at the history of validity (Angoff 1988; Ittenbach, Esters, and Wainer 1997; Kamphaus, Windor, Rowe, and Kim 2005; Shepard 1993; Thorndike 1997; von Mayrhauser 2005) refer to validity in this way. Angoff's chapter title is "Validity: An Evolving Concept."

the true sticking point for establishing writing assessment as an acceptable testing procedure. For example, in their germinal research monograph that described what came to be known as holistic scoring and set the stage for reliable writing assessments in the future, Godshalk, Swineford, and Coffman define their efforts to discover a valid test of writing:

> It looked as if the efforts to improve reading reliability had been going in the wrong direction. The solution, it seemed, was in subjecting each paper to the judgment of a number of different readers. The consensus would constitute a valid measure of writing ability, assuming of course that the readers were competent. (1966, 4)

In this discussion of reliability and validity, validity almost seems like an afterthought, in some ways drawing upon the overall history of validity in which the test authors were the supreme authority about the validity of their tests. This conflation of reliability with validity can still be seen some thirty-five years later in Galen Leonhardy and William Condon's discussion of the development of writing assessment: "eventually, newer assessments have met the challenge of scoring longer, more complex varied samples consistently. In this way, the field of writing assessment has achieved the significant goal of greater validity" (2001, 65). This conflation of validity with reliability is understandable given the great emphasis on achieving scoring consistency. For the educational measurement community, if a test was reliable (had consistency from one administration to another) and correlated to another valued measure of the same trait (had validity), then it was an acceptable or valid test. As Lorrie Shepard notes, "Thus, in the first part of the century, psychologists used correlations to learn about their tests but focused on the convergence or 'reliability' of measures as evidence of validity" (1993, 409). For the English-teaching community, which was less concerned with the statistical apparatus associated with reliability, a writing test needed to include writing that was read by teachers—in some ways what teachers wanted is what the measurement community referred to as "face" validity, that is, a test looked like it would measure the desired ability or trait. We can see references to face validity even in fairly recent scholarship, when Yancey (1999) and Leonhardy and Condon (2001) and many others in college writing assessment automatically assume more validity for portfolios because, as we all agree, a portfolio looks like a better measurement of a student's ability to write than an essay produced in twenty minutes.

Modern work in validity theory really begins in the mid-1950s with the publication of "Technical Recommendations for Test and Diagnostic Techniques" (1954), sponsored by the American Educational Research Association (AERA), the American Psychological Association (APA), and the National Council on Measurement in Education (NCME). In 1966,

AERA, APA, and NCME published a second book-length (all versions after the one in 1954 were book-length) version titled *Standards for Educational and Psychological Tests and Manuals. Standards* has been rewritten in 1974, 1986, and subsequently in 1999, reflecting the complexity of the "evolving" nature of validity.

Since the initial version of *Standards* in 1954, validity has been conceived as more than just a correlation and defined in multiple ways. At first, there were four main categories for validity because "tests are used for several types of judgment, and for each type of judgment, a somewhat different type of validation is involved" (APA, AERA, and NCME 1954, 13). In the 1966 edition of *Standards*, content, criterion, and construct validity became the three main foci for test validation. Content validity referred to a test consisting of adequate content to measure the desired ability or trait; criterion validity made sure that performance on an examination was related to other performances or valued measures. For example, a score on a writing test could be seen as having concurrent validity with a student's scores on the SAT Verbal or predictive validity for students' grades in first-year writing classes. Criterion validity has been the fount of many different types of validity referred to throughout the literature, including face, predictive, and concurrent.

The last of the three validity types defined in 1966, construct validity introduced a new concept for validity theory and test validation. It was the first time validity had been conceived of in a theoretical way. Evidence for construct validity could not merely consist of statistical correlations or an analysis of test content. As Lee Cronbach notes, when validity was defined as the degree to which a test measures what it purports to measure, the focus was on the test's truthfulness—did it do what it said it would? Later, alternative definitions that stated "that a test is valid if it serves the purpose for which it is used, raised a question about worth" (Cronbach 1988, 5). Construct validation introduced the question of whether or not a test was a worthy construct of the ability or trait being measured. Construct validity radically enlarged the scope of any investigation for test validity, although validity was never meant to be a process or concept that could be reified into separate categories or classes: "These aspects of validity can be discussed independently, but only for convenience" (APA, AERA, and NCME 1974, 26). Unfortunately, that is exactly what happened, with especially dire consequences for writing assessment.

For example, when a test, like the COMPASS (an untimed editing exam delivered on computer and used to make placement decisions) is developed, test developers run correlational statistics to establish a relationship between student performance on the COMPASS and student performance on other valued measures like course grades or scores on holistically graded essays. This information by itself might be seen as useful, but these correlations are used to make claims about the concurrent or predictive validity of the COMPASS without any attention to construct validity. These procedures allow the companies who develop, own, and market these types of tests to claim that they are valid, ignoring the theoretical principles of validity that they ironically claim for their tests. This continuing misuse of validity is especially problematic considering that by the late 1980s, Lee Cronbach (1988) and Samuel Messick (1989a), leading measurement scholars, had firmly established validity as a unitary concept. In other words, any claim for validity must address construct validity, which includes issues of content and criterion validity as well as reliability. The most recent APA, AERA, and NCME *Standards* published in 1999 supports Cronbach's and Messick's ideas for a comprehensive, unified theory of test validity. This contemporary view of validity not only includes all notions of validity and reliability, it also demands that test consequences and implications for the local educational environment be considered. Unless decisions based upon a test can demonstrate educational value for students, it is difficult to make a convincing argument for validity. Shepard illustrates the importance of testing decisions having value for students in her critique of school-readiness testing, since there is no evidence that keeping students out of school benefits them in any way. This would mean that any writing program using a placement procedure (including Directed Self-Placement[6]) for determining placement into basic writing would have to demonstrate that students profit from the basic writing experience.

Unfortunately, the combination of writing assessment's preoccupation with reliability, the use of outdated notions of validity by composition scholars, and the inappropriate reification of validity types created a situation in which validity was claimed for assessments that contain no writing at all. The necessity of emphasizing reliability to establish writing assessment as a viable form of educational measurement also focused writing assessment scholars and practitioners away from any consideration or sustained study of validity—however conceived or defined. In the inaugural issue of *Assessing Writing*, the first journal devoted to writing assessment, Huot (1994, 2) notes that in a bibliographic essay published some four years earlier, he had identified three main areas around which most writing assessment scholarship had clustered, but none of the six articles in the first issue focused on the main categories he had previously identified. Huot goes on to note that while the categories he had defined earlier permitted scholars to establish the efficacy, reliability, and viability of writing assessment, the articles in the first issue of *Assessing Writing* provided a much needed

---

6.   Even if we structure placement around decisions students make for themselves, we must still provide evidence that each decision is a beneficial educational opportunity.

critique. In some ways, it might be possible to see this transition from one kind of writing assessment scholarship to another as a move from reliability as the main subject to validity as the necessary focus of writing assessment scholarship.

This transition to studying validity can be seen in the work of William L. Smith (1992, 1993), who conducted a series of studies on the writing placement program he directed at the University of Pittsburgh. Eventually, Smith turned his attention to the way essays were scored after finding that prompts and other testing conditions had no significant effect on student scores. Although he was able to produce acceptable rates of agreement through holistic scoring, Smith noticed that this rate of agreement was misleading, since there were sets of raters who agreed and disagreed with each other on a regular and predictable basis. Once Smith realized that the rater sets he identified were usually teachers who most regularly and most recently taught the same course, he designed a rating procedure in which teachers who taught a specific course made a single determination about whether or not a student belonged in her class, producing more accurate placement and greater agreement among raters than holistic scoring.

Smith's inquiry into writing assessment, which extended beyond answering the question "How do we get raters to agree?" was made possible because earlier research had answered those questions with holistic scoring. The earlier work set the stage for Smith to ask questions about how raters agreed and what raters were likely to agree with other raters, exploring the nature of how teachers come to arrive at the judgments they do. Smith's finding echoed research conducted—and dismissed—in the 1950s. At one point, when researchers were struggling to develop procedures for reliable writing assessment, Paul Diederich (1950) published a study in which readers agreed with each other at a high rate; however, he dismissed these findings because of the small number of readers coming from the same institution, since he did not think it possible to replicate such results with large numbers of essay readers. In other words, Diederich's results were aligned with Smith's finding several decades later: readers who share similar backgrounds agree at higher rates than those with more disparate backgrounds. Unlike Diederich, Smith used his findings to develop a more effective assessment procedure for placement, as he focused on not just the reliability rates but also the adequacy of the placement, or the validity of the assessment's results. This movement away from looking exclusively at reliability has fostered a range of writing assessment procedures at various institutions (Harrington 2005; Haswell 2001a; Haswell and Wyche-Smith 1994; Hester et al. 2007; Lowe and Huot 1997) that do not involve rubrics or scores. In fact, some of the new procedures (Haswell and Wyche-Smith; Hester et al.) do not require that every paper be read twice, so interrater reliability becomes moot (Huot 2002). Instead, those using methods in which every paper is not read twice report a degree of agreement for a percentage of papers read twice, not unlike the reliability checks used to code qualitative data. In this way, it is possible to argue for instrument reliability[7] without having each paper read more than once.

One important feature of Smith's original placement procedures is that they promote both validity (accurate and adequate placement) and reliability (better agreement than holistic scoring used with the same readers for the same purpose). A single method that promotes both reliability and validity is an important breakthrough. We know from our brief history that methods such as reading student essays were promoted for their contributions to validity, though scoring inconsistency raised serious questions about the validity of decisions made on such an unreliably scored test. Indirect tests of multiple-choice questions and the next generation placement tests (such as the COMPASS) furnished "reliable" scores without even having students write anything. This is hardly a recognizable construct for writing, and hence these tests produce a questionable degree of validity for making placement or other decisions about students. Roberta Camp (1993), Leonhardy and Condon (2001), Yancey (1999), and others have both characterized the development of writing assessment through the tension between reliability and validity, with validity finally winning out in such practices as portfolios. This tension between reliability and validity has also been used to characterize educational and psychological measurement in general. For example, Michael M. Williamson (1994) in an essay on reliability and efficiency in writing assessment, makes the point—quoting Lord and Novick, two important measurement scholars—that any assessment producing interesting, relevant, and rich information about the exam takers will likely suffer from a lack of consistency; whereas, highly consistent, standardized measurements will produce a partial and perhaps impoverished representation of the ability or psychological trait being examined. Perhaps Smith's work in writing assessment could signal a new future for writing assessment—or even for educational measurement in general—in which reliability and validity work in harmony rather than tension. Figure 1 reflects the evolution of validity as a concept and its relationship to writing assessment.

---

7. Instrument reliability refers to how consistently individuals perform on an assessment, whereas interrater reliability refers to how consistently individual readers agree on judgments for an assessment.

Figure 1. Validity and Writing Assessment

Validity as a-theoretical

- validity does not appear as a term until the 1920s
- validity is best left to test writers
- specific tests can have validity
- Spearman's 1904 formula for correlation is important in establishing relationships between different measures
- Brigham defines validity in 1937 as "simply the correlation of scores on a test with some other objective measure of that which the test is used to measure."
- J. P. Guilford defines validity in 1946 saying, "In a very general sense, a test is valid for anything with which it correlates."

Modern validity theory

- early 1950s, Cronbach challenges validity as a correlation
- the focus of validity shifts from the accuracy of a measure to its value
- "Technical Recommendations for Test and Diagnostic Techniques" published in 1954 by AERA, APA, and NCME; *Standards* continues to be revised and updated
- 1966, content, criterion, and construct validity are the main foci, though not to be used individually
- inferences and interpretations, rather than tests, are validated
- by 1989, Messick and Cronbach define validity as a unitary concept, focussing on the use of a test, including its consequences
- 1999 *Standards* mirrors Cronbach and Messick

Validity in writing assessment

- validity is often conflated with reliability
- writing-less writing tests, like the TSWE and COMPASS, claim overall validity by establishing a correlative, criterion relationship
- holistic scoring and portfolios look valid (have face validity) and therefore *are* more valid ways to assess
- outmoded definition of validity as a test measuring what it purports to measure used in college writing assessments into the 1990s
- joint ad hoc WPA/NCTE white paper adheres to current validity theory

Note: Writing assessment has only recently been influenced by modern validity theory.

CONCLUSION

If testing in general and writing assessment in particular began in the early 1900s or so, then they are about a hundred years old. What's interesting, maddening, instructive, and usable about this short history is that it appears that in writing assessment, as in most human endeavors, the more things change, the more they remain the same. For example, the creation of the CEEB in the early twentieth century—if not the beginning of formal writing assessment then certainly an important development—signalled some important trends, beliefs, and assumptions that continue with us today. The only tenant from Wilson Farrand's proposal for the origination of the CEEB not accepted was to use input from the high schools along with testing information to make college admission decisions (Elliot 2005). As state-mandated writing assessments are now established for K–12 public institutions in all fifty states, the input from teachers is devalued and the influence of these assessments is visible in high school curricula and in teachers' inservice (Hillocks 2002; Murphy 2003; O'Neill et al. 2005). The impact of an untested and unexamined belief in test scores outweighs any other evidence (Moss 1996; Rogers 2003) in making important educational decisions about students. At the college level, SAT and ACT scores are still considered significant factors in admission decisions at most universities and four-year colleges, with many using these scores in composition placement. With the revised SAT and its writing section (multiple choice and timed essay) there is potential for standardized tests to have a greater effect on access and curriculum through placement. Of course, many institutions already use commercial test products, such as COMPASS and ACCUPLACER, to determine students' entry into the college-writing curriculum—even to award credit or exemption.

While this historical look at the prevailing importance of testing evidence over other forms of evidence about student progress and achievement is certainly not uplifting news, it is important information for WPAs and teachers. As supposedly new calls for accountability come down the administrative highway, we can remind deans and other administrators that teachers' notions of accountability and their evaluations of students have never received the attention they deserve, making calls for locally based assessments stronger. We also need to remember that while most assessments before the use of portfolios were designed by test development researchers, mainly from the ETS, teachers have often been able to exert pressure to change the way writing is assessed. The influence of teachers who demanded and received the English Composition Test in the 1940s was certainly a serious thorn in the side of the CEEB, given the acrimonious response of Stalnaker (Fuess 1967, 158).

In addition to being aware of the continued, unwarranted faith in formal writing assessment, knowledge of the origins of intelligence testing and the use of the Army Alpha tests to create the Stanford Binet IQ and SAT tests is also an important hedge against those who would introduce more formal, standardized, commercial testing for making important decisions about our students. First of all, we can and should point out that the impetus driving the beginning of intelligence testing and the spate of tests needed to document and improve the dire state of student writing is part of an ongoing cycle. Whenever a substantial change in student population occurs, such as after laws were passed around the beginning of the twentieth century mandating universal education, the schools experience difficulties in adjusting to teaching students who have new needs and challenges. Intelligence testing originated as a response to new student populations at the turn of the twentieth century, just as the SATs replaced essay testing as part of the war effort in the mid-1940s. Writing tests were implemented in the early fifties when colleges became inundated with GI Bill students (Elliot 2005; Yancey 1999). Later in the sixties, holistic scoring and other "direct" writing assessments were used to sort new waves of incoming first-year students, some of whom became basic writers. As the largest influx of new students during the last decade or so has been from Hispanic immigrants and other children whose first language is not English, we once again are witnessing an increase in testing. Pointing out to administrators that testing is but one way to respond to the challenges of teaching new populations of students can help make a case for an increased investment in writing centers, smaller classes, instructional technology, and learning communities for teachers and students.

Not only is testing but one response to the need for change in education in general and writing programs in particular, it is also not a very strong one. Even our cursory look at the history of intelligence testing establishes that educational measurement's first fifty years or so was pretty much atheoretical. Proof of validity was established by the author and publisher of the test. Theoretical formulae that established statistical correlations between measures and retests were the proof that the tests were accurate and valid. It is astonishing to think of the many important educational decisions based upon tests whose impact and value were never examined in any rigorous, systematic way. Fortunately, validity theory in the last fifty years of educational and psychological testing has developed in ways that now focus on making the best decisions based upon the data generated by tests. These decisions must include a rationale for using the test (Messick 1989) and a justification of the educational value for any decision based upon a test's results (Shepard 1993). The consequences for each decision must be thoroughly examined (Cronbach 1988; Messick 1989; Moss 1992; Shepard

1993). Understanding the history of contemporary validity theory provides the WPA and writing teacher with an understanding of the professional standards educational testing professionals are supposed to follow.

This kind of information about the development of validity allows a WPA or writing teacher to look at a range of statistical data offered as proof of validity and to remind her colleagues that validity is more than a row of statistical correlations. We must also remind our colleagues in measurement and testing that content or criterion validity of various ilks are not "proof" of validity. All evidence, including traditionally defined content and criterion validity and interrater and/or instrument reliability, are subsumed into one validation argument for what used to be labeled construct validity. Validity must be considered a unitary construct (AERA, APA, and NCME 1999; Cronbach 1988; Messick 1989; Shepard 1993).

Probably the most usable part of our history is the realization that the prevailing focus of writing assessment on how to make teacher/readers agree better might have been a shortsighted approach to the "problem" for writing assessment. When Gere (1980) and Faigley, Cherry, Jolliffe, and Skinner (1985) lament the lack of a theory for writing assessment because people were working on establishing the practices themselves, what they could have been saying is that focusing on reliability had prevented research on other aspects of writing assessment. On the other hand, lack of rater agreement was a serious problem—no important decisions should be based upon scores that vary widely depending upon the rater. Nonetheless, the fact that the reliability problem for writing assessment has been solved once and for all with computer scoring does not mean a blank check for validity. The limitations of computer or automated scoring have to be factored into any argument for making specific decisions based upon writing assessment data generated by computer analysis of student writing.

Of course, it was never really true that writing teachers could not agree with each other. Even Paul Diederich of ETS knew that in the early 1950s, though the small population of raters who agreed with each other in his study did not satisfy his needs for large readings (1950). Even so, the bad rap about agreement was fueled by asking a specific question and not asking other questions—such as the ones Smith (1992, 1993) asked about the ways in which readers agreed and disagreed with each other. Smith's and Haswell's (2001a) work allows WPAs to design their own assessments that depend upon local knowledge of students, curriculum, and institutions. With the theoretical and research base (Harrington 2005; Haswell 2001; O'Neill 2003; Smith 1992, 1993; Williamson 1994, and others) establishing the efficacy of designing local assessment methods, we may have come full circle from the origination of the CEEB and the initial devaluing of teacher's' local knowledge. It would be politically and practically naïve of us to say "we've come a long way baby" without qualifying that statement a great deal. Nonetheless, the amount of scholarship, including the number of books, over the last half dozen years is remarkable and is made possible by the wide range of writing administrators, researchers, and teachers working in writing assessment. One thing we know for sure, if WPAs and writing teachers work actively to create a productive culture of assessment around the teaching of writing and the administration of writing programs, the future of writing assessment will be much different from its past.

3

CONSIDERING THEORY

There is nothing as practical as a good theory.

—Kurt Lewin

Theory and practice have had an uneasy relationship in college writing assessment (much like the relationship between theory and practice in teaching). Writing assessment scholars, such as Brian Huot (2002) Pamela Moss (1998), Bob Broad (2003), and more recently, Patricia Lynne (2004), have agreed that the emphasis in assessment is on practice without adequate attention to theory. Yet, as James Zebroski (1994) and others have explained, theory supports and informs practice whether or not that theory is articulated, whether or not practitioners understand the theory. In writing assessment, practitioners need to understand multiple layers of theories—theories about language, learning, written literacy, and educational measurement—because all of these play into how we make meaning as writers, as readers of that writing, and ultimately, as evaluators of it. Practitioners of writing assessment also need to think about how these different theories intersect and fit together. The tensions among theories don't go away just because administrators ignore them or practitioners reject them. By unpacking theories associated with writing assessment, administrators can begin to better understand how to make their programs more theoretically consistent, how to communicate more effectively with the various participants in the assessment, and how to improve teaching and learning in their writing program.

This chapter begins by defining what we mean by theory and why it is critical for people engaged with assessment to think explicitly about theory. From here, we review basic theories about language and written literacy, move to discussions of theories of validity and reliability, and end with emerging theories of writing assessment. While the discussion is positioned in terms of large-scale assessment, in writing programs the classroom teaching and student learning are always a part of the conversation because the essence of a program is what happens in individual classrooms between students and teachers. In other words, the focus of this chapter (and this book) is not necessarily on how individual instructors grade students in a particular course but on assessments that occur beyond the classroom (e.g., placement, program, and proficiency evaluations). However, we see these two locations of assessment as intimately connected.

THEORY

Theory is one of those terms that evokes all kinds of associations and definitions. It can lead to heated debates, especially in English departments (the most common institutional home to writing programs and the most common disciplinary heritage of writing program administrators and instructors) where "wars" and "backlash" are just some of the recent rhetoric surrounding the term. Theory, in this context, is coupled with a particular approach and school of thought such as postmodernism, feminism, postcolonialism, or Marxism. In this sense, theory is a way of "conceptualizing, organizing, explaining, analyzing, reflecting on, and interpreting experiences and specialized knowledge gained through experience or observation" (Rose and Weiser 2002, 2). Specific theories involve a formal set of universal principles and assumptions that have been articulated and are used, for example, for analysis and interpretation of a text or event (e.g., rhetorical or pedagogical theories). Advocates of particular theories debate and discuss the finer points, but in general, scholars agree about what constitutes the theory. Theory, in this case, is positioned as intellectual, academic work, often seen as separate from—and in fact opposite from—practice. In the traditional binary relationship between theory and practice—or thought and action—theory has occupied the privileged position, especially in the university where attention to practice has been seen as "too vocational," the kiss of death in the academy (Argyris and Schön 1981, 3). Formal theory is a mainstay in the contemporary academy, with scholars often identified by their theoretical position. While in some ways we are working within this tradition as we identify and explain theories about literacy and assessment, we do not see theory as opposed to practice.

While we value abstract, theoretical work that aims at constructing formalized positions and schools of thought, we also understand theory as less formalized, more concrete: as basic assumptions and beliefs that inform actions and practices. Theory, in this sense, is intimately tied to practice, although it is often left unarticulated as such. Louise Phelps (1989) explains that there is a dialectical relationship between theory and practice (in reference to teaching writing), which she refers to as a Practice-Theory-Practice arc. Theory, in this scheme, helps in understanding practices, and practice helps to formulate theories as an instructor moves to deeper theoretical sophistication and improved practice. In fact, theory is fundamental to practices and our revision of practice. Phelps's articulation echoes, in some ways, Donald Schön's idea of "reflective practice," which involves a practitioner (not necessarily a writing specialist) who "reflects in action," becoming a "researcher in the practice context" (1983, 68). Phelps (and, by extension, Schön) is not necessarily referring to an organized, particular school of thought but rather the ideas and beliefs of an instructor that influence her practice. Thinking through beliefs and assumptions in the context of action can help the practitioner develop a deeper understanding of the action, the practice.

Other composition scholars express a slightly different view of theory and its relationship to practice. Charles Schuster, for example, argues that there is a productive tension between theory and practice and concludes that "theory is a form of practice and that practice is the operational dimension of theory" (1991, 43). Schuster still sees theory and practice as split, while James Zebroski sees a more intimate relationship:

> Theory is not the opposite of practice; theory is not even a supplement to practice. Theory *is* practice, a practice of a particular kind, and practice is always theoretical. The question is not whether we have a theory . . . but whether we are going to become conscious of our theory. (1994, 15)

Writing assessment literature, as scholars such as Gere (1980) and Faigley, Cherry, Jolliffe, and Skinner (1985) have said, has long focused on articulating practices while the theories that inform the practices remain tacit. In this chapter, we aim to articulate the theories, both formalized schools of thought as well as more informal beliefs and assumptions, informing teaching and assessment practices to argue that effective, appropriate writing assessments need to be theoretically consistent with what linguists and educators know about language, literacy, and learning and what psychometric scholars posit about testing and assessment. We are not actually formulating *the* theory of writing assessment but rather explicating the general theoretical positions and the multiple disciplinary perspectives that are relevant for those engaged in writing assessment. We are arguing for an approach to assessment that requires writing instructors and administrators to "become conscious" of the theories informing their practice as part of the assessment process. (The articulation of theories that influence and frame our practices is, after all, a critical component of validity inquiry, which we address later in this chapter.)

Shaping our understanding of these relevant theoretical positions is the change in conceptual frameworks that happened in the second half of the twentieth century. According to Lorrie Shepard in an article on classroom assessment, the early twentieth century was influenced by scientific measurement, a hereditarian theory of intelligence, and associationist and behaviorist learning theories, which supported a curriculum of social efficiency that was characterized by the scientific management of schools, differentiated curriculum based on predicted social roles, carefully specified educational objectives, and the science of exact measurement and precise standards among other things (2000, 5). Given this framework, Shepard notes in classroom assessments "various recall, completion, matching, and multiple-choice test types, along with some essay questions, fit closely with what was deemed important to learn" (5). Since the early 1900s, however, our conceptual frameworks have changed in many significant ways. Shepard explains that social constructivist frameworks, which draw on revolutionary theories in cognition and sociocultural theories, have created a contrasting set of assumptions about education, including the following: (1) society and culture influence the development of intelligence, (2) knowledge and understanding are constructed by learners within a social context, (3) metacognition is a critical component of learning, (4) prior knowledge influences new learning, (5) all students can learn and should have the opportunity to learn, (6) material should be challenging and promote higher-order thinking and problem solving, and (7) learners should be socialized into academic disciplines' discourses and practices (8). Based on these assumptions (and other positions she articulates), Shepard argues that classroom assessment needs to change to fit this social constructivist approach to learning. In this framework, assessments should address learning processes as well as products, be formative and ongoing, feed back into learning, elicit higher-order thinking, require self-evaluation, and have explicit criteria and expectations (8). Although Shepard's article is focused on K–12 education and classroom assessments, the approach to education she identifies is clearly consistent with contemporary literacy scholarship, psychometric theories, and the approach to writing assessment we endorse.[1] We argue, however, that these types of assessments are not only for classroom-based assessment but should guide writing assessment done beyond the classroom as well.

BELIEFS AND ASSUMPTIONS ABOUT LANGUAGE AND LITERACY

Linguistics and literacy research has much to offer writing instructors and assessors. Understanding basic theories about language and literacy is essential to designing writing assessments (and programs) that are informed and effective in promoting the teaching and learning of written communication. Without a sense of how language is learned and how literacy functions, an assessment may not yield information that is accurate, useful, or valid (validity is addressed in more detail below). When results are invalid, not only are resources wasted but the consequences can be damaging to students, faculty, programs, and institutions. For example, poorly designed placement tests could place students into courses that they are

---

1.   In fact, Michael Williamson (1994) makes a similar argument in "The Worship of Efficiency: Untangling Theoretical and Practical Considerations in Writing Assessment," that is specific to writing assessment, although his overview of the historical changes takes a slightly different approach than Shepard's.

over prepared for, which squanders their educational time and money and can undermine their self-perceptions and confidence, stalling or derailing their education; or they could place students into classes that they are *under* prepared for, which can result in failure, poor grades, and/or dropping out, impeding progress toward a degree. Research into language and literacy, which has grown exponentially over the last half-century and given rise to new specialties within linguistics and education, has produced critical information about how language and literacy functions and circulates, as well as how people learn to read and write. This scholarship provides a theoretical framework for the assessment of written literacy.

Literacy learning, according to linguistics and literacy scholars, is best fostered with a holistic approach, which emphasizes communicative competence. The parts of the linguistic code are learned within the framework of the whole. Linguist Roger Shuy explains that this is a constructivist approach which doesn't ignore the parts of language but which does not teach parts in isolation. Error is an important part of language learning: "[Linguists] have learned, in language teaching, that there is no way to learn a language without being wrong in it and without being *allowed* to be wrong in it as one learns the right forms" (1981, 105).

In sociolinguistics, discourse analysis, and pragmatics, scholars study language as a social activity, which is how language functions. According to sociolinguist James Gee, language and literacy only make sense within "discourses," and "discourses include much more than language" (1996, viii). Gee explains that discourses include ways of behaving, valuing, thinking, believing, speaking, reading, and writing (1996, viii). Meaning, therefore, cannot take place outside of context. Work such as Gee's demonstrates the interaction between language, culture, and society. Understanding and interpreting language requires knowledge beyond the linguistic code (letters, words, grammar). Gee explains that it is impossible to communicate in a decontextualized way because "all communication is rooted in sociocultural identities and based on shared knowledge and understandings" (156–57). Research in sociolinguistics also shows how language use influences social interactions. The context of language use influences the meaning of an utterance, but utterances can also influence the understanding of the context as well as perceptions of the speakers or about them. This approach to language has led to important research about the discourse expectations in school and how teachers and students interact (e.g., Cazden 2001, Heath 1983, Gee 1996). According to Jenny Cook-Gumperz, literacy is not merely the acquisition of cognitive skills but also a social process for "demonstrating knowledgeability" (2006, 3).

Findings from classroom research studies demonstrate that students who do not know how to participate in the discourse patterns of the classroom can be labeled as deficient or difficult. For example, Heath demonstrated that specific language practices of home cultures can clash with the linguistic norms of the school culture, making communication ineffective and negatively influencing the teachers' perceptions of students' abilities and, consequently, their educational opportunities. While Heath's work was specific to elementary-school-aged children, the implications span the academic continuum. Hull, Rose, Fraser, and Castellano explain how a student from a minority group, who has been placed into a basic writing class at the university, is considered a "problem" and her intelligence, abilities, and performance questioned by her writing instructor because she violates the classroom discourse conventions.[2] The authors describe how the instructor perceived the student's "bothersome conversational habits" as "evidence of a thinking problem—evidence that is so salient that it goes unqualified even in the face of counter-evidence that [she], in fact, wrote rather well" (1991, 311). In an interview, the instructor commented that the student was probably getting a lot of help from her parents to explain her good performance (the authors note that the student's parents did not even speak English).

In a different study, also linked to college remedial writing programs, Hull and Rose focus more specifically on how a student's "misreading" of a poem makes sense within the student's home culture and experiences. From their research, they conclude:

> The desire for efficiency and coverage can cut short numerous possibilities for students to explore issues, articulate concerns, formulate and revise problems— all necessary for good writing to emerge—and can lead to conversational patterns that socialize students into a mode of interaction that will limit rather than enhance their participation in intellectual work. We would further suggest that streamlined conversational patterns . . . are often reinforced by a set of deficit-oriented assumptions about the linguistic and cognitive abilities of remedial students, assumptions that are much in need of examination. (1990, 296)

Based on their research, Hull and Rose endorse a pedagogical model that makes "knowledge-making" central by disrupting typical school-based discourse patterns and encouraging active engagement instead. Students

---

2.   In Western schooling, according to linguistic research (Mehan 1979; Cazden 2001), the classroom talk is organized into certain patterns. The most common pattern involves turntaking in which the teacher initiates interaction (e.g., asks a question, gives a direction), the student replies (e.g., raising a hand, answering the question, following the direction), and the teacher evaluates the student response (e.g, "Okay," "Right," "Are you sure?"). This pattern is commonly referred to as IRE, or Initiation-Response-and-Evaluation. Other standard classroom patterns include lectures—the teacher lectures and students do not interrupt until there is a break for questions. In the Hull et al. research, Maria violated the classroom discourse norms. For example, she would interrupt the IRE pattern or a mini-lecture.

participate in the "real stuff of belonging to an academic community," through "dynamic involvement in generating and questioning knowledge" (297).

While Hull and Rose's research focused on classroom-based language use, it speaks directly to writing assessment. Understanding writing, like any language use, depends on the sociocultural context. While we may perceive writing as less dependent on context, accurately reading and evaluating it demands extra-textual knowledge because written language is created, read, and interpreted within particular contexts (more discussion of this occurs in chapter 4). Robert, the student in their study, needed to have knowledge about how poems are interpreted within a certain literary tradition to have accurately read and written about the poem; Hull and Rose, however, needed a better understanding of Robert's cultural context and experiences to accurately interpret Robert's writing about the poem.

As literary and language scholars, we know that extra-textual knowledge is necessary for interpreting a text and understanding the author's main idea, purpose, and even language. Even New Criticism demands that the reader understand certain conventions such as symbol systems and forms to accurately read a text. The need for extra-textual knowledge is true for published texts as well as student-generated ones. Literacy involves more than the knowledge of the grammar and code of a language. All communication demands readers/listeners use extra-linguistic knowledge to determine meaning. Students need to have opportunities to engage in authentic language use if they are going to develop into sophisticated language users. In assessments of written literacy, students are expected to produce acontextual essayist prose, which privileges logic, rationality, and dispassion, and is based on the assumption that writing can transcend social and cultural differences (Gee 1996, 156). However, according to Gee and other sociolinguists, it is impossible to communicate outside of the social and cultural context so that even concepts such as *logic* and *rationality* are dependent on sociocultural context. To get an accurate sense of students' strengths and weaknesses as language users, assessors need to allow students to engage in authentic language use. Which means that students and teachers/assessors use language for genuine communication and meaning making in specific but varied sociocultural situations. While one of these contexts may be school, that is a very narrow and limited situation that does not accurately represent the multitude of situations that students will encounter as they communicate in school and beyond it.

For professionals working within English studies, these assumptions and beliefs about language and texts, which are supported by linguistic research as well as our own experiences, are nothing new or radical. Recent theoretical positions (e.g., new historicism, postcolonial theories)

highlight particular aspects of a context that influence the creation, interpretation, and significance of a text. Likewise, characteristics of the writer and reader—including social and political positioning, ethnicity, gender, class, and sexual orientation—are considered important factors in the
interpretation of a text. As scholars examine these cultural, extra-linguistic factors that bear on a text, they debate a text's meaning, interpretation,
and significance, constructing arguments to endorse one reading over others. These theories are familiar to scholars in English studies, yet they often
are considered irrelevant in reading and interpreting student-generated
texts, especially those used in writing assessments.

In administering writing assessments, we need to be sure we think
through the way socio-cultural factors can influence not only students'
reading of a task and written response but also our own interpretations of
the responses. We draw conclusions about the student based on our interpretation of the response, which may or may not be accurate, as Hull and
Rose (1990), Haswell and Haswell (1996), and other researchers have discovered. For students whose home cultures are substantially different than
school culture, assessments can position them unfairly. In writing assessment, misunderstandings can occur when test takers don't understand
the conventions of the test or when their understandings of the task differ
from those of the test designers. Sandra Murphy (2007) summarized several studies that demonstrated how misfires can happen in writing assessment when tests are not sensitive to the particular students and their context. She relates one example with a familiar prompt that asked elementa-
ry students to write a letter to the principal about a problem in the school.
At one school students responded to the prompt with laughter, complaints,
and even refusals to write because they didn't think the principal would listen to anything they said. At another school, the students struggled because
they couldn't find any problem in the school to write about. This prompt
"misfired" because the particular climate and culture of these schools
made the given rhetorical situation seem unimaginable to students who
didn't understand the discourse conventions of testing and, thus, took the
task literally. Murphy (2007) argues that for students with linguistic and/
or cultural backgrounds different from the dominant or mainstream culture (including non-native speakers of English and international students),
these kinds of misunderstandings are more likely to occur. Arnetha Ball
(1997) makes a similar point and argues that we need to be sure to include
teachers of color as evaluators because her research revealed differences in
scoring patterns between white and African American teachers who otherwise shared similar backgrounds, training, and teaching experience. Along
the same lines, Haswell and Haswell's (1996) research into gender and writing assessment reveals how readers' stereotypes about gender influenced

their reading and evaluation of student texts. Misunderstandings are just one type of problem that can influence writing assessments. Agnew and McLaughlin's (2001) research demonstrates how the exit exam used in a basic writing program unfairly discriminated against the African American students at one institution in Georgia. Negative experiences with writing assessment, such as the ones Agnew and McLaughlin report, can be important influences in students' development because, as Arnetha Ball and Pam Ellis (2008) explain, writing assessment influences students' perceptions of themselves as writers and as students.

This research on language and literacy, reviewed by Ball and Ellis (2008) and Murphy (2007), informs statements on writing assessment published by professional organizations such as the National Council of Teachers of English and its Conference on College Composition and Communication as well as the Council of Writing Program Administrators. The statements codify the contextual nature of literacy learning and how it can or should be factored into writing assessments. Specifically in relation to teaching, learning and assessing writing at the college level, CCCC articulated basic assumptions about language that are relevant to college writing programs in "Writing Assessment: A Position Statement," which was approved by the organization in 1995 and revised in 2006. The statement, available in its entirety in appendix B, the statement explains that "writing by definition is social" and that best practice in assessment "respects language variety and diversity and assesses writing on the basis of effectiveness for readers, acknowledging that as purposes vary, criteria will as well." Writing assessment programs, it continues, "should be solidly grounded in the latest research on learning, writing and assessment."

In short, for those charged with administering a writing assessment, understanding basic concepts about language learning and the way it functions is critical. Acts of literacy are situated within sociocultural context. Attention to the context is essential to adequately understand those acts and their associated discourses. For writing assessment, this means that context needs to be acknowledged, interrogated, and considered a significant part of the assessment.

THEORIES OF ASSESSMENT

While most English professionals feel comfortable with language and literacy theories, assessment theories seem more alien because of the education and experience that keeps education and English scholars professionally separate. Most English professionals don't have a clear understanding of the key concepts in educational measurement, such as validity and reliability, nor do they understand the statistical formulas associated with psychometrics. However, understanding validity theory—and applying it—by those of us who are not psychometricians is critical in developing useful, ethical assessments and in interpreting and using assessment results. Pamela Moss, an educational measurement scholar with expertise in validity theory, suggests "that all of us who work within the field of educational research have a role that we can play in the dialogue on validity theory and to argue, moreover, that we all have a responsibility to participate in the dialogue within our own research communities in critical and generative ways" (2007, 92). Moss explains that validity theory is "socially constructed, that it reflect[s] an evolving and frequently contested set of perspectives. . . ." (2007, 92) and to fulfill this responsibility, researchers need to understand validity theory has evolved within the field of psychometrics (which we have covered in part in chapter 2).

Although many university English and composition and rhetoric professors may be reluctant to see validity theory and educational measurement as areas of interest (their scholarship), desiring to focus instead on their own specific, immediate assessment needs (practice), Moss (2007) explains how an understanding of the complex—and often contentious—development of current validity theory can open up the assessment process to alternative practices and interpretations. These alternatives, she contends, can broaden the assessment possibilities and can include different disciplinary research traditions, such as ethnographic, hermeneutic, and postmodern. For writing assessment, this means that those charged with administering an assessment should not simply adopt a test or assessment plan that someone else has developed but rather see the need for assessment as an opportunity both to explore assessment theory and practice and to conduct systematic inquiry into the validity of the results. One way to realize Moss's view of assessment is to approach it as research. That is, instead of positioning a demand for assessment as an administrative task or a service assignment, the writing faculty and administration should consider it as research, drawing on their expertise and education as researchers to help them articulate questions and methods for answering those questions. Issues of validity and reliability, which are concerns in research not just in assessment, can also be considered in a new way although they cannot be ignored or dismissed. O'Neill, Schendel, and Huot put it this way:

> By viewing writing assessment as research, as a way to ask and answer questions about our students, their writing, our teaching, our curricula and the other factors that constitute effective writing instruction, we can move beyond reliability and toward constructing a validity argument. This different orientation also provides a way to reimagine writing assessment. Instead of it being something imposed upon us, something we have to do or have done to us, assessment becomes a way we can research answers to legitimate questions about how

instructors, students, administrators, and programs are doing. In this approach, emphasis on technical concerns such as reliability is reduced. . . . (2002, 14)

Responsibly working in writing assessment—no matter what department, college, or discipline one identifies with—requires some familiarity with validity and educational research to ensure ethical, thoughtful, appropriate assessments. This familiarity also helps in communicating with other interested parties, such as the university testing office, administrators, and staff about procedures, rationales, and results. Below we provide a brief overview of validity and address other key terms such as reliability.

In educational measurement, the *Standards for Educational and Psychological Testing*, co-authored by the American Educational Research Association, the American Psychological Association, and the National Council on Measurement in Education (1999), articulates the professional guidelines and standards for those using tests. It covers the basics of test construction, evaluation, and documentation, including validity and reliability, as well as fairness in test use and testing applications. Although the *Standards* purview is clearly limited to testing—that is, the authors explain that the text only focuses on testing (a narrower term than assessment, according to their definitions)—they admit that it may be useful in other situations although not for every assessment.[3] However, because *Standards* is endorsed by three of the most important professional organizations that represent psychometric scholars and practitioners, it represents mainstream

---

3.   The *Standards* document distinguishes between testing and assessment. Here are the definitions it provides for each in the glossary:

> Assessment—Any systematic method of obtaining information from tests and other sources, used to draw inferences about characteristics of people, objects, or programs (172).

> Test—An evaluative device or procedure in which a sample of an examinee's behavior in a specified domain is obtained and subsequently evaluated and scored using a standardized process (183).

The *Standards* acknowledges that these are not mutually exclusive concepts and that in certain contexts they may be interchangeable. Educational measurement scholars, however, often seem to use these terms interchangeably. George Madaus explains that the terminology doesn't matter because the basic process is the same:

> But strip away the linguistic veneer and, regardless of what noun we choose— assessment, exhibitions, examinations, portfolios, or just plain test—all types of evaluation rest on the same basic technology. That is we elicit a small sample of behavior from a larger domain of interest . . . to make inferences about a person's probable performance relative to the domain. Then, on these inferences, we classify, describe, or make decisions about individuals or institutions. (1994, 77)

While we recognize the distinction that the *Standards* is making, we see assessment and testing more as Madaus explains it because, in part, there is no agreement on what distinguishes assessment from other terms such as testing or evaluation. We argue that the fundamental concepts and standards of validity apply to assessments (which may have results that are not reported in "scores") as well as tests.

psychometric theory and is considered the foundation of psychometric practice. Understanding how the key concept of validity is defined in the *Standards* provides the basics of the concept to build on as we move from testing to assessment, and more specifically to writing assessment. In addition to grounding the discussion of validity in the *Standards*, we also draw on psychometric scholars, many of whom participated in the drafting of the *Standards*, to explain the evolution of the concept.

Validity, according to the most recent edition of the *Standards*, is a unitary concept that "refers to the degree to which evidence and theory support the interpretations of test scores entailed by the proposed uses of tests" and is "therefore, the most fundamental consideration in developing and evaluating tests" (AERA, APA, and NCME 1999, 9). In other words, tests are not in and of themselves valid or invalid but rather the *results* are considered to be valid or invalid according to their intended use. The *Standards* emphasizes that it is the scores that are evaluated, not the test itself: "The process of validation involves accumulating evidence to provide a sound scientific basis for the proposed score interpretations. It is the interpretations of the test scores required by the proposed uses that are evaluated not the test itself. When test scores are used or interpreted in more than one way, each intended interpretation must be validated" (AERA, APA, and NCME 1999, 9). This means, for example, that standardized tests purchased by testing companies for placement into first-year composition cannot be considered valid in and of themselves; locally conducted validation inquiry is needed. Without this local research, the results of standardized exams may not be valid.

Validity inquiry involves constructing a sound argument to support the interpretation and use of test scores from both theoretical and empirical evidence. According to educational measurement scholars such as Cronbach, who was instrumental in drafting the original *Standards*, validity "must link concepts, evidence, social and personal consequences and values" (1988, 4). Messick, another influential voice in the debate on validity, argues that validity uses "integrated evaluative judgment," supported by empirical evidence and theoretical rationales, "to support the adequacy and appropriateness of inferences and actions based on test scores and modes of assessment" (1989, 5). In other words, validation arguments are rhetorical constructs that draw from all the available means of support. Validation is also ongoing and should include a feedback loop: "As validation proceeds, and new evidence about the meaning of the test's scores becomes available, revisions may be needed in the test, in the conceptual framework that shapes it, and even in the construct underlying the test" (AERA, APA, and NCME 1999, 9). The validation process starts with explicit statements about the proposed interpretation of the test, including the concepts or constructs being sampled, the conceptual framework of the test, the knowledge, skills, abilities, processes, or characteristics being assessed, as well as how each construct is to be distinguished from other constructs and how it relates to other variables (9). The conceptual framework also takes into consideration the use of the test results. Evidence used in validity arguments, as articulated in the *Standards*, should come from various aspects of the test including

Test Content: This includes the actual content and its relationship to the construct intended to be tested, as well as an analysis of the theme, wording, and format of items, tasks, or questions, and guidelines for administration and scoring and the relevance of these to the proposed use of the results (AERA, APA, and NCME 1999, 11–12). For example, in writing assessment, evidence about the topic and writing task needs to be considered.

Response Process: This type of inquiry examines the fit between the construct being assessed (e.g., writing ability) and the actual process test takers use in completing the test (AERA, APA, and NCME 1999, 12–13). This has traditionally been associated with both construct and content validity. For example, if an impromptu essay test is administered as a course exit test, then evidence about the writing process students use on the test should be compared to the process students were taught (and expected to perform) in the course.

Internal Structure: Investigation of this type examines how the structure and content among items and components, and their interrelationships, conform to the construct the assessment is intended to measure (AERA, APA, and NCME 1999, 13).

Relationship to External Variables: This type of evidence results from an examination of performances or results of other measures or tests that are hypothesized to measure the same construct; it includes convergent (based on the relationship of the assessment's results and other measures of the same construct) and discriminatory (based on the relationship between the assessment's results and measures of different constructs) evidence; test criterion (historically termed predictive and concurrent validity); and validity generalization, which may include meta-analysis of past validation studies in similar situations (AERA, APA, and NCME 1999, 14–16).

Consequences of Testing: This type of evidence is not to be confused with consequences that have to do with social policy but rather with the test itself; for example, consequences may only be considered as part of the validation process when they "can be traced to a source of invalidity such as construct under representation or construct irrelevant-components." Because it is reasonably expected that some benefits will result from the use of scores and a "fundamental purpose of validation is to indicate whether these specific benefits are likely to be realized, consequences do need to be considered." If a major rationale for a test is based on the consequences of it (e.g., student motivation will improve, teaching will improve), then it is appropriate to determine if the benefit—the consequence—is realized (AERA, APA, and NCME 1999,16–17). A focus on this type of evidence was termed consequential validity.

Sandra Murphy (2007) argues that in literacy assessment evidence related to sociocultural context also needs to be gathered and evaluated because cultural context is critical in determining linguistic competency. This type of inquiry would include not only the test-takers' language proficiency but also how they "make sense of test items and situations," moving beyond simply evaluating the responses as right or wrong (236).

Although there are many types of validity evidence and discussions of validity tend to focus on one aspect over another, or privilege just one type of evidence, it is critical to remember that validity is considered an integrated concept as we explained above. The validity argument needs to consider all of the evidence to "construct a coherent account of the degree to which the existing evidence and theory support the intended interpretation of the test scores for specific uses" (AERA, APA, and NCME 1999, 16). Validity inquiry is ongoing as evidence changes or new information is discovered and may require test developers and users to re-evaluate the test, its uses, and the interpretation of its scores. It also requires investigators to consider alternative interpretations of the results to verify that the test and its results are actually functioning as proposed.

Without the systematic inquiry demanded in the validation process, we cannot assume the content of a test is appropriate, that the scoring of it is accurate, reliable and fair, that the results are interpreted accurately and used appropriately, that the test serves its intended purposes, that the intended consequences are realized, and that other variables are not interfering with the test takers' performance or the scoring of it. For example, in composition placement testing, there needs to be clear articulation of what skills, abilities, and attributes are being tested, how these relate to the composition curriculum and course structure, how the construct is distinct from other constructs (e.g., the ability to compose an essay versus the ability to read the prompt) and what other factors may be influencing the students' performance on the test (e.g., time allowed for the test or writing in longhand instead of on a computer, when the test is given).[4] If students of color are failing in disproportionate numbers—especially when scores are controlled for variables such as GPA, academic preparation, or other factors—assessment administrators need to consider other reasons, such as cultural bias in the prompt or bias in the scoring, that are not related to the students' ability to perform adequately in a particular course or situation. The validation process needs to be ongoing and isn't something done once and for all.

Reliability is the other critical concept associated with psychometrics, and although it is often considered the twin to validity, it is in fact a much more restricted concept that refers to test scoring, which enables the quantification, evaluation, and interpretation of the behavior or work samples (25). According to the *Standards*, reliability is "the degree to which test scores for a group of test takers are consistent over repeated applications of a measurement procedure and hence are inferred to be repeatable for an individual test taker." It also includes the "degree to which scores are free of errors of measurement for a given group" (1999, 180). Reliability is a key concept in the generalizability of the test scores. In determining reliability, test users need to identify potential sources of measurement error, which are divided between those that originate in the examinee—motivation, interest, attention, and application of skills—and those that are external to the examinee, such as differences in testing sites, scorer subjectivity, or variation in scorers' standards (26). Measurement errors are considered random and unpredictable; they are distinct from systematic errors, which are consistent, not random (26). For example, a systematic error will occur if several different writing prompts are given for a placement test and one of the prompts is more difficult than the others. With this type of error, the scores are adjusted to account for the different level of difficulty. Because measurement errors are random and unpredictable, "they cannot be removed from observed scores"; however, they can be summarized and reported in various ways (27). Individual systematic differences, such as an extreme level of test anxiety that impairs an individual's cognitive functioning and therefore affects score consistency, cannot be overcome by statistical adjustment and are not considered contributors to reliability.

Key in reliability studies, according to the *Standards*, is "the identification of the major sources of error, summary statistics bearing on size of such errors, and the degree of generalizability of scores across alternate forms,

---

4.   See Smith's essay, "Assessing the Reliability and Adequacy of Placement Using Holistic Scoring of Essays as a College Composition Placement Test," for a detailed, thorough example of validity inquiry as research. See O'Neill's "Moving beyond Holistic Scoring through Validity Inquiry" for a discussion of how Smith's research functioned as validity inquiry.

scores, administrations, or other relevant dimensions" (27). Information about the population tested is also important. The standard error of measurement, which is "the standard deviation of a hypothetical distribution of measurement errors that arises when a given population is assessed," should be reported (27). Reliability coefficients are typically calculated in the following categories based on different sources of information: scores from administration of parallel forms of a test in different testing sessions (alternate form coefficients), scores from the administration of the same test on separate occasions (test-retest coefficients), scores from the same administration based on subsets or individual items within one test (internal consistency coefficients), and indices of scorers' consistency (27). This last category, what is often termed interrater reliability, has received the most attention in writing assessment. Cherry and Meyer (1993) explain that many different facets of reliability are at issue in the scoring of writing samples, including how interrater reliability, which is the consistency of scoring across all raters, is calculated.[5] Smith argues that in scoring writing samples, interrater reliability should be more nuanced. For example, Smith (1992, 1993) explains how intrarater reliability, the degree to which raters agree with themselves, can be helpful in identifying sources of error. This aspect of reliability considers how consistently one individual scores across the scoring sessions. A rater may be consistent in her scores, for example, but her scores may not be aligned with those from the rest of the scorers. Smith also examines rater set reliability, which involves comparing the two scores given by each rater in the set with the scores given by another set. Looking at how consistently samples are scored by raters across test administrations also needs to be part of determining reliability, according to Smith.

While much of the discussion of reliability for writing tests has assumed essay exams, portfolios and other sampling methods are also subject to scoring by readers. Moss reminds us that these types of "less standardized forms of assessment . . . present serious problems for reliability, in terms of generalizability across readers and tasks as across other facets of measurement" (1994, 6). Though carefully trained readers can achieve acceptable rates of reliability, Moss explains that with "portfolios, where tasks may vary substantially from student to student, and where multiple tasks may be evaluated simultaneously, inter-reader reliability may drop below acceptable

5.   Cherry and Meyer's chapter covers all of the technical aspects of reliability and the use of statistical formulas for calculating it for direct writing tests. It is very helpful for determining how to calculate and report interrater reliability for non-experts. See Hayes and Hatch for more on reliability and writing assessment. Our discussion of reliability here is an overview and introduction, not an exhaustive discussion. For more information, see *Standards*, specifically the following chapters: "Reliability and Errors of Measurement" and "Scales, Norms, and Score Comparability."

levels for consequential decisions about individuals or programs" (1994, 6). Moss concludes that "although growing attention to the consequences of assessment use in validity research provides theoretical support for the move toward less standardized assessment, continued reliance on reliability, defined as quantification of consistency among independent observations, requires a significant level of standardization" (1994, 6). However, these less standardized forms of assessment are often preferable "because certain intellectual activities" cannot be documented through standardized assessments (1996, 6). Moss (1994) suggests that we look beyond psychometric theories and practices in cases where acceptable reliability rates are difficult or impossible to achieve. She recommends hermeneutics because as a philosophical tradition, it values a "holistic and integrative approach to interpretation of human phenomena" (1994, 7). After summarizing the key perspectives of hermeneutics, Moss explains how this methodology would work:

> A hermeneutic approach to assessment would involve holistic, integrative interpretations of collected performances that seek to understand the whole in light of its parts, that privilege readers who are most knowledgeable about the context in which the assessment occurs, and that ground those interpretations not only in textual and contextual evidence available, but also in a rational debate among the community of interpreters. (1994, 7)

Key features of this type of assessment include the recognition of disagreement or difference in interpretations as evaluators bring their expertise and experience to bear on the work. Positions of individual evaluators can change as the rational debate ensues, with the final decision coming out of consensus or compromise. In supporting this approach in specific situations, Moss reminds readers that reliability and objectivity are no guarantors of truth and that they can, in fact, work against "critical dialogue" and can lead "to procedures that attempt to exclude, to the extent possible, the values and contextualized knowledge of the reader and that foreclose[s] on dialogue among readers about specific performances being evaluated" (1994, 9). While Moss recognizes that reliability standards, within the psychometric tradition, are grounded in fairness to stakeholders, she contends that from a hermeneutic perspective, reliability "can be criticized as arbitrarily authoritarian and counterproductive" (1994, 9–10). In the end, Moss is not arguing for abandoning reliability but rather advocating that alternative approaches to assessment theory and practice be considered when appropriate (1994, 10). Her position is especially relevant for those charged with writing assessments because writing is a complex, multidimensional, contextually situated activity. Importing psychometric theory and practices, especially in terms of reliability, may undermine the very usefulness of a writing assessment's results. However, psychometric theory cannot be dismissed out of hand; instead, writing assessment administrators need to draw on language, literacy, and psychometric theories as well as other interpretive traditions to design assessments.

Moss is not the only scholar interrogating approaches to reliability and its role in assessment of complex constructs. Jay Parkes recently advocated that reliability needs to be considered as an argument, much as validity is. In this approach, which is somewhat different from Moss's (1994), the emphasis is on developing methods that support the values—such as accuracy, dependability, stability, and consistency—that reliability represents. This shift to a focus on values, according to Parkes, de-emphasizes the methods, which are most often associated with statistics and quantification, that typically dominate reliability discussions. Parkes argues that methods for determining reliability should "serve as evidence of broader social and scientific values that are critically important in assessment" (2007, 2). In Parkes's approach to reliability, a "coefficient is a piece of evidence that operationalizes the values of accuracy, dependability, stability, consistency, or precision. In practice and in rhetoric, however, the methodologies for evidence reliability are often conflated with the social and scientific values of reliability" (2). If methods don't currently exist for effective assessments, then new methods need to be developed. A sound reliability argument, according to Parkes (6–7), should:

1. Determine the social and scientific values (dependability, consistency, etc.) that are most relevant and decide which ones are most important.

2. Articulate clear statements of the purpose and context of the assessment, which includes making explicit the reasons the information is needed and how it will be used.

3. Define "replication" in the particular context.

4. Determine the "tolerance" or level of reliability needed.

5. Present the evidence from the assessment, which may include traditional reliability data but also other information such as narrative evidence.

6. Pull all of the information together to make the judgment and explain how the evidence supports the final judgment.

Rethinking the approach to reliability, as illustrated by Parkes's focus on argument or Moss's (1994) on hermeneutics, provides writing assessment administrators with strategies for countering a focus on correlations and statistics promoted by others such as test developers and measurement experts. However, it also demands that we engage in discussions of reliability—and validity—in rigorous, informed ways. Asserting reliability because we achieved a .71 interrater reliability rate isn't enough to deem assessment results "reliable."[6]

The next section presents a framework for writing assessment theory that takes these various positions into consideration.

WRITING ASSESSMENT THEORY

As a field, composition and rhetoric doesn't yet have a clearly articulated and widely acceptable theoretical position on writing assessment, a result of the confluence of a variety of factors. First, the interdisciplinary nature of writing assessment makes defining "the field" and determining what research and scholarship (and by implication, what scholars and researchers) are included under the umbrella of writing assessment difficult. As Huot (2002) explains, writing assessment scholarship has been divided into two fields: the K–12 community that comes out of the education tradition, typically publishes in education journals (e.g., *Review of Educational Research, Educational Researcher, English Education*), and attends educational research conferences (e.g., AERA); and the college composition community, usually coming out of English departments, publishing in composition journals (e.g., *CCC, Composition Studies, WPA*) and attending composition and rhetoric conferences (e.g., CCCC, WPA). These two different camps are grounded in different disciplinary traditions, including different values about research and scholarship. There have been attempts to disrupt this divide or to create venues that include voices from both sides (Assesment Testing Network, *Written Communication, Research in the Teaching of English, Assessing Writing, Journal of Writing Assessment*), but that work has had varying degrees of success.[7] While some scholars, such as Brian Huot, Pamela

---

6.   For a fuller discussion of how reliability can be reframed, see O'Neill, "Reliability in College Writing Assessment."

7.   The division, however, between K–12 and college composition studies was not always so pronounced, as Russel Durst argues. In its formative years, many prominent scholars and much scholarship came out of education and its empirical research tradition. During this early period, the college K–12 divide in writing assessment was less defined. In the late 1980s and 1990s, according to Durst, as composition studies developed into a full-fledged field, it rejected empirical research, especially quantitative and experimental methodology, in favor of more humanistic methods. Writing assessment is clearly connected to education and its empirical methods and has suffered from this break. As we draft this in the fall of 2007, the National Council of Teachers of English, which is the parent organization of the Conference on College Composition and Communication, and the Council of Writing Program Administrators have assembled a joint task force to articulate principles and best practices of writing assessment (of which two of the authors are members). While this is a positive sign that the barriers between the different groups involved in writing assessment are breaking down, it is noteworthy that the American Educational Research Association—one of the authors of *Standards* and the primary organization for educational researchers—is not involved,

Moss, Sandra Murphy, William L. Smith, Stephen Witte, and Michael M. Williamson have tried to bridge this divide, most practitioners and scholars continue to operate in distinct spheres, not reading or citing work from the other side. In college composition, this divide is sometimes encouraged. For example, Patricia Lynne argues that composition should reject the education and psychometric tradition, focusing instead on formulating writing assessment theory and practices grounded exclusively in the tradition and values of composition.[8]

A second factor complicating writing assessment (and assessment in general) is another group of practitioners and researchers—outside educational testing organizations such as the Educational Testing Service, ACT, Inc., Pearson Educational Measurement, CTB/McGraw-Hill and the many others that develop, market, and administer tests. To greater and lesser degrees, depending on the organization, testing agencies operate outside of scholarly communities although many of their employees are involved in scholarly organizations or present at academic conferences, with the range of products, methods, and standards of research varying across the organizations. One of the critiques levied against even the best testing organizations is that their goal is not to contribute to the scholarship as much as it is to develop and sell tests. While this claim alone doesn't call into question their research and scholarship, it does demand that we pay close attention to their methods, purposes, and promotions. Organizations that depend on sales of their products have vested interests in supporting certain positions or methods. Ericsson and Haswell (2006) make this point in critiquing much of the research on machine scoring of writing. Testing organizations are driven more by product design and marketing than by a

---

nor were its members invited to join the task force.

8.   Lynne argues that composition and rhetoric as a field should reject educational measurement concepts of validity and reliability, which she feels are inexorably linked to positivism, and develop their own theories and terms that are compatible with social constructionist theory. In her argument, Lynne contends that psychometrics and its desire for objective measurements fails to support assessments that are compatible with composition studies. However, contemporary psychometric theory—as represented by the *Standards for Educational and Psychological Testing* as well as by measurement scholars such as Cronbach and Messick—is compatible with social constructionism. Because some people and agencies (including policymakers, testing corporations, and school districts) do not adequately or accurately apply the theory does not mean the theory is at fault, nor does developing our own terms guarantee that writing assessment practices will be any better. Furthermore, the roots of contemporary composition grew out of education and its research—and assessment. Unlike Lynne, we argue that compositionists need to become informed assessment practitioners who have some understanding of the professional standards and guidelines for assessment. Current psychometric theory, especially validity theory, is critical for those of us who need to develop useful, ethical assessments and to interpret the results responsibly and accurately. Besides, teaching and assessing writing are not the exclusive domain of college composition folks; research, theories, teaching, and assessing practices developed by education scholars make critical contributions to composition studies, and we need to value their contributions.

commitment to contributing to a scholarly tradition. Critiquing or countering the testing organizations are groups researching tests and testing practices such as the National Center for Fair and Open Testing (FairTest), the National Board on Educational Testing and Public Policy, and professional organizations such as the American Educational Research Association.

A third reason for the disjunctions in the scholarship on writing assessment is the focus on satisfying immediate, practical needs for assessments as scholars such as Gere (1980) and Faigley et al. (1985) explain. Much of the published literature on college composition assessment supports their position. For example, both Haswell and Wyche-Smith (1994) and Elbow and Belanoff (1986) note that their assessment work was initiated by institutional demands. Meeting an immediate need—developing a placement method, an exit exam, or some other assessment—consumes composition scholars' and administrators' efforts with little attention given to articulating theories that will inform and direct the assessments let alone working toward developing them (O'Neill, Schendel, and Huot 2002). A notable exception is the research that Smith (1992, 1993) conducted into his placement system. Smith explains that when he took over placement at the University of Pittsburgh, the placement system he inherited conformed to conventional standards, but he was curious about it (1992). His curiosity led him to conduct a series of studies into placement methods that culminated in the expert reader system that he developed. If he had just approached the placement issue as a practical concern, he never would have embarked on the years of research that inspired him to revamp the placement system he directed and contributed to writing assessment theory and practice. While satisfying an immediate need requires our attention, it doesn't mean we shouldn't be thinking about assessment in more disciplinary and scholarly ways, as Smith's work illustrates. For example, we need to consider how a particular placement test or program assessment aligns with literacy and pedagogical theories as well as institutional goals.

Complicating the state of writing assessment scholarship even more is the abundance of district, state, and federal governments' testing mandates, many of which have foreshortened timelines that don't allow for the development and field testing necessary to ensure writing assessments meet the standards for testing articulated by the professional organizations such as the APA, AREA, and NCME. Not all of the mandates for testing are about writing, not all are new; and while most are associated with K–12, colleges and universities are not immune to the regulations. For example, Georgia has had state-mandated literacy exams for graduating from college since the early 1970s, and Maryland has required students to pass the Maryland Writing Test (along with math and other basic skills tests) to earn a high school diploma since the early 1980s. However, the last decade has seen more testing and higher stakes not just for demonstrating basic competencies but also certifying mastery. Consequences are felt at both the individual and institutional levels. The federal government's No Child Left Behind, passed in 2001, ratcheted up the stakes, moving the assessment machine into high gear. The 2006 Spellings Commission report on higher education has jump started discussions about the need for more rigorous assessments in higher education.

In short, although some of the scholars and organizations involved in writing assessment have been working to define and delineate theoretical and practical parameters of the field, as of now there is no one, unified sense of the field and no clear articulation of a specific theory that has been endorsed. The lack of a shared sense of purpose, of common research methods, and of agreement on what constitutes assessment literature interferes with the theoretical development of the field because practitioners and scholars are not building from a large base of work but rather from a smaller, less comprehensive, understanding of theories and practices. As we explain in chapter 2, compositionists continue to use a definition of validity that is over sixty years old. Michael Williamson argues that composition continues to use psychometric concepts in simplistic and outdated ways (1993, 15), which has hampered our ability to develop effective and informed assessments and to create a knowledge base. The divisions between college composition, English education, and pyschometricians exacerbate the already difficult tasks not only of defining the field but also of building new theories and practices from a common body of scholarship. We believe that writing assessment in college—indeed college writing pedagogy and literacy studies in general—should be seen in unity with that in K–12. In fact, both would benefit from a more unified approach that includes K–16 and beyond. After all, students do not enter college as blank slates; they bring with them many, many experiences with tests of writing, whether from state or district assessments, advanced placement exams, or the new SAT.

Given this state of the field, Huot articulated basic principles for writing assessment, drawing across the various sites and traditions, first in his 1996 article, "Toward a New Theory of Writing Assessment" and more fully in *(Re) Articulating Writing Assessment for Teaching and Learning*. By situating recently developed, newer writing assessment practices within current psychometrics as well as language and learning theories, Huot identifies five basic principles for an emerging theory of writing assessment: site-based, locally controlled, context-sensitive, rhetorically based, and accessible. To the five articulated by Huot, we have added another (implied by Huot's scheme but not made explicit): theoretically consistent. Below, we explain each of these in more detail, drawing explicitly on Huot's 2002 schema:

Site-based: Writing assessments are developed in specific sites for specific needs. Procedures are determined by the specific site's resources, concerns, personnel, and other factors.

Locally controlled: The writing assessment should be controlled by the local institution, which is responsible for managing, revising, and validating the process according to the stated goals of the assessment as well as professional standards of assessment.

Context-sensitive: Writing assessments need to take into account the local context, honoring the instructional goals as well as the sociocultural environment. This is especially important for authentic reading and writing of textual communication.

Rhetorically based: Writing assignments, criteria for evaluation, readings, and other processes must adhere to recognizable and supportable rhetorical principles that are integral to thoughtful expression and interpretation of texts. Basic to these principles are the roles that audience, purpose, and context play in the production and interpretation of texts.

Accessible: The assessment program should be transparent to those who are affected by it as well as others invested in the results. Procedures, criteria, rationales, samples, and results should be available to all parties involved in the assessment, and this information should be communicated in language that is accessible to the constituencies.

Theoretically consistent: The processes and procedures of writing assessment must be consistent with the most recent research in language and literacy learning. They should also be consistent with the most recent scholarship in assessment.

Using these principles to get valid results requires those charged with writing assessment to resist standardized, pre-packaged programs. Instead, assessment needs to be considered integral to the teaching and learning that happens in a program. These principles situate assessment as a meaning-making activity that defines what it means to write well and to teach written communication. Assessment requires ongoing inquiry into the procedures, the consequences, and the results to determine how it affects teaching and learning. Huot recommends using qualitative methods for documenting teaching and learning as well as for validation inquiry. He explains that we need to think of "writing evaluation not so much as the ability to judge accurately a piece of writing or a particular writer, but as the ability to describe the promise and limitations of a writer [or writing program] working within a particular rhetorical and linguistic context" (107).

Now that we have addressed the historical and theoretical frameworks relevant to all writing assessments, we turn to a discussion of how individual contexts need to be considered. The following chapter focuses on working successfully within the realities of contemporary higher education, given these historical and theoretical frameworks.

4
ATTENDING TO CONTEXT

As scholars interested in writing, we are used to thinking about context. Contemporary theories of interpretation require that, in our analyses of texts, we consider not only what the text says but how its meaning gets "made." We examine both the local textual context—the particular genre, use of genre-appropriate conventions, how words, sentences, paragraphs, and chapters work together to create an integrated whole—as well as the larger social contexts influencing the ways texts are written, distributed, and read. Likewise, when we examine writing or reading behaviors, we consider not just the behaviors themselves but the contextual factors that can help us explain and interpret them.

Context also influences how we design studies and present results. The research questions we ask, for example, reflect not only our own scholarly interests but current disciplinary discussions and debates—our sense of the gaps in collective knowledge. Our selection of methods, whether library-based or empirical, is guided by our research questions as well as disciplinary attitudes about their appropriateness and efficacy. Moreover, the choices we make about how and where to share our findings are influenced by our purposes and audiences and by institutional perceptions about what counts as scholarship and the degree to which scholarly work should be supported through such means as travel funds and release time.

In much the same way, context informs the decisions we make as teachers. We consider not only what teaching methods are available but how they coincide with the mission of the school, whether they support the goals of a particular program or course, and how we will modify them for different groups of students. Along with factors in our immediate environments, we also acknowledge the influence of external factors: the enrollment trends and budgeting formulas that affect staffing and class size, the scheduling difficulties that result in once-a-week writing classes (where students may retain less from one class session to the next), the accessibility of technology for students, and so on.

Because writing assessment is fundamentally about supporting current theories of language and learning and improving literacy and instruction, it should involve the same kind of thinking we use every day as scholars and teachers. Unfortunately, it often doesn't. The same faculty who readily account for context in their scholarship and teaching often overlook its importance when it comes to evaluating writing for purposes such as course placement/exit, program review, and curricular revision. The same program administrators who challenge placement of students based on context-deficient ACT tests debate the pros and cons of program-evaluation methods without accounting for the history and values of their individual schools, departments, or programs; the backgrounds and goals of their particular students; and the potential implications for faculty and curricula. This tendency to neglect context when it comes to writing assessment is especially well illustrated by professional listserv postings with subject lines like "Help! Good Assessment?" and conference presentations that promote a particular assessment model or rubric, as if assessment methodology can be readily transported between schools and departments and even between disciplines.

What our experiences have shown, however, and what much of the literature on assessment illustrates, is that faculty and administrators charged with assessment ignore context to their own detriment. Beyond the theoretical inconsistencies that arise when context is ignored, there are many related practical problems. If we believe that literacy activities or events occur within—and reflect—a social context, as chapter 3 contends, then assessment (itself a literacy activity or event) must account for context in order to yield meaningful results. Practically speaking, assessments that minimize attention to specific learning situations (e.g., the specific school, students, teachers, curricula) do little to help us improve our teaching. Even worse, their results can lead to questionable decisions about student placement, graduation readiness, and curriculum—especially if there is a disjuncture between what is being assessed and what is being taught in relevant courses. In fact, an unwillingness to account for context may undermine efforts to facilitate a useful assessment in the first place. The faculty who are needed to support an assessment and apply the results, for example, may be unwilling to participate if their beliefs, values, and experiences are not acknowledged early on in the assessment process.

Similarly, upper-level administrators who are not helped to understand the reasons for and implications of a given course or program assessment may be unlikely to support it with money (to pay for data collection, analysis, and reporting) or time (in the form of course releases, for example).

In the next section, we illustrate the importance of considering context by discussing the many environmental factors that can influence the success of assessment initiatives as well as the range of methods available for accommodating these factors.

THE WRITING PROGRAM AS CONTEXT

What defines the writing program?

Where do program values and philosophies come from?

Who are the students?

Who are the faculty?

How are program values supported—or complicated—by course goals, curricula, and instruction?

What does all of this mean for writing assessment?

The way *context* is defined will affect the manner in which it is approached, interpreted, and, to a large degree, how it is assessed. With respect to writing programs—as contexts—definitions vary, as do the reasons for those definitions. What seems possible, in terms of writing assessment, will often reflect how a particular program is viewed and why. Hence, determining how a program defines itself (or has been defined by others) is an important first step toward developing context-sensitive assessments.

At the most basic level, a program can be defined in spatial terms— that is, in terms of where it is located on campus (e.g., on the 2nd floor of the humanities building) or, more typically, where it appears on the university organizational chart (in an academic department? as a stand-alone program or center? spread across the campus, as is the case with writing-across-the-curriculum initiatives?). Writing programs can also be defined in terms of courses and/or curricula. Within this framework, the first-year writing program might be described simply as the English 101 and 102 sequence or the critical reading/writing seminar. Yet, because the design, implementation, and success of any program requires people (students who will benefit from the courses, staff to arrange the physical spaces, faculty to design and teach the courses), most writing programs are appropriately viewed not as objects unto themselves (the way literary texts were read in the 1960s) but as value-laden products of real people with diverse backgrounds, experiences, opinions, levels of status/power, etc. The CCCC Certificate of Excellence for writing programs is significant here in the way that it conceives a writing program as more than just a collection of courses or set of activities. An important part of the certificate-application process involves describing "the principles underlying the program and the ways writing pedagogy grows out of those principles" as well as demonstrating the relationship between key program features and "the needs and opportunities of its students, instructors, institution, and locale" (CCCC 2004).

While discussing the multiple possibilities for defining writing programs may seem like splitting hairs, an awareness of the possibilities can help administrators understand the values that have shaped a program and anticipate the value-based challenges that may be highlighted through an assessment. For example, although the location of a writing program may seem a small factor in creating theoretically sound assessments, it can be a huge issue when it comes to designing *politically* astute assessments. An assessment designed by writing faculty, based on research and theory in composition and rhetoric, promises to work much better for a writing program housed in an English department than for one that is incorporated into a non-academic unit and overseen by an upper-level administrator (e.g., the writing center that is part of a student-services initiative) or one that is de-centralized and spread across disciplines, as is the case with WAC efforts. Similarly, though the difference between defining a program as a set of courses and defining it in terms of the people who teach and take the courses may seem small, it can have a big influence on the types of assessments imagined and supported by administrators and faculty. Though all good assessments involve matching data-gathering methods with particular "research" questions, the first type of program definition might immediately call to mind assessments that examine student achievement through student-composed products alone (e.g., sample papers or exit exams), while the latter, context-inclusive definition would more likely inspire thoughts of accounting for multiple influences on student learning by, for example, surveying and observing faculty, examining instructional materials, and interviewing students.

UNDERSTANDING CONTEXT THROUGH RESEARCH

But how do writing program administrators—especially new ones—identify and begin to understand the underlying values that define a writing program? The fact is, despite larger disciplinary encouragement to identify principles that unite program efforts, many programs lack a sense of program-ness; that is, the faculty who teach the courses have not thought about who they are—what distinguishes them as a program and why. The values are there but they remain hidden or, if visible, they remain unarticulated. This can be especially true of programs that are directed by faculty who were not trained as composition specialists, within coherent, theoretically based programs or those that rely heavily on part-time faculty who may not have been introduced to writing theory and pedagogy and may not have the time or motivation to discuss program values. In such cases, an administrator can start to put together a picture of a program by utilizing research strategies typical of academic work, including textual analysis, archival research, observations, and interviews. (In fact, this type of inquiry, in itself, can be considered a form of program assessment.) In his article on "enculturating" new WPAs, for example, Bradley Peters suggests a rhetorical method of "reading" writing programs that highlights the level of disciplinary expertise shaping program "identities" and how that may correspond with the perceived purpose of individual programs:

To read a writing program, I would propose WPAs keep four major categories in mind. These categories correspond with Richard Lloyd-Jones's schema in "Doctoral Programs: Composition": (1) those that are an extension of the English department's interests, offering practice in exegesis and the genres of critical/literary research; (2) those that are a service of remediation or standards-setting for the rest of the institution, but are not directed by "experts" in the discipline; (3) those that are shaped by one faculty member who has developed interest, or has already been trained, in rhetoric and composition and can acquaint TAs or adjuncts with reasonably timely practices; (4) those that are nourished by the collaborative participation of several faculty committed to rhetoric and composition, whose various specializations contribute to a masters or doctoral degree in the discipline. (1998, 124)

Of course, as Peters himself points out, the danger in relying too heavily on sorting mechanisms like this is that they tend to downplay the complex dynamics typical of any program—an issue we will discuss in great detail later in the chapter. In fact, because of their typical complexity, some programs may, in Peters's words, "elude" the categories "enumerated" (124). Despite its drawbacks, categorization like this which privileges coherence can be a good way to *begin* to understand the values and beliefs that have shaped a program. For instance, while it would be unfair to say that all writing programs designed by faculty outside the discipline of composition and rhetoric are somehow impoverished and all programs "nourished" by faculty within the discipline are sound (an interpretation encouraged by the word choice and progression in Peters's/Lloyd-Jones's framework), it is often the case that differences in disciplinary expertise *do* lead to different kinds of initiatives, different decisions, and different outcomes. It's important to realize, though, that there are differences within the categories that not only work to disrupt any tidy categorical framework but also influence (in both good and bad ways) any administrative initiative, including assessment.

To uncover the differences and, ultimately, the true *dynamics,* of a writing program, administrators need to look not only at points of coherence but at the tensions. That is, we need to dig beneath the surface of the "text" and conduct deeper, more sustained inquiries. One means of uncovering hidden textual meaning is to assume the role of "historian," as Ruth Mirtz did when, as a new WPA, she sought to understand both the evolution of her writing program and the roots of particular program artifacts, such as a problematic placement exam. Her methodology included reading long-forgotten graduate student files, department newsletters, administrative memos, and Faculty Senate minutes—and "interpreting" these materials in light of personal observation/experience, institutional histories, and disciplinary conversations (Mirtz 1999). Muriel Harris (1999) suggests a similar

approach for understanding the "local knowledge" that shapes writing centers (and reflects the institutions that support them), adding to the list of
relevant archival documents such materials as "yearly reports, memos, analyses of usage data, journals and notes the director keeps, tutoring training materials and curricula, proposals, [and] announcements and bro-
chures that present the center to its various constituencies" (2–3). In fact,
Harris finds archival research so essential to successful administrative work
that she urges writing center directors to "set up and maintain a research
archive" for their centers (14)—a sentiment echoed by Shirley Rose (1999)
in her call for "preserving" writing program documents as a way for administrators to "recover the values and beliefs that have informed" program
decisions so that we can, among other things, make better administrative
decisions (107–8).

To complement text-oriented program research, the scholars cited
above suggest pursuing other forms of inquiry that more directly reveal the
human dimension of writing programs. For Mirtz, it was important to "balance" textual analyses with "oral histories" gathered from students, faculty, and administrators (123). Similarly, Peters used interviews with various
groups of people to "go beneath the 'surface'" of and "deconstruct" his initial rhetorical reading of his program (125–26). Harris's menu of "diverse
research methodologies" includes student and faculty questionnaires, student interviews, and "usability testing" of sign-in sheets and online writing
center services. In fact, what all of these scholars suggest is that, like many
empirical research pursuits, understanding a writing program requires not
just multiple methods of inquiry but methods that help answer particular research questions—in this case, questions about the people who comprise a "program" and how their attitudes and experiences have shaped,
and continue to shape, program identity, program initiatives (such as writing assessments), and success of those initiatives.

What follows is a discussion of the key human components of any writing program: the students, the faculty (or, in the case of writing centers,
tutor/consultants), and the administrator(s). Given the specific purposes
of this book, we focus not just on the importance of understanding who
these groups are (e.g., their motivations and experiences) but how differences within the groups may influence the design and implementation of
writing assessments.

WHO ARE THE STUDENTS?

Context-sensitive program definition often starts with students—much as
classroom teaching begins. In fact, it is not unusual for programs to be
initiated and then labeled in terms of presumed student preparedness or
abilities. There are developmental writing programs for "developmental"

students, first-year composition programs for students who are deemed ready for college-level writing, honors composition programs, etc. Such definitions rest on the general assumptions that (1) we can easily categorize learners, and (2) the differences between groups (e.g., in ability, achievement, preparedness) far outweigh any differences among individuals in those groups. In fact, the mechanisms often used to place students into these distinct programs (e.g., standardized test scores, single timed writing samples) rest on the same assumptions. Yet, as chapter 3 underscores, there is much more to learners and learning than can be successfully captured in a single, isolated evaluation—especially if that evaluation minimizes the influence of social context. For this reason, a "developmental writer" at University A may not necessarily be the same as a "developmental writer" at University B (no matter how much the standardized-test designers want us to believe otherwise). In fact, it is often the case that there are big differences among students who are labeled "basic" on the same campus. (Again, if a standardized placement test is used to identify students as "basic," the differing reasons for the score [e.g., test anxiety/inexperience, unfamiliarity with test concepts or terminology, illness, inability to focus] are not taken into account.) For these reasons, writing program administrators should argue for multiple indicators of student performance and should carefully weigh the data generated by standardized testing with knowledge of the individual particularities, or differences, that are harder to measure but which have a significant impact on classroom learning and achievement.

Knowledge about students can be gathered through the types of research methods mentioned earlier. Again, a good starting place is often a study of written documents, such as program reports, memos, syllabi, assignments, and instructor support materials. Such study is usefully guided by questions like the following:

- Who are the (basic, first-year, honors-level, etc.) writers in the program?

- What are their similarities? Their differences?

- How are they identified as basic, first-year, honors, etc.—and why?

- What are their attitudes about education, writing, particular writing courses, the program?

- How might student identities, experiences, and attitudes shape assessment?

One of the best sources of information about students is the students themselves. As scholars like Linda Adler-Kassner (1999) and Susanmarie

Harrington (1999) have pointed out, we can learn a great deal about students' experiences with and attitudes about writing through such means as formal interviews, conducted as part of an empirical research study (Adler-Kassner); writing assignments (such as literacy narratives) that highlight perceptions about writing and the writer; and informal discussions or classroom "interactions" with students about their writing backgrounds (Harrington 100–2). While a WPA may not have the time or inclination to conduct a formal research study, he or she can certainly pursue informal, classroom-based research by teaching the courses that are most directly informed or affected by large-scale assessments (or, in the case of a writing center, to tutor on a regular basis). This is sometimes hard to do—especially if the administrative position is tenure-track and a department tends not to assign tenure-track faculty to introductory courses (or provide release time for one-to-one tutoring)—but it is one of the best means of gathering information about student experiences, attitudes, and abilities. When he was WPA at his former school, for example, Brian taught composition almost every year, even though he received little on no compensation for doing so. This experience enabled him to see students' writing for himself, to talk to students about their writing, and to use his developing knowledge of these students to challenge a placement mechanism (ACT scores) that minimized important differences among students.

Writing faculty, too, are a good source of information about students, but for reasons we discuss later, it is rare for faculty to define groups of students—and what they need—in the same way. In fact, differences in faculty perceptions of students are important to acknowledge and understand because they can have a huge impact on how an assessment is designed and implemented. At Cindy's former university, for example, there is little consistency in how faculty view developmental students and describe their needs. Some faculty view developmental writers in terms of academic preparedness (e.g., the writing skills they need to succeed in the "regular" first-year course); others define them in terms of social acclimation (e.g., the "life" skills they need to succeed in an unfamiliar social context). In fact, the first category can be further separated into, for example, those faculty who view essential skills as including mostly grammar and punctuation, and those who see overall rhetorical and analytical abilities as especially crucial. Though all of these definitions can be supported to some extent, each will call to mind a different type of assessment. Faculty who define the "developmental writing problem" as a matter of correct grammar, for instance, will likely support assessments that focus on errors in writing. Those that define it in terms of critical thinking will want assessments that highlight analytical abilities. Those faculty members who privilege acculturation may resist any kind of assessment that focuses solely on improved writing ability, without considering improvements in dispositions toward school, attendance, participation, etc. While a program director may have the freedom to design an assessment using any definition—or, more likely, definitions—he/she wants, if faculty are going to participate in it, then their definitions will need to be acknowledged, discussed, and accounted for.

Finally, program administrators can learn much about students from university administrators, such as the developmental-education coordinator, dean of students, admissions counselors, academic advisors, and institutional-research personnel. In the case of students in particular programs, often there will be an administrator who may be doing regular assessments of student achievement, retention, and progress toward graduation. Such administrators will not only be able to provide anecdotal information about students, but most are willing to share statistical data (e.g., on demographics, rate of retention, degree-completion rates) from their own ongoing assessments and from reports written by other campus administrators. In addition to developing a better knowledge of students, communicating with other administrators can help WPAs determine administrative attitudes toward particular groups of students and the courses (or programs) designed to serve these students. Such attitudes (which are sometimes based on empirical research, sometimes on personal belief) can go a long way toward explaining the particular histories of writing assessments that a new WPA may inherit—histories that may impact current and future assessment initiatives, as well as the overall effectiveness of the WPA.

Again, for purposes of assessment, it is important to understand both the similarities in how students are viewed and the differences. As we suggest above, for example, and as research makes clear, student perceptions of themselves as writers do not always coincide with faculty and administrator perceptions of these same students. In fact, self-perceptions of students who are grouped together under a single label (e.g., developmental, first-year, honors) often differ widely. One important implication for writing assessment is that there may be a gap between what one "stakeholder" (student, faculty member, administrator) believes an assessment is, or should be, measuring and what another interested party believes. Through her study of a group of "basic" writers, for instance, Adler-Kassner (1999) found that while many students perceived their key writing "deficiencies" as "unsuccessful information transfer" (79) or the inability to write about subjects that don't interest them (85), neither the placement mechanism (a timed impromptu essay) nor the required basic writing course (supported by faculty and administrators) accounted for these issues in any obvious way. The unfortunate results of disjunctions like these are frustration and even anger on the part of students who often may not know why they have been placed into a particular class or feel that the class does not address their writing needs. As Harrington (1999) puts it, as a result of not "understand[ing] their audience," many writing programs end up not being as "rhetorically effective" as they could be if they took the time to actually talk with students (105).

WHO ARE THE WRITING FACULTY?

As indicated at the end of the previous section, faculty experiences and attitudes can also impact assessment. While it is fairly common these days to see student learners in terms of context (i.e., in terms of their educational preparedness, cultural background, and attitudes toward school and writing), we typically don't adopt the same perspective toward instructors. Though theory suggests that context is key in any discussion of learning and, hence, teaching effectiveness, many universities continue to rely on standardized measures, such as institutional—or even national—student course-evaluation surveys that minimize context by asking students to comment on aspects of the course or abilities of the instructor divorced from environmental factors. In other words, we are accustomed to measuring good teaching in much the same way that we are used to measuring learning—through standardized, one-size-fits-all assessments that often provide little insight into how a particular instructor might help her particular students learn better. Teachers, like students, both reflect and are defined by multiple contexts. They have individual histories, cultural identities, and disciplinary knowledge that affect not only their general approach to teaching but also specific teaching practices.

While differences in faculty experience and expertise often make a writing program rich and interesting, they can create special challenges for writing program administrators who are trying to design meaningful assessments—especially if they believe, as we do, that faculty support or "buy in" is crucial to the success of assessment efforts. At the basis of most writing assessments is a definition of what makes writing good or effective. Yet, unless the writing program has achieved a high level of theoretical and pedagogical consistency, the ways that faculty answer this question may differ, depending on their particular teaching backgrounds and disciplinary training. Someone who is conversant with the current literature in composition and rhetoric, for example, likely would define good writing in terms of effectiveness for a particular rhetorical situation (i.e., a particular purpose and audience). Someone not conversant with current research and theory might define good writing as simply clear and correct writing. Each of these definitions would inspire a different conception of appropriate assessment methods.

Of course, even if faculty agree on definitions of assessment constructs and basic assessment design, they may interpret the results of a given assessment differently, which creates another challenge for a WPA. As William Smith (1993) acknowledges in his discussion of the pros and cons of holistic scoring of placement exams, there is a host of contextual influences on how the exams are read and evaluated. These influences include how long the readers can read and "efficiently" score, how many essays are being read, how the rating scale is designed, how raters understand the scale, and whether students clearly fit the categories designated in the scale (150–55). Similarly (and even more relevant to our present discussion), scholars like Michael Williamson (1993), Judith Pula and Brian Huot (1993), Arnetha Ball (1997), and Bob Broad (2003) have found that despite attempts at "norming" raters so that they read consistently, and in line with a published scoring rubric or guide, assessment decisions are nonetheless influenced by such environmental factors as raters' reading and writing experiences, disciplinary training, teaching experience, scoring experience, ethnic identity, and attitudes toward a particular writing assessment and/or use of results.

Beyond the influences outlined above, power relations can also influence how assessments are designed and implemented. Such relations can be institutional, reflecting differences in pay, status or rank, length of service, and job security; or they can be disciplinary, emphasizing differences in theoretical and pedagogical currency or cachet. In practice, the relations are fairly complex (e.g., an un-tenured assistant professor who is well published in a well-respected discipline may be seen as having more institutional "clout" than a tenured full professor who hasn't published in twenty years). Generally speaking, though, faculty who feel they have more institutional and/or disciplinary power will participate differently in assessment initiatives than faculty who feel they have little or no power. A useful illustration of this point is made by Allene Cooper, Martha Sipe, Teresa Dewey, and Stephanie Hunt (1999) in their discussion of an innovative portfolio-based assessment initiative designed by composition specialists to replace a questionable "minimal competency exam." During the assessment pilot, tensions between two key groups of portfolio readers (graduate TAs and adjunct faculty) arose not just due to differences in experience but because of differences in perceived status and security. The TAs, who had recently "quadrupled" in number, saw the assessment as a way to learn more about composition theory and, thus, build professional credentials; adjunct faculty, who had recently been described as "a dime a dozen" by the university president, perceived the assessment as a vehicle for exposing their weaknesses as teachers and getting them fired. Importantly, the comments on and about student writing reflected the degree of perceived threat just as much as they represented a particular teaching philosophy or approach.

Faculty differences can also affect the ultimate use of assessment data—how the results are acted upon (a process that assessment experts term "closing the assessment loop"). This is especially true when faculty most involved with assessment have one idea about what constitutes good writing and how such ability should be measured, but those actually teaching the courses important to assessment efforts have very different ideas. Data collected through holistically scored exit portfolios of revised student writing, for example, may seem irrelevant to classroom teachers who are committed to traditional single-paper grading that emphasizes mastery of discrete writing tasks and minimizes revision. A similar situation arises when, at the program level, evaluators are looking for evidence of one type of ability and classroom teachers are not emphasizing that ability. A small-scale study of the developmental writing program at Cindy's former school indicated, for example, that while the program exit exam is designed and read to emphasize analytical writing, many developmental-writing faculty do not emphasize this type of writing in their courses.

So, given the prospect of initiating assessment efforts with faculty who are diverse in many ways, what can writing program administrators do to increase the possibility of success? Again, a good starting point is to think in terms of a research project, by generating questions that will lead to helpful answers. Here's a start:

- Who teaches writing and why?

- What is the instructor's approach to teaching and what rationale does she/he provide for it?

- What are the instructor's attitudes toward students? Toward writing? Toward a particular writing course?

- How is the instructor positioned within the program, in terms of job status and security, disciplinary expertise, and experience?

- How will the answers to these questions inform assessment design and implementation?

One way to begin understanding who faculty members are (including what their theories of language and learning are, where the theories come from, and how their theories will affect assessment efforts) is to simply talk with them—especially those who teach writing regularly. This can be done in a variety of informal and formal ways. An informal means of investigation is simply to make time for one-to-one or small-group conversations with as many faculty as possible. Stopping by a colleague's office for ten minutes during posted office hours, inviting a colleague for coffee (your treat), or arranging a small-group lunch outing to the campus food-court are all good opportunities for asking questions about writing, teaching, and assessment. A more formal means of researching the faculty is through planned forums or brown-bag sessions on writing issues/questions important to the program. Such activities can be especially helpful if faculty members are encouraged to ask their own questions about program identity or definition and to work toward answers together, with the administrator serving as a facilitator.

Classroom observations, including pre- and post-observation discussions, are another formal means of gathering information about faculty. Though observations themselves can give administrators a sense of what faculty members do in their classrooms, it's the one-to-one discussions that highlight the values about teaching and learning that can influence attitudes toward assessment. It is in such discussions, for example, that WPAs can ask instructors why they have chosen particular approaches, assignments, and assessment methods. Such discussions can be complemented with review of syllabi, assignments, and other handouts. Additionally, if assessments are already underway, a new WPA can simply participate, observe, and listen as faculty readers talk about how they are assessing student writing and why. Then, following the protocol Broad (2003) suggests, the WPA might use her observations as a basis for faculty to openly discuss scoring trends and the multiple reasons for them—perhaps as part of a department retreat or lunch-hour forum.

To find out how writing faculty are positioned within a program or department (again, this will highlight the power issues), administrators will want to consider obvious factors like pay, benefits, office space, and course load along with less obvious factors, such as relationships with other faculty in the department, degree of support from the department chair and other administrators (e.g., the dean), faculty-development opportunities, and relative autonomy. Because the first kind of support (pay and benefits) often dictates the level of other kinds of support, it's good to find out as soon as possible (even before being hired) how writing faculty are compensated. If faculty members are tenure-track, they typically will be compensated at the same rate as others within their department and, by virtue of their tenure-track status, will benefit from a certain degree of institutional respect. They will usually have their own offices, some choice about their teaching schedules, freedom to experiment with teaching approach and methods, and the benefit of colleagues who, for the most part, will listen to and respect what they have to say. For writing faculty who are adjunct or part-time, or non-tenure-track but full-time, chances are very good that the level of institutional support will not be as great—and the less obvious forms of support (type of work space, degree of freedom to innovate, etc.) may reflect this. Even if the pay is the same (or proportionately the same), non-tenure-track faculty will not feel as secure in their positions and, therefore, may respond differently to assessment efforts. Along with interviews of faculty and knowledgeable administrators, review of university and departmental documents (meeting minutes, memos, relevant handbook material, etc.) can highlight more subtle power relationships. Something as seemingly benign as the use of "they" or "them" to refer to adjunct faculty in department minutes can reflect relevant power disparities and accompanying tensions.

Once a WPA determines who the writing instructors are, in all of their complexity, he or she will want to think hard about the implications for assessment. One approach that, thankfully, has become less common (largely due to feminist critiques of traditional administrative methods) is to downplay or even ignore faculty experiences and attitudes and just design an assessment in one's own image. Before an administrator adopts what is known as the "WPA-centric" approach, though, he or she should understand that it rarely works—especially in the long run. While colleagues may grant the program administrator a certain degree of expertise (especially if these colleagues are part-time faculty), they will not appreciate being told what to do (which will be the perception even if the WPA just suggests a new direction for assessment) or being excluded from discussions and decision making.

Beyond the level of common courtesy and diplomacy, there are very practical reasons for not forcing ideas on others. Again, as we suggest earlier, if there is no "buy in" on the part of key stakeholders, there will likely be no long-term success. Further, some assessment initiatives inspire wholesale shifts in views of how writers learn, the role of the teacher in such learning, and so on. The literature on portfolio assessment, for example, suggests that in moving from single-product grading to portfolio evaluation, teachers often experience a shift in how they respond to writing and interact with students, generally. Because differences in teaching philosophies often run deep, touching "founding insights, beliefs, [and] axioms" (J. Harris 1997, 42), it can be very dangerous for a writing program administrator to impose a paradigm based on a conflicting philosophy or, worse yet, to suggest that faculty members with differing philosophies are uneducated or "out of it." What seems like an innocent or commonsense effort to be more current or more "cutting edge" to the WPA can feel like a threat not only to a faculty member's teaching identity but to his or her very self-concept and worldview.

A better means of ensuring the success of assessment efforts is to investigate faculty experiences, interests, and values, and recognize similarities and differences at all stages in the assessment process. This approach allows faculty to feel included and to see their interests and ideas acknowledged, if not actually represented, in assessments. In fact, differences in experience, if acknowledged and discussed, can be effectively used to create more valid writing assessments, as Smith (1993) found through his student-placement research. Smith discovered that the accuracy of first-year student placement into composition courses improved at his school when teachers, who themselves regularly taught the courses, placed students based on their own local knowledge of student preparation and abilities rather than according to scoring rubrics that are meant to minimize the impact of teacher differences. While an assessment like this one may be based on philosophies that differ from those held by faculty, the fact that diverse experiences are acknowledged through faculty involvement can make a big difference in terms of attitude, morale, and openness to changes based on assessment results.

WHO IS THE WRITING PROGRAM ADMINISTRATOR?

Many new program administrators assume their positions with a strong sense of purpose. In fact, many people who pursue administration do so because they feel they have the skills necessary to maintain successful programs or improve weak ones. While there are indeed many WPA success stories, there are also numerous accounts in the literature of struggles and setbacks. These struggles often have little to do with disciplinary expertise or career preparation, but instead result from a lack of self-knowledge and/ or an inability to appreciate the potential tensions between how we view ourselves and how others view or "construct" us. In fact, even when program administrators have a good sense of their strengths and weaknesses, their administrative efforts may falter because the staff, faculty, and administrators with whom they work perceive them differently than they perceive themselves. To get a sense of how the WPA position is being constructed by others, it can be helpful to employ the same kinds of investigative techniques used to understand how the writing program as a whole is defined.

One way to analyze the position—or positioning—of the WPA is to think in organizational terms. Where does the WPA position exist in the institutional hierarchy? This varies greatly from institution to institution and can have a great impact on assessment. The typical institutional position for WPAs is within a department and "under" the department chairperson. (For many writing center and WAC directors, administrative positioning can sometimes be more complicated because such directors may be English faculty members who are supervised by the department chair but who report to an academic vice president or provost.) Where a WPA is located within the institutional organizational structure can have important implications for assessment because organizational structure will, in many ways, influence the flow of resources (and, as suggested above, access to resources is often accompanied by increased credibility and status). Given that the larger financial decisions are made by people highest in the hierarchy (VPs and provosts), it is not hard to imagine the many institutional layers that must be confronted by a department-based WPA looking for money to fund a large assessment initiative. Typically, a request for money would need to start with the chair and then be forwarded to the dean and then the VP or provost. A WPA who works more directly with upper-level administrators has more direct access not just to decision makers but to their financial resources. Of course, sometimes the presumed (i.e., theoretical) power relationships are different from actual practice. At some schools, for instance, the institutional position of the WPA is low, but the everyday, practical status is quite high—especially if a school is emphasizing writing and/or if the WPA is respected by faculty and administrators. If status is high, then the WPA will likely be able to get more support (financial and otherwise) for assessment. In any case, successful WPAs figure out how they are positioned and how to make effective arguments to administrators based on an awareness of their perceived status.

With respect to how an administrative position is perceived by faculty, it can help to start again with organizational charting. In programs where writing is mainly taught by adjunct faculty and graduate teaching assistants, the WPA will be positioned "above" most classroom instructors as a supervisor or manager. The challenge in this arrangement is that any administrative initiative will be seen as coming from above—even when the WPA attempts to be collaborative. Many former and current WPAs have described frustrated attempts to challenge institutional hierarchies through such means as co-directorships and collaborative mentoring (see, for example, Schell 1998 and Harrington, Fox, and Hogue 1998).

A related challenge can arise if most of the writing courses are taught by full-time faculty, as is often the case at small liberal arts schools. Here, no matter how WPAs attempt to position themselves, they will be seen at best as a consultant or facilitator. Such perceptions of the WPA can be good in many ways (e.g., they often inspire the kind of collaboration necessary for long-term success) but also may create special challenges. As Rebecca Taylor (2004) explains, full-time tenure-track faculty who support a writing program (in this case a well-established WAC program) can be fiercely independent—both in terms of their teaching and the assessment of teaching efforts (59–60). Thus, for any large-scale program assessment to work at her school, she avoids approaches that would threaten faculty members' "academic freedom or pedagogical decision making" and is careful not to be "perceived as 'overseeing' in any way" (60).

Disciplinary histories and tensions can also affect WPA positioning—particularly at the department level. Because it is sometimes still the case that faculty members outside of composition and rhetoric believe that "anyone can teach writing," it may also be the case that there will be a prevalent philosophy of "anyone can be a WPA." If this perspective is predominant, it will be difficult to get faculty teaching composition courses to take seriously what the WPA says—even (or sometimes *especially*) if the WPA is a composition and rhetoric expert. It can also be the case that a WPA is viewed differently if there is a degree program in writing or composition and rhetoric, which suggests a certain kind of status and recognition for writing, if not the discipline of comp-rhet as a whole. It is important to note, too, that the WPA can position him/herself in unproductive ways. In his analysis of a narrative written by Wendy Bishop and Gay Lynn Crossley about challenges Bishop experienced as a WPA, Tim Peeples (1999) implies that WPAs who struggle in their positions often do so because they have constructed their administrative stories in terms of a larger comp-rhet master narrative in which writing program directors are forever the victims of colleagues and upper-level administrators who don't understand or appreciate their work.

While it is true that institutional hierarchy and departmental history can play a part in perceptions of a writing program administrator, so, too, can other factors. For example, feminist compositionists such as Sally Barr-Ebest (1995), Hildy Miller (1996), and Eileen Schell (1998) have written convincingly about how larger social factors, such as a WPA's gender, can affect how her/his administrative efforts are perceived. If, as Barr-Ebest suggests, for example, a female WPA is much more likely than her male counterpart to be viewed by colleagues and other administrators as a service practitioner (rather than a serious scholar), her administrative work (including assessment) may not be valued.

To determine how a particular administrative position at your institution has been—or is being—constructed, it can help to start with questions like the following:

- Are there program or department documents that describe the WPA position? What do they say about departmental (institutional) role(s) and values?

- What do other documents, such as administrative letters and new-faculty handbooks, say about the relationship between the WPA and others?

- Is program management presented as a single person or as multiple, knowledgeable people working together to make a program successful?

Questions like these can then be explored using some of the same research techniques mentioned earlier. Interviews with former administrators, for example, can be a particularly useful way of determining relationships among key groups within a writing program. Note how these administrators talk about faculty—as colleagues or underlings? As people who know what they are doing (i.e., professionals) or as people who are lucky to have a job? Rhetorical analyses, which both highlight the multiple competing discourses that situate WPAs as well as the possibilities for negotiating these discourses, can also be helpful. By reading his position as a nexus of competing local and institutional "conversations," for instance, Peters recognized that the ultimate viability of his position and success of his work depended upon an ongoing "dialectic" between the writing program and upper-level administration (1998, 130–34). The usefulness of a rhetorical approach is underscored by Peeples (1999), who promotes "postmodern mapping" of the WPA position. Such mapping invites both an analysis of the complex factors that influence WPA positioning and an appreciation for the multiple relationships among factors. By understanding how the administrative "text" can be read differently, depending upon the factor or relationship of factors emphasized, WPAs can begin to understand how slight changes in actions and responses can reposition a WPA in powerful ways.

OTHER CONTEXTUAL INFLUENCES ON WRITING ASSESSMENT

While it has always been the case that people and policies outside of a program or department have influenced assessment, these days external entities are exerting even greater influence because they, themselves, have more at stake. It is not enough anymore to simply say that you run a good school with quality programs; you have to show it—to students, parents, accrediting agencies, and the legislators who control state funding. This increased pressure on upper-level administration to show results of student learning is now filtering down to departments and programs by means of increased demands for "measurable outcomes" and "use of results"—especially with respect to core curriculum or general education courses.

Because the perspectives on writing and learning—and on faculty and students—represented by different administrators can conflict with the perspectives of the WPA, and because these conflicting perspectives may have very different philosophical roots, the impact of external contexts on writing programs can be both powerful and challenging. This impact is typically illustrated in the comp-rhet literature by descriptions of the dean or provost who defines good writing in terms of correctness and, so, can't understand why a grammar-based placement test or exit exam is problematic. In reality, though, such conflicts are often much more complex, reflecting not just an individual's preference or viewpoint but an entire institutional culture and/or history. When, as a new WPA, Mirtz researched the genesis of the placement exam being used at her school ("a multiple choice grammar and usage test"), she discovered that the exam didn't so much reflect an individual or even small-group agenda as much as ambivalence among English faculty about having to create a placement process that would correspond with "the literal politics and the tacit ideologies" of the state legislature and educational system existing during the late 1970s and early 1980s, when the test was adopted (127).

Another related extra-programmatic challenge for a WPA can occur when administrators who appropriate money and/or release time for assessment (and, thus, feel justified in approving assessment methods) hold traditional views of assessment that do not acknowledge context and/ or are not generally grounded in current learning and teaching theories. Though accrediting agencies allow for great latitude in how faculty and directors design assessments, emphasizing, for example, that assessments must generate data that instructors can actually use to improve teaching and learning, university administrators, in the interest of gathering data that can be easily reported in a consistent form across disciplines, will often impose a standardized structure or set of criteria that makes sense to them, but not necessarily those who are conducting the assessments. One good example of this urge toward standardization is the university general education assessment for which many different disciplines are involved in gathering and presenting data, but one entity (the university general education committee, which may or may not include someone from English, let alone a writing specialist) does the final interpreting and reporting. Sometimes, such a group will even design evaluation rubrics for writing courses without consulting faculty knowledgeable about writing assessment. The typical reaction to this, captured well in Chris Fosen's (2006) article on the influence of general education initiatives on writing programs, will be feelings of indignation and exasperation with objectives that seem totally out of line with values and beliefs embraced by writing administrators and faculty.

While it can feel good to complain about upper-level administrators who may know little about writing and even less about assessment—or who may be reluctant to fund good assessments—the most successful WPAs will attempt to first understand where other university administrators or agencies are coming from and then try to see where there are openings to do meaningful assessments but still meet the perceived needs of these administrators. Fosen, for example, not only reflected deeply on the differences between the historical purposes of general education and those of most English departments and writing faculty, but he recognized the importance of resisting the temptation to simply "react" to top-down assessment mandates and to instead be "pro-active" by, for instance, encouraging knowledgeable faculty to join key university committees, including the General

Education Advisory Committee, where they could "raise concerns," "connect with faculty facing similar issues with assessment," and "learn the convoluted rhythms of upper administration" (26).

In fact, sometimes, if simply shown how a theoretically grounded writing assessment will fit university requirements, many upper-level administrators will be glad to let experienced and knowledgeable faculty spearhead assessment initiatives. As Richard Haswell and his colleagues discovered when their university's faculty senate mandated the development of both a required writing placement exam and a "rising junior" test, interested administrators, such as the dean and vice provost, "listened" to their concerns about how plans for these exams were "shaping up" (as single impromptu essays to be graded holistically) and their proposals for more theoretically sound alternatives. As Haswell and Susan Wyche (2001) explain, "We discovered the first truth about institutional assessment of writing: no one feels competent to do it. . . . [T]he administration was delighted to find writing teachers who said they had an innovative plan and were eager to get a problematic task out of their own hands" (15). Sometimes, too, with a little investigation, what looks like an assessment mandate that ignores values and beliefs shared by comp-rhet specialists may have simply been presented in an unfamiliar way, with specialized, unfamiliar terminology (e.g., "outcomes" versus "objectives" or "reporting group" versus "department/program"). Additionally, administrators, knowing little about accreditation themselves, will interpret accrediting agency language more narrowly than it should be interpreted—and they just need a department chair or program director who is more knowledgeable to explain why the interpretation can be broader (which is where a WPA's knowledge of information included in our first two chapters can be extremely helpful). That is, rather than seeing situations like these as capricious attempts to control others, it can help to view them as a natural reaction to assessment demands that upper-level administrators themselves do not always fully understand.

THE PRACTICE OF ASSESSMENT: DETERMINING WHAT THE CONTEXT WILL SUPPORT

In the ideal assessment world, all interested parties would define assessment concepts and interpret assessment needs and results in similar ways. The program administrator would simply ask what faculty, staff, and students wanted; draw upon his or her knowledge of current theory and practices; design a meaningful assessment; and secure immediate moral and financial support from upper-level administration. Yet, as we have illustrated throughout this chapter, this type of agreement rarely occurs— even in departments with long historical commitments to writing and to composition and rhetoric as a discipline. Most often, there are disagreements and/or differences in priorities that must be openly acknowledged and carefully negotiated. And even in the most congenial of circumstances, compromises of one kind or another must be made to insure that the important work of assessing writing gets done at all.

In the following chapters we discuss three major focuses for writing assessment (students, programs, and faculty) and offer ways of applying knowledge of assessment history, theory, and contextual factors to practical assessment problems. We try to be both idealistic and realistic in our approach, knowing that often the best assessments are those that demonstrate attention to current theory and practice while also acknowledging the constraints of the local assessment context.

5
ASSESSING STUDENT WRITERS— PLACEMENT

Placement is one of the most common reasons WPAs and writing teachers become involved in writing assessment outside the classroom. Many writing programs offer more than one starting point for students to satisfy the written communication requirement (or its equivalent) for their undergraduate degrees. Having multiple courses requires a selection process so students receive appropriate instruction. As we have noted throughout the volume, a fundamental practice of using information from writing assessment in a principled and valid way is to document that the decision(s) based on test data have positive educational benefits for individual students. This documentation of a use of writing assessment is called *validation inquiry* or a *validity argument*. For writing placement, important evidence for a strong validity argument centers on the performance of the student in the class in which she was placed. Because we believe that making good decisions about assessment for placement is a local, contextual activity requiring local knowledge and expertise (because all curricula, students, and institutions are not the same), we cannot be theoretically and practically consistent if we recommend specific procedures over others. However, we certainly favor those approaches that are consistent with the theoretical framework of this book, such as the use of student writing to make important decisions about students' writing instruction. In addition to the obvious need for developing procedures that examine student writing according to criteria relevant to the courses in which students are placed, the assessment procedures have to be realistic in light of the needs and challenges of the students, the teachers, the curriculum, and the missions of specific institutions. Our purpose for this chapter is to outline various approaches available in the literature, highlighting how each can be used to make the best placement decisions and to provide some explanations and models for documenting these decisions through validity inquiry.

WRITING-LESS PLACEMENT

It is common to refer to procedures for assessing writing that actually contain no writing at all as *indirect writing assessment*.[1] These kinds of assessments have long been used for placement. For example, over fifteen years ago

---

1. We resist using "writing assessment" or even "indirect writing assessment" to describe any set of procedures that do not involve students actually writing.

Brian Huot surveyed around 1,100 writing programs and found out that about half of them still relied on placement procedures that did not include teachers reading student writing to make placement decisions (Huot 1994). Probably the most common source of information used to make placement decisions is the verbal score from the standardized college admissions exams, ACT or SAT. The exams primarily examine a familiarity with an academic vocabulary and have a statistical relationship to success in college, though there is reason to believe that their statistical relationship to success in first-year writing courses is questionable. The advantage of using SAT or ACT verbal scores is that most colleges require them anyway, so there is little or no associated cost or effort in using them. Of course, there are also some problems with using ACT or SAT verbal scores. These scores, by themselves, are not recommended by testing developers and companies for placement purposes.

A common measure used to make placement decisions without looking at student writing is a test of grammar, usage and mechanics. At one point the Test of Standard Written English (TSWE) was the most commonly used example of this type of measure. The value and appropriateness of these exams depend upon how much emphasis an individual program places on mechanical correctness in its curriculum. Like other measures that do not use writing, tests of grammar, usage, and mechanics are practical, convenient, and relatively inexpensive and cost-efficient.

The COMPASS placement exam is a popular writing-less procedure for placement that represents a departure from traditional approaches. It is advertised that COMPASS places over 750,000 students a year and has been adopted by whole state systems as their primary placement procedure. The COMPASS is untimed and taken on a computer. Students are given a passage to edit, and their scores are tabulated based on the correct number of edits for a given passage. Again, the appropriateness and accuracy of a set of procedures that makes placement decisions based upon a student's ability to edit a passage she did not write depend upon the emphasis and importance of editing as an independent skill in the curriculum. There is some evidence that exams like the COMPASS are not effective for placement in courses which emphasize rhetorical skills and writing as a process. For example, during a one-year period, at an institution where Brian oversaw the placement process, students were required to take the COMPASS because it was a mandated placement procedure for the community college to which basic writing had been outsourced. Students took the COMPASS, and the writing program also considered the ACT verbal and teacher examination of a single or portfolio sample of their writing.[2] The

---

2.   For a fuller explanation and discussion of this placement system, see Hester et al.

COMPASS placed over 400 more students in basic writing than the other methods. Around 250[3] of these students selected the higher placement and enrolled in the regular writing course at the four-year institution. Around 70 percent of these students earned As or Bs and over 90 percent earned Cs or higher. Clearly, COMPASS did not accurately place students at the four-year institution, but what is more troubling is that thousands of students throughout an entire state's community college system received basic writing placements when an overwhelming percentage of them could have passed regular composition at a four-year school. Tests like the COMPASS are inexpensive (less than a dollar per student) and easy to administer. Those interested in placement procedures that do not include writing might consider them an improvement over timed multiple-choice tests of grammar, usage, and mechanics.

TRADITIONAL WRITING ASSESSMENT

The next group of procedures we consider involves students supplying a writing sample that is read for placement purposes. As we detail in the history chapter, traditional procedures for reading and assessing student writing like holistic, analytic, and primary trait scoring provide a means for a consistent scoring of student writing. Analytic and primary trait scoring ask raters to give separate scores for different traits exhibited in a piece of writing. Analytic uses a generic notion of writing quality, whereas primary trait scoring asks raters to evaluate an assignment-specific writing quality—for example, the clear use of chronological or sequenced order in writing directions or instructions. These different scores can be aggregated to supply an overall score for a piece of writing. Individual scores can also be weighted. For example, content and/or organization can be worth more than the use of transitions. The primary difference between holistic scoring and the other types is that with holistic scoring, raters are asked to designate a single score for the entire paper based on an overall impression and not on an examination of individual features. A holistic rubric typically provides a general description for each score point that identifies the salient features for the texts that fall into that range, but it doesn't expect raters to be evaluating each trait individually as in analytic scoring nor is it focused on only the defining features of the type of writing required as in primary trait scoring.[4] Research comparing holistic, analytic, and primary trait scoring does indicate that analytic and primary trait are a little more

---

3.   The other 150 students either enrolled in other institutions or did not enroll that semester.
4.   See appendix C for sample scoring guides. Additional examples, as well as help in creating one's own rubric, can be easily found through a Google search for "writing assessment rubrics."

consistent and accurate, but the small difference between the scores often does not warrant the possibly considerable increase in expense (Veal and Hudson 1983). Trait scoring does offer the advantage of providing detailed information about what a student's writing strengths and weaknesses might be. In this way, trait scoring has a much stronger diagnostic value, since the student, her teacher, and the institution would have a stronger idea of the student's writing and her instructional needs. However, if an institution making placement decisions does not need or will not use detailed diagnostic information, then holistic scoring is probably the best choice of the three procedures for placement scoring. Because of its efficiency in time and money, holistic scoring is probably the overwhelming choice among these three methods. Holistic scoring is still a viable option for institutions wanting to include student writing in efficient and relatively inexpensive placement procedures.

EXPERT READER SYSTEMS FOR PLACEMENT

Over the last two decades, local experimentation with methods for reading student writing and making decisions about placement for students has spawned a number of placement programs that involve the reading of student writing but do not require the use of holistic or other traditional types of scoring. Practically speaking, placement programs that ask for readers to make a decision rather than give a score require much less paperwork and labor, both in terms of the effort involved in reading student writing and the amount of administrative work required to translate raters' scores into student placement into specific classes. Using traditional scoring for placement creates the need to sum the scores from the two raters and to set a cutoff score for each one of the placement decisions. Scoring leaders have to read a wealth of the papers to be scored to locate sample, or anchor, papers for each one of the score points. For each of the score points, the scoring leaders write a description, based on the samples and anchor papers they have reviewed, that articulates the types of texts that fall into that category. Readers have to be calibrated and recalibrated to agree with each other before and while live papers are read and scored.

In contrast, expert reader placement scoring systems call on readers to make a placement decision directly, rather than to score a paper. Peggy O'Neill (2003) notes that giving a paper a score and making a placement decision based upon the reading of a paper are very different activities. While teachers might disagree on the quality of a paper, they can still agree on a placement. Scores require an additional level of abstraction beyond the relevant content knowledge and experience teachers normally possess for reading student writing to make educational decisions in and outside of the classroom. Two studies (Huot 1993; Pula and Huot 1993) that asked holistic raters to talk aloud while reading for placement demonstrated that teachers made placement decisions and then looked for the appropriate numerical score on the rubric. It makes sense that teachers would feel more confident making a decision about what class a student might profit from than they would about a numerical score from a rubric with which they had been trained to agree. This research establishes the theoretical and psychological efficacy of asking teachers to read student writing and make direct decisions. In addition, work done by William L. Smith (1992, 1993) at the University of Pittsburgh (we've discussed this work in detail in the history and theory chapters) established a placement scheme in which teachers who were experts for specific classes made one placement decision about the class for which they were most expert. Smith compared the placements from holistic scoring with those using the same readers in his direct-decision method and found that readers were more accurate and reliable when they made placement decisions directly. Talk-aloud protocols of teachers reading student writing for placement (Huot 1993; Pula and Huot 1993; Smith 1993) and for classroom purposes (Edgington 2005) contrast sharply with those in large-scale assessments (Wolfe 1997). Edward Wolfe (1997) found that raters who agree with each other at a higher rate read in more focused and narrow ways than those who agreed at a lesser rate in large-scale writing assessments using holistic scoring.

Expert reader systems can take many forms, depending upon the number of placement decisions individual institutions need to make. For example, one of the earlier expert rater programs used at Washington State University required that all essays be read by a single reader who was expert for the most regularly enrolled class (Haswell and Wyche-Smith 1994). Readers made a single decision about whether a student's writing placed her into that class or not. In this manner, 60 percent of students were placed into a class on a single reading. The remaining 40 percent of students' writing received an additional reading that placed students into the remaining classes in the curriculum. Expert reader systems also have been used to read portfolios, and because these reading schemes do not necessarily require second readings, calibration training, and additional administrative work, they are cheaper overall (Hester et al. 2007). Hester et al. (2007) reported on a multi-year placement study in which portfolios were read for under four dollars apiece, a price that's less than what many programs using holistic scoring pay for reading a single sample of student writing.

In addition to being cheaper, expert reader systems for placement are also potentially more flexible. Holistic scoring requires constant calibration training and ongoing rubric revisions based upon the use of different prompts, which requires being in contact with a group of raters. An expert reader system, on the other hand, assumes that the training and rubric are within the readers themselves, based upon their experiences teaching and reading student writing for placement and other purposes. Their preparation[5] is their expertise. They read appropriately and make reliable and valid decisions about students because they know the curriculum, the students, and the art and craft of teaching writing. Of course, an expert reader system relies on a writing program having shared values in terms of teaching, learning, and evaluating. Without common expectations and standards across sections, results from an expert reader system may be idiosyncratic and inconsistent, because each teacher would be representing his or her individual expectations instead of the program's.

Since expert readers do not need to be trained, placement systems have been developed that do not require all readers to convene in a single room to be calibrated, read anchor papers, or discuss a specific rubric or its revision. Instead, some of these expert reader systems have used the Internet so that teachers could discuss writing through e-mail (Allen 1994) before making decisions. Other systems have been designed so that students could compose online. Readers could then access student writing electronically, read the writing on their own time, and submit their decisions directly online. Administrators could have student writing read for placement without having to have some common face-to-face reading (Harrington 1998). This flexibility and the potential of putting the placement program online can be crucial for many institutions that need to be able to collect writing samples and produce placements in a short period of time during summer orientation or other periods when time is at a minimum. This virtual scheme for placement also allows individuals to interact and talk about their readings, keeping the best of placement scoring without the labor and effort involved in scheduling common reading times when all placement readers must be present.

Not only do expert reading systems reduce costs and increase flexibility of how the scoring can be accomplished, they also introduce the possibility of only having a single reader for some placement decisions. Although Smith's (1992, 1993) original scheme used two readers, subsequent placement programs have relied on one reading of a piece of writing by an expert who made a single decision (Haswell and Wyche-Smith 1994; Hester et al. 2007). While holistic scoring is usually associated with reading and scoring single samples of student writing, it has also been used to score portfolios for placement purposes (Daiker et al. 1996; Willard-Traub et al. 1999). Nonetheless, placement schemes that do not require two readers for

---

5.   Expert readers are prepared, not trained. In the same way, we call those who give scores *raters* and those who make decisions *readers*—it is, we believe, an important set of distinctions based upon a more social, interactive, and realistic notion of the way human beings make meaning with and through texts.

each student sample of writing need not report interrater reliability, which refers to the consistency of scores given by two or more raters on a single student performance. Instead, we recommend like Hester et al. (2007) that such programs report on instrument reliability, using student samples from other years or using samples read by other readers to give a sense of how reliable the overall placement program is. As we have discussed in other parts of the volume, it is important to monitor and insure reliability, whether instrument or interrater; otherwise, it is difficult to make a convincing argument for using the results of an assessment to make important decisions about students.

DIRECTED SELF-PLACEMENT

One of the more innovative approaches to placement to come along in the last few years— actually it's ten years ago since the first article was published—is Directed Self-Placement (DSP), which is sometimes called Guided Self-Placement. DSP was invented and first used by Dan Royer and Roger Gilles (1998). DSP was developed at Grand Valley State University because they were unhappy with the results of their placement process. Instead of traditional placement procedures that look at student performances like tests, scores, sample essays, or even portfolios of student work, Royer and Gilles decided to ask students to decide on their own placement. At orientation, a representative of the writing program would talk to a hundred or so students about DSP, distributing a checklist which asked students to think about their experiences with writing in and outside of school and to make a decision about whether or not the student thought she would profit from a basic writing course before moving on to the most commonly enrolled course in the curriculum. While Royer and Gilles (1998) reported a drop in the number of students who enrolled in basic writing courses, they were, nonetheless, happy with their system and the placements of their students. Clearly, a placement system that involves students in the decision-making process has many potential advantages. Several schools have adapted DSP, and an entire edited collection (Royer and Gilles 2003) features the various schools using it and the different versions that have evolved.

In addition to the version of DSP spawned and promoted by Royer and Gilles (1998; 2003), there are other versions that allow students to make their own decisions but structure the process a little differently. David Blakesly (2002) describes a program in which students make their own decisions but only after an appointment with an academic advisor. Blakesly notes that while the proponents of DSP tout how inexpensive it is, the program he describes did not save the institution any money, since funds spent for teachers to read student writing were diverted to pay the academic advisors who helped students make placement decisions. Other institutions have expanded the process students go through to make a placement decision. A system for a large urban commuter institution that calls itself Guided Self Placement (Harrington 2005) has students navigate a process over the Internet that gives them information about how they might reflect on their reading, writing, and learning experiences in terms of each course offered in the curriculum. For an urban, commuter school or other institutions at which students cannot always be on campus, putting the process on the Internet makes great sense because students do not live on campus and only visit campus to attend classes. In the Guided Self-Placement system (Harrington 2005), students receive a detailed account of each of the courses they might place into, complete with writing samples that indicate to students what kind of writing is expected at each level of the curriculum. In addition, students are given a list of frequently asked questions and are prompted to contact the writing program so that they might speak to a writing teacher should they have trouble making their decision.

AN INTEGRATED PLACEMENT MODEL

Although we have so far considered the attributes of the major types of writing placement procedures singularly and on their own merits, it is also possible to use such methods in combination with other forms of placement. For example, a school that did not want to use a writing placement test for all students could consider students' SAT or ACT verbal scores or scores from another writing-less measure, exempting some students from further placement procedures if they scored above a certain level. In this way, writing-less placement procedures could reduce the number of students that a school would have to test for placement. In other words, depending upon the first-year writing curriculum of a specific school, a writing-less measure could be an effective screening device for students who would be successful in the most commonly offered, credit-bearing course for first-year writing students. Placement decisions for students who are candidates for basic or remedial courses according to the writing-less method, would be determined by an evaluation of a writing sample, ensuring that students are not placed in remedial, developmental, or non-credit-bearing courses based solely on their knowledge of grammar or vocabulary, their ability to edit another person's writing, or some other writing-less measure.

Multiple measures for placement can be structured in other ways and include procedures like DSP, portfolios, writing samples, homegrown writing tests and other procedures that furnish a full picture of student writing ability and suitability for a particular curriculum. In addition, as we discussed earlier, some of these procedures might be available for students through the Internet or in other digital formats. As a culmination of the section of this chapter on various approaches to assessment and the different kinds of procedures postsecondary institutions use and can use, we provide a model for a writing-placement program at a large institution, since great numbers of students who need placement information for registration within strict time limitations are often a major dilemma for schools who want to collect and use robust information about student writing while at the same facing daunting fiscal and logistical problems in providing such information.

In our model program at Phantom U, students begin the writing-placement process online, accessing a placement portal that they can navigate to successive Web sites, depending upon a host of factors, since no two students' journey through the placement process need be identical. We narrate a fictional pathway that highlights the many possible activities and interactions a student might access, though in no way do we mean to imply that every student would engage in all of the activities we demonstrate in our model placement program, or that a student would have to follow the path we outline below. To complete the placement process, students would choose the path that most suits their needs and understanding of the institution.

A student starts at a site that provides her with an overview of the writing courses first-year students take, complete with sample assignments, curriculum, course goals or objectives, and requirements for each of the courses. Such a site might also include statements, reflections, and comments from students and teachers about each of the courses in the curriculum as well as samples of student work and the criteria teachers typically use in determining student success and progress in specific writing courses. This site, as all others in the portal placement system, allows students to ask questions of composition teachers and former composition students or take part in a chat session about the courses offered at the institution with teachers and former students. As at every site in the system, students have the option of making virtual, face-to-face, or phone appointments to meet with teachers and/or advisors.

Once our mythical student determines she knows the curriculum and range of courses that make up the possible placements and has had all of her questions answered, she can then proceed to access her relevant academic information, including high school grades in English and scores on standardized tests like AP, ACT, or SAT. She would also be able to complete a profile and checklist of her experiences and interests with reading and writing in and outside of high school. The site also provides statistical information about the placement of other students with similar grades, test scores, and profiles and their levels of success in each of the choices of writing courses in the curriculum. Again, the student could ask questions over e-mail, take part in a chat with other students and/or teachers, or make an appointment with a teacher and/or advisor to discuss her past accomplishments and experiences and her suitability for one of the placement choices.

Up to this point, the system we have been describing looks like a virtual DSP program with access to more information about curriculum and individual academic records, not to mention the access to students and teachers. Depending upon the curriculum, the experience, and the academic record of our mythical student, the next Web site would allow the student to submit a writing sample—either by composing a piece of writing in response to a given prompt, a portfolio of previously composed writing, or a combination—for feedback from teachers who know and teach the curriculum. The feedback options could include the possibility for the student to sit down with a teacher face-to-face or in a virtual mode, whichever is most convenient for her. There is, however, no logistical reason why this type of online system even needs to require that students complete a writing-less placement procedure, because, in our view, the best way to determine students' placement is actually to look at student writing. The placement decision itself could be regulated by a number of institutional factors or guidelines, including or limited to teacher feedback, academic record, and writer's profile, or the completion of a writing sample and positive feedback from teachers. All of the specifics could be governed by the institution, including the possibility of the student making her own decision after receiving as much feedback, including having her writing read and responded to, as she deems necessary to make a good decision. This model, it seems to us, incorporates many of the major means for placing students within a manageable, flexible environment controlled by the student and tolerable to the institution, including its resources.

VALIDATION

At this point, we have probably exhausted most if not all of the ways institutions can structure the placement process. Regardless of how placement decisions are made, it is incumbent upon individuals using any form of assessment (even student self-assessment) to offer some evidence that the educational decisions being made by or for students are profitable to the students involved. While we have talked already about the concept of validation and its importance to all assessment procedures, it's important for us to situate validity inquiry within the specific context of placing students into college-composition courses.

One of the first kinds of evidence necessary to make a compelling argument for the degree of validity of the placement decisions being made by a placement system should focus on the courses students are being placed into. It is important to establish that all of the courses in the curriculum, including and perhaps especially the alternate basic writing course, provide a sound, consistent, and coherent educational experience for students who place into it. Questions such as, "How well do students who place into basic do in other writing courses they take at the university?" and "How well do basic writing students' performances in other writing courses and in their university careers compare to students who do not take basic writing?" are important questions to ask for validation research. We should also ask questions about how well students are profiting from the other courses in the curriculum, although basic writing is probably the most crucial site for this kind of inquiry because a basic writing course requires students to do extra work, often requires them to pay for a class that might not count toward graduation, and frequently carries a stigma that a student isn't smart enough or ready for college. Unless we can present evidence that all of the choices of a specific placement program provide sound educational experiences for the students who take such courses, we will have difficulty making an argument that our placement program produces valid decisions—that is, it provides sound educational experiences for students.

There are different kinds of evidence crucial to making a case that a placement system is generating valid[6] decisions. One common way of marshaling evidence for decisions based upon a placement program is to compare placement with grades or other valued measures. There are two common ways to consider various influences and relationships between a student's placement and other indicators such as grades. We can calculate the percentage of students who earn a specific grade (or other measure—we'll discuss some possibilities later) with a specific placement or use a t test to produce a correlation statistic.[7] There are probably not a lot of reasons to use a correlation, since it cannot by itself predict probability or isolate a specific variable, though we can run more than one t test, depending upon the number of variables. If you want to use inferential statistics, we recommend using a regression analysis[8] because it allows a more nuanced treatment of the statistical relationships between variables and can consider the various influences of different variables while at the same time providing a p value (a percentage of the probability that results are not due to chance). We favor using simple percentages and have found that even for reporting

---

6.   We use the term *valid* to mean all of the necessary kinds of information including, but not limited to, the reliability of the decisions to be made on behalf of an assessment.

7.   Offices of institutional assessment or measurement or colleagues in psychology or education can help WPAs and writing teachers without expertise in setting up and calculating inferential statistics.

8.   The 1999 *Standards for Educational and Psychological Testing* is very clear about the preferred use of regression analysis over correlations: "Regression equations are more useful than correlation coefficients, which are generally insufficient to fully describe patterns of association between tests and other variables" (1999, 21).

instrument reliability at statistically savvy meetings such as the American Educational Research Association, percentages were perfectly acceptable.[9]

While grades are certainly the most common way that placement can be verified, we, like others (Smith 1992, 1993; Hester et. al. 2007), are not convinced that they should be the only means used to determine accurate placement. Grades are determined by student performance, which is influenced by a variety of factors such as attendance and engagement. In our experience, many of the students who do poorly in first-year or required writing courses fail not because they have been inadequately placed in terms of their writing competencies, but because they have failed to attend class regularly, submit work on time, or complete assignments. Using grades, then, will indicate that anyone who did not do well in class was inaccurately placed, which may not be true, giving the sense that the placement system under review is doing a poorer job than it really is.

Another common practice, one we endorse (though not necessarily as part of validation inquiry), is to have all students in required writing courses compose an essay on the first day or in the first week, so that each teacher can make sure that the placement for each of her classes is relatively accurate. We endorse this practice because it can help teachers move students into more appropriate courses in the beginning of the semester to insure students receive the most appropriate instruction. However, as Smith (1992, 1993) found, this method is not really a good measure of how well teachers believe students are placed because many teachers find it difficult to suggest alternative placement once students are already in their classes. This method does give teachers the opportunity to move students who are particularly unsuited but can't really be used as evidence that students have been appropriately placed.

Smith (1992, 1993) explored various possibilities for providing evidence that students had been adequately placed and found that a survey given to teachers around the sixth to eighth week of a fifteen-week semester worked best. Querying teachers earlier in the semester didn't appear to give them enough experience with students' writing, and waiting until the end of the semester made teachers unwilling to question student placement (and decisions were more likely to be influenced by other factors and to reflect final grades). Hester et al. (2007) also employed this method over a six-year period. Evidence from teacher surveys is more compelling than grades alone because teachers are making a judgment about student suitability for the courses they are teaching without the confounding variable of how hard students work. In addition to asking teachers about the suitability of

---

9. Our advice to use percentages is in direct opposition to some like Hatch and Hayes (1999) who favor more complicated statistical formulae like the Spearman Brown or Product Moment for calculating interrater reliability.

placement, both Smith (1992, 1993) and Hester et al. (2007) queried students about the suitability of the courses into which they had been placed, asking them about the level of difficulty in relationship to their level of preparation. Information from students, combined with information from teachers and course grades, provides the most comprehensive form of evidence about placement procedures. While we have so far referred to surveys, there is no reason why other kinds of data might not be collected. For example, focus groups of students and teachers separately and together might yield information about the suitability of individual placement and provide important feedback about other aspects of the placement procedures, such as student ease with the placement times, locations, writing prompts, and other affective issues that could be modified or revised to improve student use and overall comfort and satisfaction with the system.

It's important to keep in mind that validation inquiry is a crucial part of using any assessment, whether it be a commercially developed test bought off the shelf or DSP in which students make their own decisions. What's necessary in any writing assessment situation is that the student profit from the decision made through a specific set of procedures. In placement, this means that it's important to document that students benefit from the structure and procedures used by a particular program to make placement decisions. Validation is an ongoing process (Cronbach 1988; Huot 1996, 2002; Moss 1998) not unlike reflective practice in which practitioners continually monitor their own actions to make sure that the assessment produces results that profit students and do no harm (Moss 1998). Consequences from specific placement procedures that might unduly reward students whose home-language literacies most resemble the prestige dialect used in school or procedures that help reinscribe gender and/or other inequitable power relations by encouraging students to under- or overestimate their abilities on a regular, systemic basis (Schendel and O'Neill 1999) need to be monitored, examined, and mitigated. It's crucial to keep in mind that validation inquiry is essentially empirical research and that all forms of data-driven inquiry start with questions. Given the various forms placement can assume, our validation questions should also vary, as we illustrate above. As a further example, consider the Internet-based model we outlined above. Certainly, an important set of questions for that model would revolve around students' access to technology and their ability to navigate a complex portal containing several Web sites. In addition to information provided by students about their experiences with the system, it would also be important to look at the number of Web sites students usually navigate and how many of these sites are actually used to make the placement decision. Just as this chapter has assumed that there is no one-size-fits-all placement, there cannot be a uniform set of procedures for validation, although students, teachers, and administrators should all be consulted in terms of the questions that drive validation for placement.

Our intent for this chapter was to provide a wide range of possibilities for placement procedures. Any decisions about placement should be rooted in the principles we outline in chapter three and elsewhere, which argue that appropriate writing assessments should be locally controlled and site-based. This is especially important for placement procedures since they are inextricably connected to the courses offered and the curriculum within these courses. The choice of placement procedures is fairly daunting, ranging from writing-less scores produced by college admission tests to checklists or surveys through which students can make their own placement decisions. Nonetheless, any of the various placement procedures enact certain attitudes and assumptions about literacy, learning, and the teaching of writing. While it is a truism that placement procedures need to fit institutional mission, student population, and teacher vision, it's also important for an institution to align theoretically its placement procedures with the goals and objectives of the program itself. Whether an institution decides to use a combination of writing-less and traditional or expert reader procedures, it should attempt to see its placement procedures as an extension of its overall educational goal(s) for students in writing classes. While the model we suggested, which allows students to electronically navigate various ways of achieving accurate placement, might seem at present beyond or unnecessary for some institutions, we are confident that technology will play a larger role in the years to come. In addition, while we have not recommended one kind of placement over another because of our belief that placement and other writing assessment choices should be local matters, we feel as if we have given WPAs, teachers, and other administrators enough information about placement to make informed decisions about placement and to use validation procedures to insure that placement programs support accurate and educationally sound placement decisions.

6

ASSESSING STUDENT WRITERS— PROFICIENCY

In this chapter, we discuss how to design appropriate assessments for evaluating writing proficiency. Like placement, discussed in the previous chapter, this type of assessment evaluates the performance of individual students beyond the classroom. Proficiency testing can be done for a variety of purposes—for example, exit from developmental or first-year composition courses, certification for writing in the major, graduation, or exemption from required writing courses. Sometimes a proficiency exam is tied to a specific writing course—such as a portfolio produced in a developmental writing course that is assessed beyond the individual course instructor to determine students' readiness for the credit-bearing course or a WAC portfolio that draws on writing completed in courses across the curriculum that certifies students' accomplishment of more advanced academic writing. At other times, this assessment involves writing produced outside of a course—such as a stand-alone impromptu essay written under standardized test conditions. In some cases, both types of writing samples may be used—writing done during regular courses as well as an extracurricular writing test. Regardless of the evaluation methods used, however, the primary purpose of proficiency assessment—like placement—is to make decisions about individual students. Naturally, proficiency assessments can also serve secondary purposes, such as contributing data to a program review (see chapter 7) or to the evaluation of instructors and instruction (see chapter 8). These secondary purposes, as we discuss elsewhere, do not demand that each student be assessed and that the consequences of that assessment be directed toward the student as with proficiency evaluation. In designing and implementing a proficiency assessment, then, it is critical to keep in mind that the primary function is to evaluate students as writers or their writing abilities.

As we have discussed in previous chapters, the purpose of an assessment is a critical factor in determining its design and implementation. When consequences are high stakes—and let's face it, almost any assessment can be considered high stakes for those who experience the consequences directly—we have an even greater responsibility to ensure that the methods are appropriate and theoretically sound and that the results are valid; that is, they improve teaching and learning. Specific writing assessments, including proficiency, need to be determined by local context but informed by what we know about language and learning as well as by psychometric theory. Our goal, in this chapter as well as the book as a whole, is not to give you a recipe that provides step-by-step directions for your writing assessment needs; instead, we are trying to help you learn about the basic ingredients and how you can use them to make informed decisions about your own assessments. As we explained in chapter 5 about placement, we believe that making good decisions about proficiency is a local, contextual activity requiring local knowledge and expertise. Because curricula, students, and institutions are not the same, we would not be theoretically consistent if we recommended specific procedures over others. However, in proficiency as in other writing assessments, we favor approaches that use student writing to make important decisions about students and instruction. In addition, we realize that writing-proficiency-assessment procedures also have to be tolerable—that is, they must consider the needs and challenges of the students, the teachers, the curriculum, and the missions of specific institutions.

Because assessment methods can be used for a variety of purposes, the specific details—such as what will be examined, how it will be evaluated, how the results will be used, what are the consequences for all participants, and how will the results be validated—need to be determined for each particular situation. For example, a portfolio of student writing can be used for placing entering students into the writing curriculum or for certifying proficiency for graduation. However, the specifics of the portfolio will differ dramatically depending on the purpose. The entering students' portfolios, as explained in chapter 5, will be read according to the specific curriculum in each course in the first-year program. Likely, the readers will be the teachers of these courses, and the consequences will be that students will take a specific course based on the evaluation results. Ongoing validation will consider (among other things) how adequately the courses meet the students' needs or how students perform in subsequent writing situations. As you can imagine, for proficiency assessments the specifics will be vastly different. While placement is trying to determine where the student should enter the writing curriculum, proficiency usually determines if the student is ready to exit the curriculum or if the student is competent for the next stage of writing challenges. For example, a portfolio used as a graduation requirement will have different types of writing, different evaluative criteria for judging the writing, and different judges, than one used for placement. First, the portfolio contents will be different because the writing will draw from the students' college experiences. Second, the evaluative criteria will also be different because it will be aligned with the curricular goals of the college. Third, the readers should represent not just the entry composition courses but also the next stage of the students' education, such as a writing in the major course or even the workplace.

Although there are differences between placement and proficiency, as we have explained, proficiency assessment shares its general purpose with placement (i.e., assessment of the individual student) and some methods (e.g., portfolios or impromptu essays), and in some situations, it may also overlap with placement. For example, students transferring from other institutions may need to demonstrate proficiency in writing through a portfolio because the curricula and requirements between the two institutions don't match up exactly. However, depending on the results, the assessment may also function as a placement test if it indicates the student needs to take the first-year composition course.

As in the previous chapter on placement, our goal in this chapter is not to say one method is always better than another. However, we do explain why some methods are preferred in most cases or why some are less likely to be useful in certain situations. In the remainder of this chapter, we discuss questions to consider before implementing a proficiency exam and follow that with general types of writing-proficiency assessments. We conclude by addressing validation inquiry.

GENERAL CONSIDERATIONS

If you do not already have a writing-proficiency exam in place but are considering one—or if your institution already has one and you are reviewing it—it is important to explore whether or not you need to have one. Consider what effect the proficiency exam will have on curricula, writing instruction, student learning, and the writing program. Are college writing administrators pressuring you to construct a writing-proficiency exam? Is the impetus coming from faculty across the disciplines? Does the state policymaking board require a writing-proficiency assessment? Questions such as these are important to consider, and responses to them may not be easy or mutually exclusive. Finding out why a proficiency exam in writing is needed—or why some people think it is needed—can help you in other ways. For example, the investigation may reveal that the institution or program does not need a separate writing-proficiency exam because, by and large, students are exiting the program or university with the requisite writing competencies. Or you might discover that testing is not the best way of determining proficiency. Maybe requiring a course of all students—such as a writing intensive course in the major—is enough and no formal program for assessing individual students is needed. Maybe the inquiry will determine that the call for a rising junior writing exam is connected to a lack of effective writing instruction across the curriculum and that focusing on an effective WAC/WID program would be more effective and efficient at improving student writing than mounting an institution-wide writing assessment. Maybe you will discover that without a formal writing-assessment requirement for all students, the institution—i.e., the majority of administrators, faculty, and students—isn't willing to make a serious commitment to writing instruction.

However, if a writing-proficiency assessment is required by the state governing board or some other agency, then you may not have a choice about whether or not you need to do it. In some cases, you may not have any input into the assessment, as was the case at all public colleges and universities in states such as Georgia, Florida, and Texas that have required state writing assessments. However, you might also be in a situation similar to the one Richard Haswell (2001) and his colleagues at Washington State University faced in which the state required writing assessment but didn't mandate the specific test or procedure. In a situation like this, the best interest of the students and the writing program may depend on you to take the lead on this, as they did at WSU, so that you can make the most of the situation for improving teaching and learning. After all, if a proficiency assessment is required, the institution will have to have one, and it might opt for a national, standardized, machine-scored, impromptu essay that is relatively cheap but probably not aligned with the teaching and writing done in your curriculum. A test like that won't have the potential to impact teaching and learning in the same ways that a locally administered writing assessment has.

By articulating the need—even gathering evidence to determine if you need some sort of writing proficiency assessment—you can begin to determine responses to some of the other questions that are key in planning an assessment such as

- How do we define proficiency?
- What evaluation criteria will we use?
- What are our resources?
- How will the results be used?
- How will it serve teaching and learning?
- How will we conduct ongoing validation inquiry?

In responding to these questions, remember that you need to balance what theory and research indicate for best practice with local needs, resources, and expectations. Given your particular curriculum, how is writing proficiency defined? It isn't effective to just import a rubric or assessment wholesale from another program. As Broad (2003) discusses in *What We Really Value*, answering these types of questions is an opportunity for your program to articulate its own values through discussions, review of student work, and other activities associated with assessment. However, learning from other institutions' experiences can help you understand the range of possibilities available to you and provide insight into ways to accommodate the constraints of your own situation. Remember that any writing assessment needs to be tolerable to its local context and improve teaching and learning. As you plan, therefore, consider long-term goals as well as short-term ones that will contribute, over time, to the long-term goals.

Below, we review some of the basic types of writing proficiency, which can help you discover ideas to adapt in designing and implementing a writing assessment that satisfies your local needs and is also theoretically informed.

COMMON PURPOSES OF PROFICIENCY TESTING

Our aim in this section is to identify the major purposes for proficiency assessment, such as exit testing, transfers, and mid-career evaluation, outlining various approaches. As we have explained, the same basic method can be used in a variety of ways, but the particular parameters of it will be determined by the specific context, including the purpose for the assessment, the resources (including time, personnel, money, and expertise) available, and other local features such as curriculum, staffing, student demographics, and institutional mission and policies.

Exit Testing

Exit testing typically comes at the end of a course or sequence of courses, and is most often associated with first-year composition. Students must pass the exit assessment—in addition to passing the course or courses—to demonstrate mastery. (In some cases, failing the exit exam translates into failing the course.) Sometimes developmental writing programs have an exit exam to certify that students are ready for the credit-bearing, first-year composition course. In this case, the exit assessment functions as a placement exam—by passing the exam, the student may be placed into the credit-bearing course. Sometimes, an exit assessment is the culmination of the required first-year composition curriculum.

In the past, composition exit exams were frequently timed impromptu essays that were holistically scored by program faculty. One of the issues with these exit exams, especially once the writing process movement spread throughout the composition community, was that they did not align with the best practices in teaching and learning to write. In a process-based course, peer response, revision, and other activities are emphasized. Students are considered writers and are encouraged to engage in activities writers engage in, including developing a topic and a purpose and writing for specific audiences. Impromptu essay exams, in spite of attempts to specify an audience and/or purpose, don't allow students to use the effective writing processes they developed in the course and don't engage them in authentic writing tasks. Peter Elbow and Pat Belanoff, who changed their institution's essay exam to a community graded portfolio and popularized portfolios in the college composition community in the process, explain that proficiency impromptu essay exams

> undermine good teaching by sending the wrong message about the writing process: that proficient writing means having a serious topic sprung on you (with no chance for reading, reflection, or discussion) and writing one draft (with no chance for sharing or feedback or revising). (1986, 336)

They continue their critique, citing Charles Cooper: "[W]e need at least two or three samples" of student writing "in two or three genres at two or three sittings" to determine a student's proficiency (336). Research also shows that the task influences writers' process as well as product (e.g., Ruth and Murphy 1988; Witte and Cherry 1994). In other words, writers' performances vary depending on the task addressed so that the results of a test that only requires one type of writing task are not adequate to make decisions about students' writing competencies in response to other tasks or in other contexts (see Murphy and Yancey 2007, 370–72, for a review of the research).

Adaptations or revisions to the basic format of the impromptu essay have been developed to try and compensate for its limitations. For example, a program can require a common assignment, given at the end of the term as part of the regular course (an embedded assignment), across all sections and mandate that it counts as a certain percentage of the course grade. Other changes may include extending the writing process for the impromptu so, for example, students may be given the prompt during one class period and then be required to write their response to it during another period (sometimes they are allowed to bring in notes for a draft). Another adaptation includes having students write a self-reflection, which attempts to get at issues of process, self-evaluation, and revision, along with a response to the standard prompt.

While attempts such as these have been made to revamp the timed essay exam, compositionists recognize that privileging the score of a single essay test over the instructor's course grade not only undermines the composition curriculum but also calls into question the authority of composition instructors (not to mention contradicting what we know about effective assessment and writing development and competency). In response to the critiques of impromptu essay testing and its revised formats, several composition programs abandoned exit exams while others (many of which are required by state or institution policies to administer an assessment) turned to using a portfolio of writing produced during the composition course as the exit assessment or in place of an exit exam (e.g., Elbow and Belanoff 1986; Durst, Roemer, and Shultz 1994; Smit 1994). These portfolio assessments have taken various forms, but most share some common features: the use of multiple writing samples written during the course; instructors of the course as evaluators of the portfolios; and a self-reflection, introduction, or cover letter.[1]

The details of each portfolio system, however, are determined by the local context. For example, Durst, Roemer, and Shultz (1994) explain that after conducting pilot studies with the various constituencies of instructors in their program, they designed a system that used trios—teams of three instructors that traded student portfolios and graded them. In some programs, trios or grading teams only review each others' borderline or failing portfolios because the strong students are clearly passing, so they determined no need to read and evaluate every single portfolio. While some programs, such as Grand Valley State University's, have grading teams actually scoring or grading each other's portfolios, others simply have the teams determining "pass" or "no pass." Grand Valley's system is based on the premise that the group of instructors meet and discuss the course, assignments, student work, and evaluation throughout the semester to "agree about what is an A, B, C, D, and F paper. The goal of the instructors in the group is to set fair and accurate grading standards." In other cases, the teams only review midterm and/or end-of-term portfolios. In most situations, programs conduct group norming sessions to help faculty determine the characteristics of passing versus failing portfolios. These discussions, in both the smaller grading groups and the larger norming sessions, can be extremely useful in making criteria and values of the program and its faculty explicit (e.g., Broad 1994; Elbow and Belanoff 1986; Smit 1994).

Portfolios have become popular exit assessments because, in general, they align with what is considered best practice in both the teaching and assessment of writing (as described in chapter 3 and in the CCCC position statement in appendix B). Portfolios are also flexible—they are defined by the local program and its curriculum. They provide ongoing opportunities for writing faculty to discuss student writing, curriculum, and instruction. However, any kind of exit assessment functions as a gatekeeping device. It presents another hurdle besides the passing of the course for students—and instructors and programs—to overcome before students are allowed to

---

1.   Writing portfolios have generated a large body of scholarship that covers a range of issues, methods, etc., which is too extensive to review here. Instead, our purpose is to use examples to illustrate different points we make and different uses of portfolios at the postsecondary level. Because of portfolios' popularity, we draw many of our ideas from this literature. For more information, see Hamp-Lyons and Condon (2000), Belanoff and Dickson (1991), and Black et al. (1994), among others.

continue. Even when a proficiency assessment is considered as a gateway—that is, it is designed to ensure that students get the appropriate instruction they need to be successful when confronted with future writing demands—the reality is that the proficiency exam can still function as a barrier. Although some administrators or policymakers see the exit assessment as a way of demonstrating the importance of writing in college education, this type of testing also sends a clear signal that instructors' in-course grading of student performance is not enough to certify achievement of the goals. Smit explains that his use of an exit assessment was necessary because of staffing practices in his writing program. Using program portfolios, "forces our weaker instructors to confront the fact that someone else" will be reading their students' papers and that "puts a certain amount of pressure" on the instructors to "learn what the standards of the group are and to help their students as best they can" (1994, 312–13).

Granted, as Smit explains, exit assessments also provide a valuable means of faculty development because the writing faculty evaluate the assessments (which is a similar argument made for local placement). However, faculty development and norming sessions do not require every student be assessed, nor do they require that the consequence be borne by individual students if they happen to have had an ineffective instructor. In other words, the use of exit assessment can penalize a student for not developing the necessary writing competencies to pass the exit exam, but the reason for not passing may reside in the instructor, not the student. Staffing issues (including salary, benefits, job security, and due process) are real concerns in composition programs, which are often dominated by contingent faculty who have little institutional status and security. (Even in liberal arts colleges, there may be a higher percentage of contingent faculty teaching FYC than introductory coures in most other disciplines.) Imposing an assessment to maintain quality seems to be a way of disciplining the program, not just the students. This is an important aspect of exit testing to keep in mind because, if the issue is the quality of the instructor, it seems unethical to penalize the student for the institution's failure to provide adequate instruction by qualified instructors. Our point is that you need to determine the main purpose of the exit exam and then consider if in fact an assessment that functions as a gatekeeping device for students is the best way to achieve that purpose.

Transfers

When students transfer into a college or university, they may not have taken a course comparable to your institution's composition course or courses. For example, some schools have replaced the English composition course with a writing-intensive, first-year seminar course (Horner et al. 2002). Depending on your composition curriculum, the course descriptions may not be enough to determine if the student has had the requisite writing instruction to meet the expectations of your program. In this type of proficiency assessment, students are usually evaluated on an ad hoc basis depending on the particular need. Your institution may already use a national exam, such as the College Level Examination Program (CLEP) offered by the College Board, or you may establish a set of in-house procedures that students can opt for in place of a course when circumstances warrant it. You might not have much choice if your institution already uses CLEP although there are several different options available for composition. The two composition exams, English Composition and Freshman College Composition, each have two options: a multiple-choice test or a multiple-choice section and a timed essay component. The two exams focus on different material although they share some common ground. They also differ in terms of the writing components: the English Composition version has just one 45-minute timed essay that is scored by college faculty through CLEP; the Freshman College Composition test has two 45-minute essays that are scored by local faculty. If you are required to use CLEP, or if you are considering it, you should review the material for the two exams and find out which is most appropriate for your needs. As we have said repeatedly, we favor local, context-specific writing assessment that uses student writing over standardized national exams, but we also think that local writing programs are the most qualified to make decisions about what is best for them.

If you are not restricted in terms of proficiency assessment for transfers, you need to consider what kind of assessment would work given your program and your transfer population. For example, if you have few transfer requests, you might consider requiring a portfolio that includes three to five pieces of graded writing from college courses along with an introductory essay that explains the writer's process and approach to the texts included in the portfolio. Or, you might use a combination of a timed impromptu essay administered at certain points in the year in conjunction with a portfolio. The portfolio might be scored by a team of writing instructors, the writing program administrator, or both. Or, if the number of students eligible for the portfolio option is manageable, the WPA may review the portfolio and meet with the student to discuss the contents and ask probing questions about the student's process and competencies. The first-year writing program at the University of Maryland College Park, for example, uses a writing portfolio to determine whether students transferring need to take the UMCP writing course or not. They have articulated clear guidelines for assembling the portfolio as well as evaluation criteria that are available to everyone via their Web site. Regardless of the specific approach used to certify proficiency, the criteria for evaluating the work should be grounded in the writing program's learning aims and criteria. The goal is to make sure that students who would benefit from the composition course take it while those who have demonstrated achievement of its outcomes are not made to spend time in a course that isn't going to challenge them. We'll discuss more specific ways of determining if your method of proficiency assessment for transfers does in fact sort the students effectively below in the validation section.

MID-CAREER WRITING ASSESSMENTS

Mid-career writing assessments may go by many different names, such as a rising junior exam, a writing-in-the-major proficiency or even a general education graduation requirement. Typically these types of tests are expected to be completed during the mid-range of a student's academic career. In some situations, students who don't pass the exam (or don't take it) may be automatically required to take an additional course. Other times they may be blocked from enrolling in courses at the junior level. Sometimes the students need to satisfy the proficiency requirement after completing sixty hours and before completing their degree requirements or they will be blocked from graduating, not earning their diploma until the proficiency requirement is successfully completed. Some graduation requirements include writing a senior thesis or creating a capstone portfolio. These are typically linked to majors, and although writing is required, they aren't writing assessments *per se* so we don't address them here.

While mid-career assessments can take many different forms—a timed impromptu, a portfolio, or some combination—they typically function to demonstrate that students are prepared for the writing challenges they will meet in advanced courses in their major. Typically students who don't pass are offered (or required) additional opportunities for developing as writers. For example, at Washington State University, all students are required to submit a portfolio of writing (which includes three essays written in courses accompanied by instructors' signatures) as well as take a timed essay exam that requires writing two essays (one based on an excerpt from a text and one that is self-reflective) after accruing sixty credits but before graduation. The portfolio requirement is a "junior-level diagnostic to determine if [students'] writing abilities have advanced in ways that can handle the writing demands of upper-division courses and courses in [the] major," according to the information available on the university's Web site. Portfolios are sorted into three categories: Needs Work, Pass, and Pass with Distinction. Washington State's junior portfolio, which has been extensively written about (Haswell 2001a) is a general education requirement and part of the university's WAC program in which students take two writing-in-the-major courses. If students do not pass the portfolio, they can be required to take an additional writing course or a one-hour writing center tutorial offered in conjunction with their writing-in-the-major course. Because the WSU portfolio is tied to the WAC program, readers for the essay portion are drawn from faculty across the campus who teach writing in the major courses and/or other advanced-level writing courses and the writing-center tutorials. Based on a two-tier expert reader model (see Haswell 2001b, and discussion in chapter 4), all essay exams are read by an instructor of the relevant courses. If students received either a "Needs Work" or a "Pass with Distinction" by the first-tier reader, their entire portfolio is reviewed by second-tier readers who determine if the collection of papers in the portfolio supports the tier-one readers' evaluation. If students receive a "Pass" from the tier-one readers of the essays, the collection of papers is not read.

The WSU Junior Writing Portfolio, which has been in place for well over a decade, is clearly situated in the curriculum and the university. It grew out of a state mandate for general education assessment. Other colleges and universities also have portfolios, but they do not replicate the WSU system. For example, Carleton College, a selective, small liberal arts college, also requires that students complete a writing portfolio as a graduation requirement. However, this portfolio is markedly different from WSU's. Carleton's portfolio is a sophomore requirement; it requires three to five papers from courses that satisfy specific writing tasks (e.g., one paper that demonstrates the ability to analyze complex information) and a reflective essay in which the students argue for their "accomplishments on the writing tasks listed below, using [their] papers as evidence" (Carleton). As with WSU's portfolio, faculty and staff from across the college read and evaluate the portfolio, and students who do not pass are provided support. However, at Carleton, the support is not a required course or tutorial; instead, according to the writing program, "the Writing Program Director or another writing professional will work individually with students to agree on the problems, propose solutions, and resubmit the portfolio during the next term the writer is on campus."

Although the details of these two portfolios are different—and the administration of them differs—both function to identify students who need more support to be successful in upper-level courses, both have been designed to function within the local culture, both are grounded in best practices of teaching and learning to write. In both cases, the writing programs are tracking and analyzing the information about the teaching of writing in their respective institutions gleaned from the student portfolios, and they use this information to revise or reconsider the writing programs. For example, Haswell (1998, 2001c) explains how he shared information with faculty and administrators about which classes students drew their portfolio papers from to provide professional development support for faculty in majors that were underrepresented in the submissions. As you can imagine, the writing portfolios also provide information that is useful for the assessment of the undergraduate educational outcomes in general that is required for accrediting agencies. Both of these writing programs have also been recognized for the excellence of their program; in fall 2005 Carleton received the Conference on College Composition and Communication Writing Program Certificate of Excellence Award; WSU Writing Program, including the Junior Writing Portfolio, was recognized by *U.S. News & World Report* for distinction from 2000–2006.

As we mentioned above, sometimes the specific requirements for a proficiency assessment—even the specific test—are determined by policymakers far removed from your campus, but in many cases you may have control over the exam. Remember, power resides in all assessments, whether imposed from policymakers or developed in-house from the ground up. Writing assessments—whether an exit test from first-year composition or a mid-career writing portfolio—will define what is meant by "good writing" and who are considered "good writers," as well as how writing is taught and the role it plays in the curriculum. Clearly, it is in the best interest of writing programs—their staff, students, and curricula—to be part of the assessment conversations when writing proficiency is under discussion.

VALIDITY INQUIRY

Part of participating in discussions about assessment requires that you be not only informed to discuss issues such as validity and reliability but that you be prepared to conduct validation studies. As we have explained in chapter 3 and more specifically in terms of placement in chapter 5, writing assessments demand ongoing validity inquiry because without it, we cannot be sure that the results of the assessments are used in positive ways (to improve teaching and learning) and that any negative effects are minimized or negligible.

In general, validation requires gathering evidence—empirical as well as theoretical—to construct an argument in support of the interpretation and use of the assessment results. For proficiency testing, validity inquiry needs to begin with articulating the purpose of the assessment, the assumptions about writing and learning to write that it is based on, as well as the intended use of the results. For example, if your purpose in having an exit test for the first-year composition curriculum is to ensure that students who pass the composition classes are writing at an acceptable level to be prepared for entry-level writing requirements in their major, you will need to determine if those passing the test are prepared to begin writing in the major. To answer this question, you need to systematically collect a variety of information. You might hold focus groups of faculty who teach writing in the disciplines, or conduct structured faculty interviews that ask specific questions about writing. You might collect samples of student writing from the relevant courses and evaluate them with a group of faculty from across the campus. You could also survey students in the senior year to ask about their experiences with the writing in upper-level courses, and you could even ask the campus writing center about the needs of students as they enter their major courses. As you investigate these kinds of questions, you need to consider other issues, such as what kind of instruction and support students receive as they move from first-year composition to writing in the major. Are instructors in the major courses—as well as other general education courses—building on what students learn in the composition curriculum as they provide instruction in writing (not just assigning writing but teaching students how to adapt to the new situation and demands they are encountering)?

If you are conducting validity studies of your assessment program for transfer students, your questions and approach will be different. For example, you may need to determine how students are performing in writing-intensive courses (either general education or major courses). How do the students who receive additional support compare to those who don't get this support if controlled for other variables? How do transfer students as a whole compare to those who go through your own composition curriculum? Are there any patterns in this data? Maybe you can conduct focus-group interviews or surveys with the transfer students about their experience in managing the writing requirements in their courses at your institution. Jennie Nelson and Diane Kelly-Riley (2001) conducted an investigation such as this on transfers at WSU and their experience with the junior portfolio. Their inquiry revealed that students' experiences didn't always play out as the writing program anticipated. As we mention in chapter 5, approaching the validation process as research will help you to form questions and methods for answering the questions. And, as in all aspects of assessment, you need to tailor your validity inquiry to the local context.

As you conduct a validation inquiry, you need to be attentive to both the intended and unintended consequences of the assessment. Administrators often make claims that the use of one method over another is preferred because of its positive influence on teaching and learning, which is a strong argument in support of an assessment. Claims, such as those made by Durst, Roemer, and Shultz as they moved to portfolio evaluation at the end of the first-year composition sequence, are common: Portfolios "had the potential to empower teachers," to decentralize the program, to give teachers more say in determining standards, and to provide more opportunities for teachers to meet and discuss writing (1994, 288; see also Roemer, Shultz, and Durst 1991). While many of the benefits that Durst, Roemer, and Shultz claim may have been realized, they didn't provide much in terms of evidence to support their position. Shane Borrowman, like many others who developed placement portfolios, made similar claims about the benefits of a placement-portfolio program, but again he didn't provide evidence to support his claims. These claims—made by administrators with experience and knowledge—may be true; however, in validity inquiry, assertions are not enough. They need to be supported with evidence because without evidence, we don't know that the intended consequences are actually achieved. For example, Broad, who has experience as a portfolio reader and researcher at several different institutions, notes that participants "complain of a contradiction between their experiences in the 'calibration' or 'norming' sessions" and the way administrators represent them (1994, 270). He concludes that often instructors' "sense of professionalism, dignity, intellectual activity, and community" can be undermined through their participation in the types of assessments that the Cincinnati administrators praise. Likewise, a portfolio assessment may not encourage the kind of writing and writing pedagogy that the administrators envision if the teachers implementing the portfolios do not understand or buy into the philosophy (Murphy and Camp 1996). For example, based on her ethnographic study of a portfolio system at a community college, Alexis Nelson identified several concerns about implementing department-wide portfolios: "Foremost . . . is the importance of any given teacher's understanding of this methodology. Students will understand portfolio assessment in the way their teacher presents it to them" (1999, 248). In other words, if teachers conceptualize and present the portfolio assessment differently from each other (and from the program's intention), then students will have different conceptions and experiences with it, and this experience may not be what is intended. In fact, it might even compromise the basic theoretical rationale used to select portfolio assessment. Xin Lui Gale (1997) argues that the benefits of a mandated programmatic portfolio system—such as those reported by Elbow and Belanoff (1986), Smit (1994), and Durst, Roemer, and Shultz (1994)—may not be realized. Without research, however, there is no way to know what stakeholders experience and what the consequences of an assessment are. Nelson and Kelly-Riley (2001), for example, found through case-study research that students' experiences with the Washington State University Junior Writing Portfolio did not always match up with the program's goals and that the consequences anticipated by the program were not always realized. Some students noted that the writing tutorial required did not necessarily provide the support that the portfolio assessment had indicated they needed. Other students, especially transfers, experienced the assessment more as a barrier exam than a mid-career diagnostic as the program intended so that it became a high-stakes test. These findings and more, including those reported by others (see Haswell 2001a), were used to make changes in the assessment system as they explain:

> [W]e were able to gather useful information about our program that we could not have obtained from other stakeholder populations or from our regular data collection. The information allowed us to identify easily solvable problems in our assessment. (Nelson and Kelly-Riley 2001, 158)

In other words, administrators charged with assessment need to conduct research into the assessment, which includes all stakeholders and considers its consequences, to determine if in fact the benefits expected are being realized and if unintended consequences are compromising these benefits. Even an assessment method such as a portfolio, which is touted to be theoretically aligned with what we know about teaching and learning to write, to support writers and teachers of writing, and to provide reliable and valid results, needs to be regularly investigated through multiple methods. Research should be used to adapt, clarify, and improve assessments so that they produce valid results that improve teaching and learning. Developing and maintaining a proficiency assessment, like any other writing assessment, is a dynamic process that requires ongoing research because local contexts and conditions are also dynamic. An assessment that doesn't respond to the local context not only can outlive its usefulness, but even worse, harm teaching and learning.

7
CONDUCTING WRITING PROGRAM ASSESSMENTS

Program assessment differs from other types of writing assessments because the focus is not on individual student performance but on collective achievement. So while a program assessment might include evaluation of student writing as a data-gathering method, it requires that the writing be considered in terms of what it says about student learning generally and how that learning is supported by curricula, instruction, and instructional materials. Also, though program assessment often incorporates information from one-time, episodic tests of student learning, it is most usefully viewed as a long-term enterprise, extending far beyond any one student's first-year composition experience or any one WPA's administrative tenure.

Because program assessment is based on the assumption that all parts of a learning context interact, it offers the best means for understanding not only what is happening in our programs but what aspects are working, how they are working, and, to a certain degree, why. For this reason, responsible program administration necessitates a commitment to ongoing, systematic assessment. Unfortunately, due to increasing calls for accountability by upper-level administrators, such assessment may be seen as a way to satisfy demands that originate outside of a program rather than a means for answering questions or addressing concerns important to those most directly responsible for, or affected by, the program. This perception is solidified when outside requests for assessment data are accompanied by directives about how to gather the data and report results that make little sense to writing program administrators, staff, and faculty. In such situations, a question such as, "Why conduct a program assessment?" is too-often answered with a statement like, "Because the dean told us to."

While we do not wish to discount the feelings of frustration that accompany requests to do something one did not plan to do, is perhaps not prepared to do, and may not be fully supported for doing well, we want to suggest that, for programs not already engaged in regular, self-initiated assessment, a top-down request can be viewed as a chance for writing administrators and faculty to serve their own local purposes—to understand what is happening in a program and how it is supporting instruction and student learning. What we offer in the following section is a way of articulating guiding questions for assessments that will serve the interests of those directly involved in a program as well as the needs of external audiences.

WHERE DO WE START?

The great temptation in any kind of assessment process is to start with a consideration of methods. While doing so will not *necessarily* lead to a poor assessment, it easily can lead to an assessment that generates data that are not very useful. Starting with methods themselves makes it easy to bypass not only questions of purpose but underlying beliefs or values and relevant definitions. As we discuss later, for example, student portfolios of writing are often favored over single writing samples for program-assessment purposes. Yet, an assessment team that collects writing portfolios without first articulating what they hope to learn from the portfolios may end up wishing they had used another assessment method or, even more likely, multiple complementary methods. While portfolios might help answer a question such as, "How successfully can students integrate source material?" the usefulness of the answer will depend upon how instructors are defining *success*. Further, simply evaluating portfolios will not necessarily provide insights about the teaching methods that help students use sources or why two students enrolled in the same course demonstrate different levels of facility with source integration. Of course, it may be the latter issues that administrators and faculty are actually most interested in examining because these are the issues that, when addressed, can lead to improved programs and, in turn, increased learning.

In short, then, attention to methods themselves, though certainly important, is not as crucial as careful consideration of what the results of the methods will mean—how they can be used to generate useful data and make responsible decisions. If we see program assessment as a type of research, a view we encourage in earlier chapters, then the methods we select will depend on what we are assessing (or researching) and why we are assessing it (our research questions).

How Is Our Program Defined?

As we discussed in chapter 4, individual programs not only have their own defining characteristics but their boundaries may be marked in a variety of ways, depending on institutional context. At some institutions, for example, a writing program may be defined simply in terms of one or two required general education or "core" courses. At other institutions, however, the writing program may be viewed as extending far beyond introductory composition courses to encompass upper-level writing or writing-intensive courses offered in multiple departments. At still other schools, the concept of "writing program" is less course-based, encompassing all writing-based initiatives, including, for example, the writing center.

What can make program definition difficult is that, unless the parameters have been clearly demarcated (through past discussion, documentation, assessments), there may be disagreement about what, exactly, the program consists of and what makes elements cohere or work together to provide a sense of "program-ness." Should a non-credit, developmental writing course taught outside the English Department by English faculty be considered along with credit-bearing English courses as part of a writing program assessment? If the campus writing center is funded by the provost's office but offers one-credit "studio" courses for developmental English students, should those courses be part of the assessment? What about honors composition courses taught by English faculty but offered through the honors college? Perhaps the program will be defined in terms of who has responsibility or authority over staffing or funding. Maybe it will be defined in terms of the specific student population served. While there are no set answers to questions like these, they need to be discussed, up front, among the people who will be designing and facilitating the assessment, and the answers should be based on reasoning that all interested parties find convincing. The principle to remember here is that the object of assessment must be defined before it can be appropriately assessed.

What Do We Want to Know and Why?

Once the program parameters have been delineated, those responsible for the assessment should consider what it is they want to know about the program. Here are some general questions that can be used, together or alone, as starting points for more specific, context-based assessment queries:

- What is currently happening in the program?
- Is what we see happening in the program what we expected to see?
- What about the program seems to be working?
- What about the program seems not to be working?

A possible follow-up to "what questions" like these is *Why?* That is, "*Why* do we want to know x?" or "*Why* does some aspect of the program seem to be working/not working?" Ideally, the answer to questions like these will be immediately, and locally, relevant. The program administrator and faculty need to better articulate, for themselves, what their goals are, so they can improve efforts to meet them; or, they may want to know if a recent innovation (such as a new textbook, new assignment sequence, or new approach to tutoring) has helped students achieve at a higher level than before. (In fact, answering questions like these is itself a form of assessment.) More often these days, though, there are external assessment demands that need to be answered. Maybe a dean or vice president wants to know how the program is helping the college or university meet its strategic goals. Or, at a more basic level, perhaps an upper-level administrator simply wants to understand what the program is trying to accomplish because its aims and methods have never been clearly communicated beyond the department.

Sometimes, as is the case with a new writing initiative, program administrators and faculty must start at an even more basic level—with questions such as, "What do we want our program to achieve in the first place?" These more basic questions will then lead to articulation of program goals. Of course, it is sometimes the case that those responsible for shaping new programs need examples of the kinds of questions that lend themselves to articulating program goals. One of the best sources for such questions is the self-study heuristic offered by the Council of Writing Program Administrators (WPA), "Guidelines for Self-Study to Precede a Writing Program Evaluation," which is available to members on its Web site (http://www.wpacouncil.org/consultant).

What Information Do We Already Have?

Like many academic initiatives, program assessments often fall prey to the "reinventing the wheel" syndrome. This is especially the case for programs that lack long-term stability (e.g., directors coming and going, new faculty replacing veteran faculty) and, thus, some degree of institutional memory. It is also the case for programs whose faculty and staff are, for whatever reason, isolated from discussions going on around campus about relevant issues such as recruitment, retention, developmental education, and graduation rates.

Before launching into a program assessment, it's a good idea to find out whether any of the questions generated during the early stages of an assessment have already been answered, in full or in part, by past assessments or by research conducted by other departments or programs on campus. For example, if part of an assessment will be devoted to examining how well curriculum is serving a particular group of students, those responsible for the assessment will want to get as much information as possible from the office(s) on campus that track demographic information such as gender, ethnicity, economic status, etc. Data about student perceptions, experiences, and expectations are also often available through offices that conduct first-year surveys or facilitate placement examinations containing background questions. If effectiveness of instruction is a concern at an institution in which standardized teaching evaluations are used, it may be possible to get

reports on relevant student feedback in the aggregate—that is, without identifying faculty members or sections of a class. An institutional research office
can also provide information on hiring trends, which might include, for
example, comparative data on part-time/full-time hires or degrees held.

WHAT RESOURCES ARE AVAILABLE FOR GATHERING DATA—AND HOW DO I GET MORE?

Another important part of the assessment process is determining available
resources. While it is helpful to start with the ideal assessment scenario, in
which multiple methods are used and multiple people are involved at all
stages, the reality is that assessments are often only as comprehensive as talent, time, and money allow. Again, because we discuss resources extensively in chapter 4, we will use this section to review the most relevant points
made earlier. Generally speaking, the most important resources needed to
conduct a program assessment are committed, informed personnel and
the money to compensate them.

Personnel

As with other aspects of assessment, it is helpful to start with a few basic
questions when considering personnel issues: Given the purpose and scope
of the assessment, how many people are needed? Who is willing to help?
Of these people, who is knowledgeable enough about available assessment
practices and relevant theories to jump right in, perhaps taking a leadership role in proposal writing, assessment design, and/or reporting? Who
may need professional support in the form of articles, books, or money to
attend a local assessment workshop? When will the greatest number of people be available to participate? How representative is this initial group of
participants, in terms of experience, expertise, and position? Is there resistance to assessment? Why?

In the ideal world, all potential participants will want to help, and they will
all be knowledgeable enough about assessment to contribute productively
to the effort. In the real world of program assessment, though, this is rarely the case. As suggested throughout this guide, many factors prevent people from volunteering to help with assessment efforts. People who do not
understand the potential benefits of program assessment—or suspect that
benefits will never materialize—will not want to participate in it. Another
factor that may inhibit participation is the time required to conduct and
follow through with assessments. It can take an extraordinary amount of
time to gather materials, analyze and interpret the data, report results, and
use the results to revise programs. Plus, in order to be meaningful, assessment needs to be regular and ongoing. Sometimes, too, the expectation is
that assessments will occur during a winter or summer break—when most

faculty do not wish to be on campus. Among tenure-track and tenured faculty, there may be an additional source of resistance: the sense that any funds used for assessment are funds that will not be available for other departmental or program needs. According to Gail Hughes (1996), "If evaluation is viewed as diverting money from the program, it is likely to generate resentment and undermine its basis of support" (171). With respect to contingent faculty, reluctance to participate may stem from insecurity about status within the program and misconceptions about the purposes of assessment.

Because lack of participation—or committed participation—affects not only assessment design and implementation but use of assessment results, it is important that constraints on participation be acknowledged upfront. If sources of resistance—or reluctance—are known, these can sometimes be easily addressed through departmental correspondence, one-to-one conversations, or informal meetings. If, as Hughes suggests, the program administrator is able to maintain separate pools of money—one for general program needs and one for assessment—then a quick e-mail to the department explaining this fact may be all that is necessary. Other sources of resistance may take more time and effort to address. In terms of resistant tenure-line faculty, one-to-one meetings may be required to reiterate why full participation is necessary and what the benefits are of assessment for the department, program, faculty, and students. Informal brown-bag meetings may offer fearful contingent faculty a chance to ask questions and to be reassured that the assessment will not be focusing on them (their students, sections, or individual materials)—but on the program as a whole. A simple invitation to participate in the design and implementation of the assessment may be all that is needed to alleviate fears.

Money

Perhaps the best way to encourage participation is to emphasize the value of faculty (staff, student) time and talent by compensating them. Compensation should at least be equal to the hourly or daily rate that the school would pay the individual. In cases where this rate is embarrassingly little (as it may be for graduate students and part-time instructors), a rate closer to the full-time faculty rate can often be obtained—especially if it is clear that the participants will be doing roughly the same kind and amount of work. Though some faculty members may say (and administrators may expect) that they will do assessment work for no additional compensation, we encourage writing program administrators to resist this situation. If good assessment is important to a university, they should be willing to pay for it.

Beyond compensating faculty for their time, those involved with assessment design will want to consider other potential expenses. Depending on the methods used, an assessment may require money to cover expenses for copying materials (e.g., surveys, student papers/portfolios, articles for faculty) or for paying for assessment resources or travel to conferences. It may also require providing refreshments to faculty who attend workshops or planning sessions. Sometimes, as in the case of assessments that include use of surveys or interviews, money will be needed to cover the costs of mailings, incentives for completing surveys (e.g., gift certificates), and long-distance phone calls. Fortunately, much of this can now be done electronically, which can save money.

Sometimes, too, space is a consideration. On a very basic level, space is needed to conduct the assessment—whether it be online space or real-time, physical space. What kind and amount of space is needed? What space(s) are available? Will there be costs associated with using the space? Another factor that is often forgotten is storage space. Though technological advances have made it easier to store and distribute large amounts of text electronically, doing so may be more feasible at some schools than at others. Can your university support electronic storage of assessment materials, or will you need to procure an extra metal filing cabinet? Whatever the situation, it needs to be explored early on, before the assessment is designed and funded.

Possible Funding Sources

Ideally, the institution will be committed to assessment, and this commitment will be demonstrated through a willingness to provide necessary resources. Where money for assessment is available, an upper-level administrator or assessment office may require a proposal before allocating funds. Such a proposal may ask for an overview of the project, description of potential methods for both gathering and analyzing data, rationale for the assessment, and a budget. If the proposal writers have experience with assessment or have read this guide, the first few elements of the proposal should be easy to draft. For those new to assessment, the budget can sometimes be tricky. It is difficult to know, for example, whether to calculate the least amount of money necessary to do a respectable assessment and ask just for that amount or to design the best assessment possible and ask for whatever that assessment will cost—even if the amount seems exorbitant. The approach used, as well as its success, may depend on the type of person currently in charge of the money. If possible, the people writing the proposal should consult with someone from the office or agency selecting proposals for tips on how to write all portions of it, including the budget. It always helps to ask for samples of proposals that have worked in the past and to speak with their authors about strategies used.

If funding isn't readily available for assessment per se, there may be ways to get support for assessment through other means. Sometimes, for example, it is easier for a department chairperson or dean to provide release from teaching responsibilities for assessment projects than to provide cash. For many academics, time to do the assessment is actually more important than money. It is also possible to fund certain parts of an assessment by framing them in terms of initiatives that are being prioritized on campus. For example, if student retention is a concern, there may be money available for an assessment that looks at the connection between writing program activities and retention. Another priority for many campuses now is diversity. Looking at how a writing program serves students from diverse backgrounds may also provide insights about the program generally. Though these indirect approaches to securing assessment funding may help to support efforts in the short-term, they should not be regarded as an acceptable long-term solution for supporting program assessments. Whenever possible, program administrators, along with department chairs, deans, institutional-assessment personnel, and provosts should push for budget lines devoted exclusively to assessments—particularly if those assessments are being initiated outside of the programs themselves.

Another short-term option is to pursue funding outside of the university. Though grants for projects in the humanities are far scarcer than those supporting initiatives in the sciences, they do exist. Most universities have resource people on campus who can help with obtaining grant information and working through the sometimes-difficult proposal-writing process. Within composition and rhetoric, two possible sources for funding are NCTE and WPA. These organizations often advertise small research grants that can be used for assessment projects.

The Need to Scale Back

If limited funds become an obstacle, the assessment will either need to be narrowly focused or involve little time on the part of faculty. That is, what might begin as a blueprint for a comprehensive program assessment will become a proposal for a targeted study. Small-scale, targeted studies don't necessarily need to be viewed in a negative way but instead can be seen as first steps or "slips" toward building a larger picture or "quilt" of what is going on in the program (Morgan 1997). Such a study might also be seen as a pilot that could then help make the case for a larger future assessment.

DESIGNING THE ASSESSMENT: MATCHING METHODS TO GUIDING QUESTIONS

Once the guiding questions and available resources have been determined, it is then appropriate to begin the process of deciding which methods will help achieve the purpose, or purposes, of the assessment. Matching methods with assessment questions requires not only a familiarity with the range of available practices and an awareness of possible contextual constraints (e.g., lack of sufficient personnel or funding), but an understanding of the theory and history associated with various approaches.

Beyond understanding that assessment methods can be categorized as "direct" or "indirect," something we discuss in previous chapters, it is helpful to know that methods are often identified as "quantitative" or "qualitative," depending upon the degree to which they acknowledge contextual influences. It is also helpful to know that the documented history of writing program assessment is often portrayed as a fierce negotiation between more qualitative assessment methods, usually preferred by writing practitioners, and the more quantitative methods embraced by the larger academic community. From Steve Witte and Lester Faigley's 1983 analysis of four sample program assessments in *Evaluating Writing Programs* to Ed White's outline of "four general models of program evaluation" in his 1985 *Teaching and Assessing Writing* to Neal Lerner's more recent (2003) account of the history of writing center evaluation, the conflict between evolving theories of writing and learning that privilege context and complexity, on the one hand, and widespread support (both within and outside of the discipline) of de-contextual, seemingly reductive assessment methods, on the other, is palpable. In fact, such conflict has been so prevalent and frustrating that it drove White to assert in 1989 that, "In relation to program evaluation, we must simply recognize that there is no replicated design in existence for demonstrating that any writing instructional program in fact improves writing, if we define writing in a sophisticated way" (178).

As White's proclamation implies, one source of tension in discussions about assessment methods is that the seemingly simple questions upper-level administrators are most interested in (e.g., "How does your program help students write better?") are difficult to answer definitively—no matter what methods are used. A student may participate in a program and may show improvement in writing, but that improvement may be based on many factors, including positive changes in attitude or normal cognitive development. While we agree with White's sentiment and are, ourselves, uneasy with assessments that seek to show simple cause-and-effect relationships, we can't ignore the ongoing pressure to demonstrate such relationships to administrators who fund our programs. For this reason, we suggest that, at the same time WPAs and writing faculty continue to promote the complexity of writing across campus, they explore whether assessment methods might be usefully combined to *tentatively* suggest connections between curricula and/or instruction and overall student achievement of learning outcomes. For example, while a complex phenomenon like writing development simply cannot be measured adequately through such means as course grades or pre- and post-tests, the results of such methods might be considered with other data to reasonably imply the positive (or negative) impact of a program. After unsatisfactory attempts at illustrating writing-center "effects" through traditional grade-use comparisons, for instance, Lerner designed a more meaningful scheme that requires additional types of data analyzed over many years. By keeping initial SAT scores of students constant (something he did in early studies), but adding high school GPA and overall first-year GPA to data about grades earned in first-year composition, he was able to illustrate "a pretty powerful relationship" between writing center use and both FYC grades and overall first-year GPA (2003, 69). In the same way, writing samples, collected early and then later in a term, can indicate more about improvement when combined with other data than they can when examined alone. Lerner discusses, for instance, the possibility of recording the conversations that take place during writing-center tutorial sessions and then examining student revisions to see the extent to which the advice was used (70–71). These types of data can then be considered along with attitudinal data gathered from interviews and surveys. Larry Beason and Laurel Darrow (1997) suggest, for example, that while their particular methods of "listening" to students and faculty through surveys and interviews "do not conclusively prove that WAC works," they can still indicate levels of "support" and "satisfaction" that, from their perspective, directly affect ultimate program success (115).

Sometimes, an effort to show cause and effect relationships to upper-level administrators will lead program evaluators back to key questions, underlying definitions (e.g., "What do we mean by improvement?"), and foundational program objectives. As the work of Haswell and his associates at Washington State University revealed, connections between instruction and learning are easier to establish when the program being assessed is centered on clearly articulated learning objectives or outcomes. Though obviously wary of drawing definitive conclusions about the data, Haswell (2001a) describes a longitudinal "value added" study of student placement samples against samples written, by the same students, for a junior proficiency exam. Because the prompts for the two exams were deliberately coordinated, and because there had been efforts on campus to advertise and discuss characteristics of good writing as part of a larger WAC initiative, the statistically significant improvements seen in student writing samples could at least "confirm existing practices" if not definitively prove a "direct causal path from particular writing courses" or the campus-wide "writing system" as a whole (122).

Taking the lead of scholars mentioned above, we promote an overall assessment approach that recognizes the value of collecting both quantitative and qualitative data in a variety of ways consistent with guiding questions and underlying goals important to those designing and conducting the assessment. We also recommend that, when possible, data be collected not only about the program itself but about the broader institutional and community context. That is, data gathered from writing-center assessments should ideally be compared or combined with results from other program assessments on campus to create a fuller picture of the state of writing on campus, generally. As Muriel Harris (1999) argues, beyond benefiting the program itself and, if it is published, the profession at large, "locally produced knowledge also can contribute to the inquiry of other writing program administrators within the institution" (3). Finally, we suggest that, when faced with directives to answer assessment questions that make little sense to us, as writing administrators and faculty, we look for ways to reframe the questions so that our assessments can be better aligned with current theory and research—or to provide responses that acknowledge the complexity of teaching, learning, and writing.

Available Means of Assessment

There are numerous methods used to assess programs, many of which overlap with methods used for placement and exit testing, as discussed in chapters 5 and 6, and for faculty evaluation, as described in chapter 8. Some of the most common methods include surveys, interviews, analysis of teaching materials, analysis of student writing, and teaching observations. Because these methods are commonly employed in empirical research, we encourage readers to supplement the brief overviews we provide here with more in-depth descriptions of the methods provided in research guides such as MacNealy's *Strategies for Empirical Research in Writing* (1999). We also advise contacting colleagues on campus who have established expertise in empirical research. These colleagues may include faculty but also will likely include administrative staff of research-oriented offices on campus.

Surveys

A survey is comprised of a series of questions targeted at a specific group of people. Surveys are routinely distributed online these days, often through an institutional assessment office, which makes them a relatively easy and inexpensive data-gathering tool.

In some cases, a survey that is already being used on campus can offer insight into issues relevant to the writing program. Examples include standardized teaching evaluations; first-year student surveys; or routine feedback forms, like those used in writing centers or at the end of WAC workshops. In other cases, a WPA or assessment team may want to design an original survey with specific questions directly tied to program-assessment concerns. The advantage of creating an original survey is that different versions can be designed for different groups, according to the particular purpose of the assessment. While most of the questions would be the same, some questions might be modified to solicit information about the specific experiences or perspectives of the individual group. A survey targeted at students, for example, might focus on how well they felt a program helped them succeed in subsequent writing situations; a survey intended for faculty might focus on perceptions of student preparedness for advanced writing tasks.

While approaches to writing surveys vary, one good rule of thumb is to keep the survey itself—and the questions it comprises—as brief as possible. Ten short questions are usually all a busy person will take the time to answer. To increase the response rate and helpfulness of the survey, we suggest conducting a pilot, whereby a small group of people, representative of the larger survey population, completes the survey and then provides feedback on such issues as comprehensibility and document design. Response rates are also improved when efforts are made to keep results anonymous. Online surveys designed through an institutional effectiveness or research office can be set up to guarantee anonymity. If the survey will not be conducted electronically, precautions can be taken, such as including a statement encouraging respondents to word-process answers and to eliminate any details that would identify them to others. If there is a desire to conduct follow-up interviews based on survey results, a simple invitation for an interview can be extended at the end of the survey, with room for name and contact information. Finally, any survey should be proofread carefully by multiple readers. There's nothing that undermines the hard work of survey construction faster than grammatical or mechanical errors. (Please see appendix J for examples of surveys used for program assessment.)

Interviews

Like surveys, interviews can involve students, faculty, and/or administrators. Because they are usually conducted in person or by phone, they offer a kind of flexibility that surveys don't allow. In addition to questions prepared in advance of an interview, there is room for follow-up questions that may lead to more detailed and often more helpful answers than those encouraged by surveys.

One issue to consider with respect to interviews is who will conduct them. A formal interview can often be intimidating—especially for contingent faculty. If formal interviews are desired, then it might be good to try to get an outside party to conduct the interview and report results in the aggregate (i.e., as representative of a particular group and not individual students or faculty members). Another factor with interviews is time. If done individually with a large number of subjects, interviews can be very time-intensive. One way to address this issue is to conduct small-group, or focus-group, interviews. (See appendix K.) These are typically harder to arrange, but the increased efficiency is often worth the trouble. If there is a good deal of trust within a program or department, interviews can also be integrated into a regularly scheduled meeting, with the participant's permission. For example, questions about curricula or teaching philosophy might be easily incorporated into routine meetings between the program administrator and faculty member.

Teaching Materials

Much can be learned through simply collecting and reading teaching materials, including course syllabi, assignment sheets, miscellaneous handouts, and course readings. Depending on the purpose and scope of the assessment, one type of material can be collected and analyzed alone, or various types can be analyzed together. Ideally, given the importance of attending to context throughout the assessment process, program assessors will want to look at as many materials—at as much of the teaching and learning context—as possible. One of the best methods we have found for gathering and analyzing multiple types of documents for context-sensitive program assessment is a course portfolio. Though course portfolios seem an obvious choice for evaluating course-based programs (e.g., first-year composition, WAC), they easily can be adapted for writing-center assessment. Materials would include those most commonly used by tutors and center directors: instructional handouts, conference write-ups, student surveys, and observation notes.

When used to evaluate a course-based program, the portfolio approach involves first asking instructors to compile portfolios for the courses they are teaching. The portfolios should include copies of *all* instructional materials (i.e., all syllabi, all assignment sheets, all handouts) for the given assessment period (e.g., quarter, semester) and an end-of-term self-reflection on the course. (See appendix G for sample course portfolio directions.) This reflection can take a variety of forms, but, if it is to be useful, it should address questions or issues important to the assessment. If the connection between course content and program learning outcomes is a concern, for example, then instructors can be asked to reflect on the ways that their course supported these outcomes. Portfolios might also include reports of peer or supervisor observations and samples of student writing, completed in response to assignments and activities. If the assessment questions require randomization of sample student work, instructors can be asked to provide samples of writing from a certain number of students selected, in a systematic way, from their course roster. For example, the WPA could ask all faculty to include writing from the fifth, tenth, fifteenth, twentieth, etc. student on his/her roster—or random numbers (simply pulled from a hat) could be given to each faculty member with directions to include writing from the students whose names appear next to those numbers on the class roster.

Like other methods, the use of course portfolios can be modified if resources are limited. Unless there is resistance among faculty to compiling portfolios (something we address below), the collection process is relatively simple. The time-intensive part is reading, analyzing, and discussing them. Beyond random sampling of the portfolios (a common approach to evaluating student writing), there is an easy way to reduce the amount of time required: identify one key issue to focus on during analysis. Instead of being guided by a general question such as, "What is going on in our program?" for example, the question might be narrowed to something such as, "What is going on in terms of the students' researched arguments?" Specific follow-up questions might then focus on how faculty and students seem to be defining *argument* and *research* and demonstrating their definitions in syllabi and papers. (See appendix H for a sample reading guide.) Because the portfolios can be stored, other issues can be considered later, when more time and/or funding becomes available.

If resistance among faculty is a problem, there are ways to make the portfolio-keeping process relatively unobtrusive. First, instructors should be provided with basic materials. Such materials might include a two-inch accordion folder with three or four slim manila file folders, each labeled according to type of material (e.g., "syllabus," "assignment sheets," "student papers"). Instructors also should be encouraged to make one extra copy of each required document at the time that they use it during the term, and then place this extra copy immediately into the relevant folder. If they wait until the end of the semester, compiling the portfolio will feel like an extra burden. Finally, to eliminate any concern that individual instructors will be evaluated, it is important that all identifying information (names, section numbers, etc.) be eliminated from materials—either by the instructors and students themselves or by the assessment coordinator or his/her staff.

Student Writing Samples

Most truly comprehensive assessments require an in-depth consideration of student writing that isn't readily achievable through the sampling of papers that may be provided in course portfolios. To ensure greater representation, those responsible for assessment will want to ask for all student work—weak, strong, complete, incomplete—submitted for a course or a particular assignment/assignment series. A sample of these materials can then be read and analyzed.

When determining sample size, it will be important to remember that there is continuing disagreement about appropriate percentages, based on differences in perceptions of "meaning-fulness," or the extent to which results can be generalized. Scholars like Huot and Schendel (2002) suggest, however, that a smaller sample, such as 10 percent, that is read in depth can offer greater insights into a program and, thus, more useful information. As they explain, "By focusing on a smaller number of students, it is possible to generate a richer amount of information in ways that are more consistent with the manner in which students and teachers work together in the classroom" (221). If a larger sample seems to make more sense—or is required by the institution, accrediting agency, or other organization— evaluators will need to recognize that, unless they have endless amounts of time (and money), the reading will have to proceed quickly. A compromise position, suggested by scholars like Haswell (2001a, 40–43) and Elbow (1996, 123–25), is a two-phased approach which involves reading a large sample very quickly, sorting it into a few categories (e.g., low, medium, high), and then reading the papers in one of the categories (typically the "low" category since these students need more help) in a more focused way. Though these scholars' immediate concern was placement of individual students, their scheme can easily be adapted for a program review.

Whatever the sample size, because theory suggests that context is important, the writing that is evaluated should not only be written for a particular rhetorical purpose and audience but should be embedded within the course, as a regular assignment—not required as an extra assignment for external evaluation purposes. Though it is often the case that single writing samples are collected and read by evaluators, for the purposes of program assessment, reviewers should examine as much varied writing as possible (reflecting the variety of actual assignments), in the form of student portfolios. Again, since the program is being evaluated (and not individual students and instructors), all care should be taken to remove any identifying information. Additional protection for students can take the form of a brief statement, included in course syllabi, explaining the purpose of program assessment and how their work will be used (e.g., anonymously, for program review only, etc.)

Teaching Observations

Because we discuss this methodology fully in our next chapter, we offer only basic considerations here. First, we have found that it is difficult to draw conclusions about what is happening in a program—or what is/isn't working—without actually observing teachers (or tutors) in action. Much about program instruction can be gleaned from informal discussions, teaching materials, student evaluations, and instructor self-reflections, but there is sometimes a gap between what is illustrated on paper and what is actually happening in classrooms or tutoring sessions. Additionally, we have found that observations for program-evaluation purposes work best if instructors are involved in determining the focus of the observations—to the extent possible, within the stated parameters of the assessment. While it is difficult to observe individual instructors anonymously, it is possible to report results of observations without identifying instructors—especially if a standard observation form, based on assessment priorities, is used.

Outside Consultant Reviews

Though most program assessments are designed by administrators and faculty within a department or program, they often include external review. Assessment by an outside (and, presumably more objective) group can be very helpful in cases where there are few writing experts to make the case for program establishment or revision, if the department experts feel they may be too invested in a program to objectively consider its strengths and weaknesses, or if an upper-level administrator feels wary about insiders gathering the data that he or she will use to make decisions about a program. Such assessment can be arranged, individually, with any number of willing composition or writing-assessment experts across the country. It can occur in person and on-site, or it can happen via cyberspace, with a program making sample materials available to experts electronically. External program assessments can also be conducted more formally, and typically more thoroughly, through the Council of Writing Program Administrators. As described on the WPA Web site, the "consultant-evaluator" service will help program administrators and faculty coordinate a multi-stage process that involves a guided self-study, an on-site visit by "leaders in the field," a written report of the "program's unique strengths and weaknesses," and a follow-up report. The costs for the service include travel expenses and honoraria for the consultants. Although the WPA consultant-evaluator service is used more rarely for writing-center assessment than for assessment of FYC or WAC programs, it is an available option for supplementing internal methods and perspectives.

An alternative to inviting off-campus experts to review a program is the on-campus review conducted by people who may be familiar with the program but not personally invested in it. This group might include faculty from disciplines outside of English, administrators or staff members from relevant campus offices or programs, and even students. In fact, this type of inter-campus review can serve as a helpful complement to an outside-consultant visit. Martha Townsend (1997) offers a good example of combining a thorough internal review with the WPA consultant-evaluator service.

ANALYZING DATA

Like common assessment methods, means of analyzing the data gathered through an assessment are similar to those used for any empirical research project. Typically these means will fall into one of three categories: systematic, organic/phenomenological, or a back-and-forth negotiation between the first two approaches. The more systematic approach is often characterized by a rubric whose categories are determined before the data are analyzed; the more organic approach might involve a bit of early hypothesizing about possible categories but allows for new categories or data trends to emerge as the data are read and discussed. It's often most helpful to start with a very general sense of possible categories that can then accommodate new categories as they arise. With respect to teaching portfolios, for example, trends might include patterns in operational definitions that faculty are using (e.g., "most faculty seem to be describing academic writing as [*xyz*]"), patterns in kind and/or number of assignments, or in what student writing indicates about content of particular sections. In terms of student writing, categories often highlight stated learning outcomes or agreed-upon qualities of effective writing, such as "audience awareness," "clarity of organization," etc. (Please see chapters 5, 6, and 8 for more information on analyzing student writing and teaching materials.)

For program-assessment purposes, it will be important to remember that analysis of individual components of a writing program should always be considered within the context of the program as a whole and, if possible, within the larger context of the institution and local community. Intersections within and between contexts are being examined—not individual achievement or performance. Also, as with other areas of program assessment, it is important to involve as many people as possible, and appropriate, in discussions about how data should be analyzed.

PROGRAM ASSESSMENT SCENARIOS: BALANCING THEORY, PRACTICE, AND CONTEXT

Beyond the various considerations discussed above, the nature of the program—its history, mission, and goals—will influence the assessment approach. That is, assessing the effectiveness of a writing center will not necessarily involve the same approaches or methods as assessing a first-year composition program or a WAC initiative. For one thing, each of these programs will affect and/or answer to different groups of people. Another consideration is the size or scope of the individual program. For very large and/or very complex programs (such as a WAC program), targeted assessments, with results that are pieced together over time, may be the only realistic approach. Consistency in staffing is also an important issue. When faculty turnover is high, as in first-year composition programs and writing centers that rely heavily on TAs and part-time instructors, then a slower, multi-phased approach may not lead to meaningful results. If faculty members change every two or three years, data gathered one year may not mean the same thing four years later.

Still, we suggest that whatever the specific mission or purpose of the program—and however the methods may change depending on the purpose—the applicable theory will remain constant, as will the range of theory-based questions that will help guide those who are designing and facilitating assessments and using the results. Acknowledging that any program assessment "needs to be tailored to the program to be evaluated," Huot and Schendel (2002) identify three general areas that should be "looked at" to determine the overall health of a writing program: curricula, instruction, and student writing (220). Below, we offer some examples of context-sensitive assessments that will generate meaningful data in all of these key areas.

The First-Year Composition Program

Because first-year composition programs differ so much, in terms of number of courses, number and kind of faculty, and institutional positioning, it is nearly impossible to imagine an assessment approach that would work the same way in all FYC contexts. Our best advice is to thoroughly consider all of the factors that make the particular context unique and then adapt the most appropriate methods to the context. Again, generally speaking, the more methods used, the better for compiling an accurate program profile.

One issue that composition program faculty and administrators often don't anticipate—or actively resist—is that while English or writing departments usually staff introductory composition courses, they don't really "own" the courses—at least from the perspective of faculty in other departments. First-year (and often second-year) writing courses are typically integral parts of general education or "core" university programs and, thus, justifiably can be seen as everyone's territory (even if everyone does not wish to teach the courses). Chris Fosen quickly recognized this fact when, as a new program administrator, he found that he and his composition colleagues did not have full authority over curricula and assessment. As he explains, "We realized that we didn't own the course we regularly teach, couldn't fully control how our course would be institutionally assessed, and didn't understand why (as writing teachers) we couldn't simply revise the GE documents we found wanting" (2006, 12). It helped Fosen to come to terms with the fact that it was "not solely our course" (12) and try to understand why other people outside the department might view the purpose of the course differently than he and his colleagues did.

An example of how one method typically used for composition program assessment can inspire productive interaction among faculty across campus is the "three-tiered approach" for assessing student writing, described briefly by Huot and Schendel (2002, 221–22) and, then, in more detail in Huot (2002, 183–87). The approach relies on the expertise of instructors who regularly teach a particular course or courses and, thus, is consistent with the expert-reader course placement method developed by William L. Smith and outlined in chapter 5. It also promotes an organic, context-sensitive process for designing criteria during the reading process—not before reading begins. Finally, because readers outside of the English department are ultimately involved, the process encourages consideration of the larger campus context for writing and community-building among faculty from diverse disciplines.

The first assessment tier comprises a representative group of current instructors, including, for example, teaching assistants, part-time faculty, and full-time faculty, reading approximately 10 percent of student writing generated in a particular time frame (year, semester). The instructors divide into three teams to read and grade one-third of the sample. Each team then discusses and articulates criteria for each grade category they used (e.g., A, B, C) and writes a report about the characteristics of student writing in the sample and the process of working together. The second tier then involves a smaller group of readers examining a sampling from the first-tier reading. This second group would typically include the WPA, an instructor or teaching assistant who regularly teaches the course(s) being assessed, as well as faculty from disciplines outside of English. Similar to the first-tier reading, the second-tier reading involves discussing the writing samples, assigning grades, and discussing what the grades mean. Though some WPAs, constrained by limited time and/or resources, may need to stop after the second-tier reading, comparing and analyzing similarities and differences in results from the two readings, Huot and Schendel (2002) suggest a third tier, which involves taking the writing beyond the program and institution to be assessed by writing experts from other institutions. This can be done electronically, using the same reading/evaluating process employed in the first tiers, and then the results can be compared across tiers. The comparisons, then, form the basis for the program-assessment report.

Other methods can be similarly adapted to acknowledge—and account for—the role that first-year composition generally plays in university-wide initiatives such as general education programs. Surveys can be employed, for example, to gather information about faculty attitudes toward the first-year composition program, disciplinary differences in definitions of academic writing, and the amount and kinds of writing being assigned in other departments. Depending on the assessment questions being asked, data might then be used to simply raise awareness among writing faculty about attitudes on campus or to inform revisions of course objectives and/or curricula.

WAC Programs

One of the most obvious characteristics of any campus-wide program is its multidimensionality. Such programs attract many different faculty members with different disciplinary perspectives on not just writing per se but on the relationship between writing and meaning-making that manifests itself in particular written forms or "particular kinds of doing" (Carter 2001, 389). They also will feel different levels of commitment to helping students develop as writers. Students, too, will interpret writing assignments and expectations differently, depending upon where they are in their degree program and what their major discipline is. Finally, because WAC initiatives are often supported outside of departments, by, for example, a provost or VP, faculty and student interests often must be accounted for alongside interests of upper-level administrators. The complexity of campus-wide writing programs necessitates getting all "stakeholders" involved throughout the assessment process—from helping to set goals for the assessment to determining methods and interpreting/using outcomes (Morgan 1997, 147–48). It is not uncommon, for example, to see assessments of WAC programs undertaken by a representative university committee, as opposed to a single department-based administrator, or, if guided by a single administrator, for that administrator to act as a facilitator or consultant of fellow colleagues, rather than as a "director."

Given the multiple facets of WAC programs, the most widely accepted assessment approach for answering broad questions about overall effectiveness is one that includes various methods. Much like the methods that might be used in comprehensive assessments of first-year writing programs or writing centers, these methods might include surveys (of both faculty and students) to ascertain amount and kinds of writing happening on campus, how such writing is contributing to student learning (see Beason and Darrow 1997), as well as attitudes toward writing; samples of assignments and activities gathered from various departments; samples of student writing completed at various points (e.g., first year in college, first year in major, senior year); and interviews with faculty and students. Again, gathering data through these various means can be especially useful when starting a new program, as a way to establish benchmarks for measuring success in future years. After a program is established, another useful method is to count the number of new faculty becoming involved, the number of new courses, or, in the case of courses already in existence, any commendations given. At the University of Massachusetts, for example, one way of evaluating the success of WAC involves triennial review of department-based initiatives, focused on curriculum, instruction, and faculty participation, and subsequent ranking by a university writing committee. The number of initiatives that fall into "exemplary" or, at the other end of the spectrum, "experiencing difficulty" or "ineffective," then becomes a way of gauging "overall program health" (Moran and Herrington 1997).

In light of the preceding discussions, it will come as no surprise that the method for evaluating student writing promoted by WAC scholars and practitioners is portfolio assessment. Referencing other well-known WAC practitioners, Huot (1997) outlines the many advantages of using writing portfolios for WAC assessment. In addition to allowing students to showcase a "range of rhetorical and linguistic" abilities used to different degrees in different courses, "the multiple samples let evaluators consider the growth exhibited by students during a specified period" (71). Also, because the portfolios are comprised of work completed for actual writing-intensive courses certified by a WAC or general education program, they eliminate the need for separate proficiency tests and allow for a view of other elements in the program besides the final written product (e.g., kinds of assignments being given) (72). In addition, as William Condon (1997) points out, the "truly cross-curricular portfolio" that is readily supported by WAC illustrates to students connections among their work in various disciplines. As he puts it, "Combining WAC and portfolio-based assessment, even within the confines of a single course, provides a bridge from one learning experience to another, a means both for tying the experiences together and for creating a document that encourages learners to reflect on the ways those experiences reinforce or build upon each other" (209). Many of these same benefits are experienced by the WAC faculty who read the portfolios. Condon, for example, notes how discussions surrounding student portfolios can inspire both heightened standards for writing and increased "awareness among all faculty for the kinds of thinking and writing that occur" across the curriculum (210). Huot (1997) attests to the positive value of engaging numerous faculty in the assessment process. In encouraging faculty to read student work together, he sees "the beginning of a partnership with content area faculty that encourages them to look at the writing they are requiring, at how well their students are writing, and at what faculty response to this writing says about their individual goals as teachers and the overall goals and mission of their programs" (76).

Sometimes, as in the case of the university about which Huot (1997) writes, the portfolios are collected and submitted by the instructors of writing-intensive courses for the sole purpose of assessing the WAC program. In other cases, the portfolios are composed and submitted for reasons other than program assessment, but, because writing curricula and instruction are well-aligned across campus, they can be used successfully for dual purposes. In their account of WAC initiatives at George Mason University, for example, Christopher Thais and Terry Zawacki (1997) explain how they use portfolios submitted for exemption from a WAC-based advanced composition course for more general WAC assessment purposes. The portfolios, submitted by thirty-five to forty students per semester, typically include a "research-based paper" from a course in the student's major, three or four "other works" from courses taken above the 100-level, and a "reflective 'process' essay" on selected portfolio contents (80, 94). Though the exemption portfolios haven't been used to "directly assess" writing initiatives across campus, they have provided helpful insights about the kinds of writing students are doing in their courses, the criteria faculty emphasize in their courses, and the attitudes students have about their writing and about themselves as writers (87–91).

One challenge for administrators and faculty who wish to read portfolios as part of a campus-wide program assessment is coming up with an evaluation scheme that will make sense to people from a variety of disciplines. If the WAC program is run by a committee or advisory board comprised of members from diverse disciplines, the group, guided by national statements on college-level writing (like those provided by WPA and NCTE), can discuss and design a rubric based on general rhetorical concerns such as purpose, audience, genre, idea development, and organization. If greater attention to disciplinary differences is desired (as may be the case with a WAC program that supports upper-level major courses), evaluation criteria may need to be more specific. An alternative to the one-size-fits-all rubric is a method offered by Huot (1997). Faculty from representative departments are paid a stipend to share samples of student writing which would fit into typical assessment categories (e.g., acceptable, unacceptable, exceptional) and work with other faculty in their disciplines, as well as WAC staff, to design "discipline specific" scoring guides that are then used to evaluate writing portfolios submitted for WAC assessment (73).

Writing Centers

Because the mission and goals of a writing center will be somewhat different from those of other types of writing programs, the questions and means of answering them will be different. One obvious difference that should be accounted for through assessment design is that writing center directors typically answer to a wider range of constituencies than do most first-year composition directors. Writing centers are often funded, at least in part, by offices outside of an English department and even outside the college (e.g., by vice presidents of student affairs, university programs, grant agencies, etc.). Additionally, though some writing centers do serve mostly (or even exclusively) students who are enrolled in English courses, others are important components of WAC programs. Writing centers that are part of larger campus-wide initiatives often need to gather data to justify external funding for people who may have little background in the humanities, let alone in English. Because they control the funding (and, thus, the continued existence) of a writing center, external agencies often feel that they not only have the right to demand a certain form of assessment report but the prerogative to dictate assessment methods and participants. Not surprisingly, then, the most typical methods for assessing writing center work have been those that translate readily into quantitative reports—methods such as "usage data" collection (i.e., counting the number of students who use the center), student and faculty surveys, objective pre- and post-tests of mechanical skills, and course-grade correlation (Lerner 2003, 60–61). The problem with methods that generate numbers, according to writing center scholars like Neal Lerner and Muriel Harris, is that, because they are often unaligned with current theories about learning and teaching, they may not provide information that will actually help center directors and tutors improve their work with students. The challenge, then, is to either combine more quantitative methods with qualitative ones or to make the quantitative methods more qualitative by contextualizing them.

For writing center directors and staff members who have the luxury of formulating their own questions and wish to start with a broad query like, "What is going on in the writing center?" or, for those proposing a new center, "What should our center look like?"—a large-scale approach that allows for collection of as much data as possible is ideal. With respect to the first question, in addition to the methods mentioned above, such an inquiry might include examining textbooks and assignments from writing-intensive courses across campus (to determine the kind of information students are getting about writing outside of the center); observing and/or audio taping tutoring sessions in light of national "best practices" and/or against rubrics developed by writing center staff; interviewing tutors, students, and faculty one-to-one or in small focus groups; and analyzing tutor self-reports. Student writing samples can also be gathered, with permission from students, to determine overall strengths and weaknesses of particular populations using the center. To answer the second question, some of these methods (e.g., examination of textbooks, assignments, student writing, and interviews) can usefully be combined with collection of data about the larger university, disciplinary, and academic context. Both Lerner and Harris suggest, for example, careful consideration of university goals (and how a writing center can help support them) and institutional data related to those goals (when available), review of literature on writing center design and/or assessment, and surveys of other WC directors (e.g., on design, assessment, and costs).

Because writing centers have traditionally been vulnerable to budget cutting for reasons having to do with how they are positioned on campus (usually as a support service for first-year composition programs), how they are funded, and how they are staffed (typically with low-status instructors like graduate assistants and term faculty), it has become even more important for them to attempt to show that their services make a difference for students. Thus, for writing center directors, questions that guide assessments often must focus on how many students are using the center, why students are using (or not using) the center, and what difference the center makes for students who use it. Again, the challenge here is trying to answer these questions in a way that is meaningful (for the writing center) and useful (for upper-level administrators or outside funding agencies)—and to resist the temptation, discussed earlier in the chapter, to engage in either-or thinking (i.e., either we use quantitative methods to satisfy others or qualitative methods to satisfy ourselves). With respect to the question on student use, the usual data collected from simply counting the number of center visits is not often very helpful to WC directors and "not exactly a selling point" for administrators because most writing centers "see no more than 10 to 15 percent of their student bodies" (Lerner 2003, 61). However, this data becomes more meaningful when combined with other, more qualitative, data (gathered through sign-in sheets or simple questionnaires) about the needs of students who visit and reasons why students use or don't use a particular center. By considering not just the raw usage numbers but demographic data (e.g., year in school, whether native or non-native speaker), statistics can be used to demonstrate how a center is supporting wider campus goals. If, for example, a university's priority is supporting diversity, then the fact that 60–75 percent of those students who use the writing center are ESL learners (the statistic that Lerner provides for his own center) will mean more to writing center directors and upper-level administrators than just an unqualified usage statistic. It may also be possible to conduct a survey in combination with counting students. Through a survey of students who did not use the writing center on his campus, Lerner found, for instance, that students were not, as he suspected, dissuaded by a "remedial definition" of writing center work, but that they felt the hours of the center were "inconvenient" (65). The raw usage data combined with the more qualitative data together offered evidence to suggest that with some changes (e.g., different hours of operation, introducing online tutoring), the writing center would attract more students. Depending on time constraints, such surveys could be supplemented with focus group or individual interviews.

Writing Majors

A growing trend in composition and rhetoric is the writing major, which typically allows undergraduate students to both practice different types of writing and study disciplinary history, theory, and research. Though program-level assessments of writing majors may not necessarily be the responsibility of writing program directors, they most likely will be designed and conducted by some of the same writing faculty who have been called upon to facilitate reviews of other writing-based programs.

While the overall approach to assessing a writing major (question-driven, multi-modal, context-sensitive) will be similar to the approaches outlined above, the values and perspectives that must be accounted for will likely change. Depending on how the major has been designed, program assessment may need to take into account not just the interests of composition and rhetoric faculty, but those of technical writing, creative writing, and sometimes journalism faculty as well. Interestingly, the differences between English subfields can sometimes seem more difficult to negotiate than differences between English and other academic fields that are highlighted in WAC assessments. While a comp-rhet specialist will likely prioritize audience and purpose, when discussing student learning outcomes for a writing major, a creative writer may have other priorities for students—an understanding of genre conventions or stylistic choices, for example. Similarly, tech writers, though convinced of the importance of audience awareness, may prioritize knowledge of design elements or software programs in ways that other writing faculty may not. The theories embraced by each subfield may also need to be negotiated. In their discussion of how creative nonfiction courses might be incorporated into a writing major, for example, Linda Shamoon and Celest Martin (2007) describe the negative attitude that compositionists trained in social or critical theory might have toward courses with words like "creative" or "expressive" in the title (53). Sometimes, conflicts can be traced to basic worries about disciplinary identity (and implied issues of departmental status and distribution of limited resources). Thomas Peele (2007) explains that his department's writing major is a site of contention because of disagreements between creative writers, composition and rhetoric specialists, and technical writers over how writing should be defined and who should be responsible for which courses.

HOW SHOULD RESULTS BE REPORTED?

Most program assessments culminate in a report with recommendations for future action. The particular format for the report will depend on many factors including the purpose of the assessment, who will get the results, and how the results will be used.

In terms of purpose, if the assessment has been conducted, at least in part, to satisfy an external request for data (from a dean or grant agency), then there may be a standardized reporting form, or reporting conventions, that need to be followed. Ideally, directions or models for reporting results will be provided, and some leeway will be given for disciplinary differences (i.e., humanities-type disciplines will be allowed to submit more descriptive data). Yet, as we have been emphasizing up to this point, assessment rarely occurs in the realm of the ideal. It will very likely be the case that a program administrator-evaluator will be asked for data but will not be provided with clear directions about how that data should be reported or that the directions will privilege certain disciplines (usually the hard sciences) over others. In this case, a greater effort will be required to consider other aspects of the rhetorical situation.

For example, White (1995) asserts the importance of considering "the kind of evidence that is likely to fit the assumptions of the audience [for our results]" (134). Along these same lines, Haswell and McLeod (2001) suggest that the data that interest program administrators won't necessarily interest upper-level administrators—and that, with this latter group, there will be differing priorities. That is, administrators more directly involved in program funding may want to know about specific problem areas and what is necessary to fix them, while a president or board of regents may just want a general sense of what is happening (178–82). From their perspective, a good initial step in determining the contents of a report is simply asking the relevant administrator, "What do you want to know?" (177). Additionally, the strategies used to report the results will need to be different depending on personal (often discipline-based) preferences. As they point out, for example, the "hard scientist" wants "clean facts" (179). In essence, then, the data may need to be presented in multiple reports, adjusted for differences in reader needs and interests.

Though some audiences may desire data in numerical (versus descriptive) form, it is important to resist selecting methods based solely on preferred reporting mode. Again, the purpose of the assessment (which should somehow be related to improving teaching and learning)—and accompanying research questions—should determine the methods. So, taking White's lead, a WPA can use his or her knowledge of writing theory to "ask [the] audience to adopt new assumptions about what counts as evidence" (1995, 134) or, if that doesn't work (the chances are better if the WPA understands not only writing theory but assessment theory), then he or she can attempt to provide results generated through qualitative methods in a numerical form.

The results that are most obviously quantifiable are results that are easily and readily tabulated: years (or kind) of teaching experiences of instructors, types of teaching methods, pass rates, retention rates, number of tutoring sessions, etc. The more important fact, though, is that if simple numbers are all that a dean or agency needs (or wants), then almost any information can be quantified—even information about student writing performance gathered through direct methods like portfolios. The truth is that the most descriptive, context-oriented scoring guide can result in a numerical report (perhaps written as an additional report to complement the context-rich report written for program purposes). The evaluators simply count how many students' papers or portfolios fell into a particular category and put the results in an easy-to-read graph or chart.

That said, it is important to note that more and more administrators (especially deans) are being asked by their institutional-effectiveness offices (who are being asked by accrediting agencies) not only to gather assessment data about their departments and programs but to make sure they are used in a "feedback loop" to improve student learning. So, while they may prefer reports that are more quantitative, they will need enough qualitative (contextual, descriptive) information to understand what the data really mean, how they can be used. That is, "the arguments that may convince them to change" (White 1995, 134) their perspectives about evidence are changing—and mostly for the better. Writing program administrators and faculty who know assessment theory (the same theory now guiding accrediting agencies) will be at an advantage when it comes to determining which results can be easily quantified without undermining the integrity of the assessment and which results might need to be presented in more descriptive terms.

If the results are going to be circulated within the department or program only, then the options for reporting may be much more numerous and flexible. Depending on the purpose of the assessment, it may be enough to simply report results orally at a meeting and schedule follow-up discussions about implications and possible program revisions. If a more permanent record is needed, then a formal report may be required. A common approach is to follow the tradition of scientific report writing, beginning with a statement of the problem or key questions, a description of methods (including approach to data gathering, analysis, people involved, etc.), presentation of findings, discussion of findings, and recommendations. Though often the leader of the assessment ends up writing the document, it's more effective, for the sake of buy in, to write it collaboratively, ask for feedback, and then make required revisions.

USING RESULTS

Because one of the biggest sources of resistance to assessment is the feeling that results will never be used, it is crucial that program administrators and faculty find ways of utilizing data to either support claims about the well-being of an already effective program or to make a program better. Even if an assessment was inspired by an external request and the person making the request is disinclined to act on results or recommendations, program directors can still make sure that something is done locally with the information that is gathered.

Along with the difficulty of demonstrating direct relationships between data and student learning, which makes it hard to confidently articulate implications and/or guarantee recommendations, there are often practical circumstances that make it difficult to implement assessment findings. For example, a program assessment may reveal that under-prepared writers would be better served by self-placement or mainstreaming, but state legislation requires placement in "remedial" classes for all students who earn a certain score on a standardized test. Similarly, an assessment might reveal systemic problems with instruction that could most easily be resolved by attracting more faculty members with credentials in writing. However, the money and other perks needed to attract such faculty may simply be unavailable.

As with program assessments themselves, which sometimes must be scaled back due to lack of resources, the findings may need to be implemented slowly, over time. While it may not be possible to mainstream low-scoring students into standard first-year writing courses, for example, it may be possible to restructure remedial courses so they require less time and expense. With respect to faculty, though money may not be available for new hires, it may be possible to pay current faculty to attend workshops and conferences.

Finally, as with data collection, it's important to see use of assessment results as something potentially long-term—something that may not happen in one WPA's tenure. Echoing Muriel Harris's call for all writing center directors to "set up and maintain a research archive" (Harris 1999, 14), we suggest that writing program administrators accept, as one of their responsibilities, the archiving of assessment records. As Harris argues, such records are not only necessary for determining the present condition of a program, they are essential to preserving the "institutional memory" that can be lost through administrative turnover. Additionally, they allow for the ongoing reflection needed for long-term strategic planning. A side benefit is that an archive that is maintained over a number of years can serve as a "testimonial" to how much we do, and how hard we work, to run our programs effectively.

8

EVALUATING WRITING FACULTY AND INSTRUCTION

Evaluation of faculty is not usually considered part of the domain of writing assessment because its purpose is to assess teachers' effectiveness, not students' writing or writing programs. Yet, the faculty deliver the writing curriculum, conduct classroom evaluation and—within the framework we present in this book—participate in writing assessments beyond the classroom (e.g., placement testing, program review, or exit testing). Faculty are arguably the most significant factor in a program's effectiveness and in students' learning; therefore, a robust system for evaluating teachers and teaching is critical to an effective writing program and in assessing a program. We are not alone in thinking that instructors and instruction are significant factors in program assessment. Evaluation of teaching materials, curriculum, and faculty is directly addressed in the self-study guidelines for writing programs published by the Council of Writing Program Administrators. Practitioners and scholars also agree that these are important components of program assessment. Edward White's text *Developing Successful College Writing Programs* (1989) includes a chapter entitled "Supporting, Evaluating, and Rewarding Faculty." Stephen Witte and Lester Faigley (1983) identify curriculum and instruction as two of the five general components of writing program evaluation.

We see these two components—curriculum and instruction—as intimately connected, joined, in fact, by the faculty. For example, a program might have a published, standard curriculum; however, if the faculty delivering the curriculum do not do so effectively, then the value of the curriculum is undermined. Or, instructors in the same program might interpret curricular guidelines, assignments, or activities in very different ways, which may result in very different student performance and achievement. For instance, if a program requires students to engage in academic research, the ways to approach assignments or courses vary. What academic discipline is going to be privileged? Does the instructor and instruction focus on developing research questions and using both primary and secondary research methods to answer the questions? Does the instructor limit the research to textual research only? How are electronic research methods incorporated in the course? Will students be writing for general, academic, or specialized audiences? Likewise, instructors' decisions about enacting the curriculum have consequences for students' development as writers, which are related to other features of the program. For example, if a program has a proficiency or exit assessment, but a teacher does not include assignments and feedback that prepare the students for that assessment, then students might perform poorly on the exam in spite of doing well in the instructor's course. Effective instruction can also have consequences for placement results; if some instructors are not teaching in ways that meet the program's expectations, accurate placement of students into courses may be compromised because the efficacy of placement will depend much more on the particular section the student is enrolled in rather than on which course the student is placed into.

Faculty, in short, are key to students' experiences in a writing program because they carry out a program's learning goals or outcomes, create learning opportunities, apply evaluation criteria, and determine individual student grades. While teachers in all subjects are critical to students' learning, writing instructors' performances may be even more critical than in some other disciplines because student achievement depends in large part on teachers' response to students' writing, the classroom activities orchestrated by the instructors, and student-instructor conferences, according to position statements published by the National Council of Teachers of English and the Conference on College Composition and Communication (1982, 1989). In most writing programs, however, the expertise and experience of faculty vary greatly; some are staffed completely by graduate students and part-time lecturers while others may consist of full-time, non-tenure-line faculty, and still others may include a mix of graduate students, adjunct, and tenured faculty. In addition to the diversity of rank, a writing program's faculty typically hold various academic degrees and represent a wide range of specialties. Strong faculty evaluation programs can help writing program administrators effectively cope with the diversity of instructors to ensure students experience appropriate learning opportunities across sections of the same course without undermining the benefits that a diverse faculty can bring to a program. A strong faculty evaluation system provides information about students' achievement of the program goals and how instruction facilitates this achievement. Students' opportunities to develop as writers should not hinge on which section of the course they enroll in (and who is assigned to teach that section), but on students' abilities, efforts, and performances. The effectiveness of a writing program depends on individual instructors and their classroom teaching; therefore, it's important to design effective, theoretically informed, faculty evaluation programs that include both formative and summative evaluations.

The rest of this chapter offers a theoretical framework for approaching faculty evaluation and describes various types and methods of evaluation, including student ratings of instruction, classroom observations, and teaching portfolios. We close by addressing some of the challenges assessors may confront in faculty evaluation.

EVALUATING FACULTY

Review of teaching and teachers can, like all assessment, be approached in various ways. Because we see the evaluation of teachers and teaching as critical components of writing program assessment and closely tied to teaching and assessing writing, we advocate an approach to faculty assessment that is based on the principles of writing assessment we outlined in chapter 3: site-based, locally controlled, rhetorically based, context-sensitive, accessible, and theoretically consistent. Applying this framework for faculty evaluation means that evaluation should be controlled by the local program and institution, which is responsible for managing, revising, and validating the process of faculty review according to stated personnel policies as well as professional standards. The assessment of writing teachers and teaching also needs to take into account the local context, honoring the program's instructional goals as well as the socio-cultural environment. This is especially important for reading and interpreting teaching materials and student-generated texts and in addressing the diversity of rank and status of faculty who may be teaching in a writing program. Considering the individual characteristics of the program is critical because the teaching of writing is not a one-size-fits-all endeavor. Teaching is a communicative act, and the teacher needs to respond to specific writers, in terms of specific instructional goals, in the specific context.

While local context is important, the processes, procedures, and criteria for evaluating faculty must also be consistent with what we know about effective teaching of writing and assessment. To be legitimate, faculty assessment must produce valid results, which means it should lead to improved teaching and learning, and it should differentiate between more effective and less effective practices and instructors. Finally, a faculty-assessment program should be transparent to all faculty involved, regardless of rank or institutional status. Procedures, criteria, rationales, samples, and results should be available to all, and this information should be communicated in language that is accessible to all as well.

Applying these basic principles requires a writing program to provide both formative and summative evaluations. Formative assessment, the goal of which is to focus on improvement, is frequently covered as part of the scholarship of teaching (e.g., Bain 2004; Seldin 1997; Seldin and Associates 1999; and McKeachie 1984) as well as the literature on preparing writing teachers—typically graduate student teaching assistants (Pytlik and Ligget 2001; Chase 1996; Morgan 2002) or faculty involved in writing across the curriculum (Bean 1994; Kinkead 1997). Formative assessment, as explained by Christine Hult in the introduction to *Evaluating Teachers of Writing*, "is designed to provide information that may help" writing teachers "to alter their teaching in ways to improve student learning" (1994, 4). The stakes are low in this type of evaluation; that is, the consequences are aimed at improving teaching and learning, and will not be used for conferring rewards or sanctions. In contrast, the purpose of summative evaluation is to determine merit or worth, or as Hult says, "judge overall teaching performance" (1994, 4), and the stakes are typically higher. Summative evaluation should come at the end of a process or program, or at designated intervals. For example, new teachers may be evaluated at the end of a semester or the end of a year to determine if they will be renewed, the distribution of merit raises, or who will receive a teaching award.

Formative and summative evaluation are often presented in opposition to each other, as Hult does in her discussion. She argues that too often "in teacher evaluation, because formative is not separated from summative, the two goals of accountability and improvements are conflated when they are not necessarily compatible" (1994, 5). However, we believe that these two forms of evaluation should work together, which is recommended in some of the composition literature (e.g., White 1989; Schwalm 1994; Weiser 1994) as well as the more general scholarship of teaching (England, Hutchings, and McKeachie 2007, 13–14). Formative assessment techniques may be used throughout a semester to not only improve teaching but also to demonstrate a commitment to teaching and innovation. Based on the formative activities, a peer, mentor, or supervisor may write an overall summative assessment report, detailing the activities, growth, and effectiveness of the teacher over the semester or longer time frame. Or, a teacher may use formative assessment results for more summative purposes, as part of a teaching portfolio to submit to a teaching review committee or as part of a tenure and promotion application. Formative assessment is also a type of faculty development because the goal of it is to provide support for faculty to improve their practice or to expand their pedagogical repertoire. In designing formative opportunities, programs should consider the professional guidelines and published scholarship. According to accepted practice in the teaching of writing, teachers should create student-centered classrooms with many opportunities for students to write with instruction tailored, in many ways, for individual students and their texts. White articulates it this way:

> The best writing teachers often appear to be doing relatively little teaching or grading by conventional definitions. They will be working very hard devising appropriate writing tasks, responding to student drafts, talking with students

about their writing, helping them evaluate and revise their work, presenting and challenging ideas, grading presentation drafts of papers, and the like, but they may never give a lecture. (1989, 165)

Professional organizations agree with White and others. According to a variety of position statements published by the Conference on College Composition and Communication (1982, 1989), its Committee on Teaching and Evaluation (1982), and its parent organization, the National Council of Teachers of English (2004), writing instruction needs to be student centered, with the teacher providing opportunities for guided practice in all phases of the process; and writing instructors need to be writers who also have a strong disciplinary understanding of language development, rhetoric, and writing as a process. As White explains, "Essentially, the teaching of writing requires a different kind of relationship between student and faculty than most other courses do, and calls for a much more steady pressure on the teacher to respond sensitively to student work" (1989, 165).

Part of the commitment to an effective formative and summative evaluation system that adheres to the principles of writing assessment includes explicit criteria for judging effective teachers and teaching (Jones 1994). In 1982, the CCCC Committee on Teaching and Its Evaluation in Composition identified seven components of teaching and learning to be considered in evaluating writing instruction—and by association instructors: (1) preliminary reflection and analysis (referred to earlier in their document as a theoretical framework), (2) planning of the curriculum and writing activities, (3) classroom activities engaged in by students and teacher, (4) instructional activities engaged in by students and teacher outside the classroom, (5) learning activities students engage in independently, (6) performances—especially writing—students engage in after instruction, and (7) students' recollections and feelings about their experiences (26).

These components, anchored in the program's mission or stated learning goals and in student performance, need to be considered as well as specific evaluation criteria tailored to local programs. However, a caution is in order. Student performance needs to be defined contextually, and evaluators must take into consideration the institution's mission and student body as well as support both students and writing faculty receive. For example, how many students are in a first-year writing class? Is there a writing center available for students? Are faculty provided with opportunities for professional development, especially related to responding to and evaluating student performance? Of course, evaluation criteria also need to be theoretically consistent—with the program's goals, with scholarly research on literacy and language, and with assessment theory (as we discuss in chapter 3). Developing students as writers and improving their written texts is complex, multifaceted, and time intensive. If a program's stated outcomes are process oriented, emphasizing multiple drafts, deep revision, editing, and proofreading, student performance on an impromptu essay exam is not an accurate indicator of their achievement of these goals. Likewise, if a composition program's learning goals address rhetorical concepts of audience and purpose and developing flexibility to address multiple rhetorical situations, a single writing sample is not enough to determine achievement. In short, as discussed in the program assessment chapter, examining student work is a critical component—but not the only one—of determining the effectiveness of teaching and learning.

As with any complex performance, the evaluation of writing teachers—and teaching and learning—needs to include multiple sources of evidence that are systematically collected and reviewed. Relying on only one data source—or on a haphazard collection of data—may not provide the kind of information needed to make a sound assessment decision about the quality of the instruction and the faculty's performance. Results of assessments of instructors also need to be considered contextually, in light of the program, the institution, the students served, and a myriad of other factors than can influence both the faculty's and students' performances. The evaluation of teachers should acknowledge that there are multiple ways to achieve the stated learning outcomes, teachers have individual strengths and weaknesses, and teachers have their own classroom personae. The goal of these assessment activities is not uniformity in teaching and materials but rather developing a shared understanding of what effective teaching and learning means in the particular writing program so that individual instructors make the most out of their strengths as teachers of writing, benefiting all students in the program.

By examining multiple sources of information about an instructor's (and a program's) performance, an evaluation system can allow for variation while still achieving its goals. Multiple sources of data allow evaluators to contextualize information and develop a more complete understanding of an instructor's performance (Baldwin and Blattner 2003). This is similar to triangulation, a basic strategy for enhancing internal validity in qualitative research, which uses multiple investigators, data sources, or multiple methods (Merriam 1998, 204). For example, if the surveys or student ratings of instruction are generic and not tied to the writing program's specific goals and criteria, those results may need to be viewed even more critically and within the context of other evidence, such as observations of instruction, student writing samples, and course materials. It is also essential, as we say above, that writing programs make the criteria and processes for assessment accessible to all faculty regardless of rank or status. The ultimate goal of any assessment program is to improve teaching and learning; however, if faculty are apprehensive because assessment is perceived as a threat, the criteria are not articulated, or they don't know how the results will be used, the potential benefits of the assessment program are jeopardized.

METHODS OF EVALUATION

As we have said about other aspects of writing assessment, using what you know about research is useful in approaching assessment of instruction and instructors. Evaluating instruction—as with research—requires asking questions and finding answers that are supported by evidence. When researching complex performances, scholars recommend multiple methods and data sources, and the same is true for evaluation of faculty and teaching (e.g., Hult 1994; Bain 2004, 167-8; Chism 1999, 4; England, Hutchings, and McKeachie 1996). Relying on one measure or one data source provides only partial answers and can, in fact, minimize important aspects of both teaching and learning. Teaching writing (like all teaching) is a complex, multidimensional activity that cannot be accurately accessed by one method or at one moment in time. Multiple methods allow for evaluation of the range of skills, activities, and teaching practices experienced faculty use and for variety in documenting the results.

We address below various common methods used in evaluating teachers and teaching. The list is not definitive nor is our discussion of each exhaustive. Many of these methods, such as student ratings of instruction and teaching portfolios, have large bodies of published literature associated with them. Instead, the list is a place to begin to think about how you can approach this aspect of a program review. As we discuss each method of evaluation, we include ways these can work together, and we remind you that many overlap with other methods, such as those in chapter 7 on program review. Obviously, we are not suggesting that all of these methods should be used all of the time. Faculty and program administrators need to decide what is best in their particular program given the local context, resources, expectations, and purposes. Including peer review in these methods emphasizes the focus on effective teaching and learning because the instructors will both give and receive feedback, learning from each other as they develop a better understanding of the program and how their teaching contributes to it.

Remember, the focus is not on the evaluation of individual instructors for personnel reviews, although many of the results of methods directly contribute to this, but rather on how teachers and teaching contribute to a program's effectiveness. By compiling the results of individual faculty evaluations, assessors can get a better understanding of the effectiveness of the instruction in a program. For example, reading through observation reports of all of the instructors—maybe even categorizing them according to certain criteria such as desired classroom activities described in the reports—can provide evidence of the type of classroom activities used in a program. This kind of review can also provide insight for determining topics for faculty-development workshops (as well as leaders for the workshops). Or, by reviewing student portfolios and detailing the type of writing represented in them, a program can provide specific evidence about the genres students write as well as how well they perform.

Student Survey

Student evaluations, commonly referred to as student ratings of instruction (SRIs), are the most common and consistent form of evaluation of instructors and instruction. These are typically completed anonymously by students at the end of the term, using a computer scan form with minimal opportunity for open-ended response. However, the quality and content of the rating systems can vary widely. Some instruments are designed locally and can range from those that are carefully developed and monitored by psychometric scholars to those that are hastily written by individual instructors; others are marketed nationwide and developed by psychometricians with national norming data provided to individual institutions and instructors. Some of the commercially available student surveys are standardized while the instructor or institution tailors others. Most use a form of the Likert Scale, and results are typically reported numerically. SRIs are likely the most-researched form of evaluation of instruction besides being the most common. Research on the surveys is mixed, complicated by the fact that there are so many different forms available. There is a large body of work on the effects of factors such as gender of instructor, size of class, time of day, and level of class on the validity and reliability of the results of these instruments.[1]

---

1.   The literature on student evaluations is extensive but often inconclusive. For overviews of the literature see the following: Abrami, Theall, and Mets (2001); d'Apollanio and Abrami (1997); Greenwald (1997a); Hobson and Talbot (2001); and Wachtel (1998). The spring 2001 issue of *New Directions in Institutional Research* focuses on student ratings of instruction; besides offering an overview, it also addresses specific issues such as validity (Kulik; Ory and Ryan), use (Abrami, "Improving" and "How to Lie"; Theall), and bias (Theall and Franklin). The literature also covers an assortment of other factors that can influence student evaluations, such as gender (e.g., Basow and Montgomery 2005), workload (e.g., Greenwald 1997b), perceptions (e.g., Sojka, Gupta, and Deeter-Schmelz 2002), and academic freedom (e.g., Haskell 1997), among others. In fact, Wachtel (1998) identifies the following factors from the body of research that can affect student evaluations: administration of the surveys, including timing and stated purpose; course characteristics, such as electivity, class meeting time, level of course, class size, subject area, course workload; instructor characteristics, such as reputation, personality, research productivity, gender, minority status, and physical appearance; characteristics of students, including interest, gender, expected grade, and leniency hypothesis; student expectations; and other issues such as student and faculty reactions to the results and publicizing student ratings. Less formal ratings,

While we can see some value in these student ratings, we also realize that the validity of SRI results needs to be determined for each particular case. It is important that so-called objective measures, such as student surveys, be interpreted within the context of the program and the institution. The data from surveys and questionnaires, especially those that do not allow for explanatory comments, are not enough to determine effectiveness. Teaching and learning are situated, contextual activities, so just because a survey works at a small liberal arts college doesn't mean it produces valid and reliable results at the state college down the road. Or, survey results that prove valid and reliable in large lecture classes may not prove so in small seminars. Determining if the results are valid demands the examination of the results in terms of other measures of effective teaching and learning. The goal is to ensure that the results of the SRI accurately distinguish effective teaching from less effective teaching. After all, in our experience, one of the biggest problems with SRIs is that faculty can learn how to "work the numbers" to make sure the ratings are good, which doesn't mean the instruction is effective (White 1994). In addition, instructors' assumptions about the surveys can influence how they teach a class. For example, although research is mixed in terms of the effect of rigorous grading on survey results, many faculty believe that tough graders get lower SRI numbers. This kind of institutional myth can affect how faculty members, especially junior faculty, non-tenured instructors, and others who feel vulnerable, grade students' performances. It is important, then, to be sure to conduct ongoing, systematic research into the SRIs and the use of them.

Depending on your local situation, you may have more or less flexibility in terms of the instrument used for the official end-of-semester SRIs. In some places, departments or individual instructors can determine the content of student surveys while in other places, college or university committees make these decisions. In any case, the standard forms can be replaced or supplemented with a survey tailored to the specific program, as Irwin Weiser describes what his program did to tailor the student evaluation to address the program's specific goals and expectations (1994, 141–43). This type of course-specific form can provide data that address the expectations and outcomes specified for the courses as well as feedback to instructors and program administrators that links directly to improving teaching and learning. New survey software, whether for online surveys or paper and

such as ratemyprofessor.com undoubtedly have some effect—if only by contributing to an instructor's reputation and students' expectations—but have not been addressed substantively in the research as of yet. Student ratings are also addressed as part of broader discussions about teacher effectiveness (e.g., McKeachie 1984; England, Hutchings, and McKeachie 2007). In the literature specific to writing instruction, there also is discussion of student ratings and the role they play in evaluating faculty (e.g., Elbow 1994; Weiser 1994; Strenski 1994; Willard-Traub 2002).

pencil, can make it easier to tailor evaluations to individual program needs. This software can make compiling and analyzing the results—even open-ended comments—easier than ever. For an example, the first-year writing program at one of our institutions developed a student survey of instruction, in collaboration with the institutional research office, based on the goals of the first-year writing program. The form was created with Class Climate software, which allows users to write their own questions, create their own scale, and collect student comments for each question to help explain the response. Both the quantitative and discursive results are compiled and reported for individual faculty, and reports can be generated for results across the program. Here is a sample from the form:

> *Evaluate the success of this course in helping you learn how to formulate an original thesis, focus, or controlling idea and support it.*
>
> Not Successful □ □ □ □ □ □ □ □ □ □ Very Successful
>
> Explanatory Comment

This type of form not only focuses more on teaching and instruction and less on the teacher as a personality, but it also provides information that can help teachers to improve their teaching. (See appendix E for a complete example of this type of survey.) In other words, it can provide information that is both formative and summative. As one instructor said in an e-mail to the composition director after switching to this form for SRIs over the more traditional one: "I appreciate the new student evaluation forms for WR100. I got mine today and was amazed at the insight they offer into the REASONS why students give the ratings they do. . . . I'm a little excited here because I think these new evaluation forms will give me much more precise feedback about the ways I need to rethink/revise my courses." The goal of any evaluation system, including student surveys, should be to improve teaching and learning, as discussed throughout this book. This approach to surveying students not only enhances the formative aspect of the evaluation for the individual instructor and the program, but it also works to make the assessment align with the particular context of the program since the survey is tailored to the course and program goals.

While most of these surveys are done at the end of the semester, programs can also use less formal, shorter surveys during the semester for formative assessment (Aultman 2006). The questions need to be tailored to the course and program. For example, in a course using a final evaluation form such as the one described above, a mid-semester survey might ask students to respond anonymously to questions such as:

1. Which learning goals do you feel you are making progress on? Why?

2. Which goals do you still feel uncomfortable with or unsure about? Why?

3. What questions or concerns do you have about the course so far?

While many writing teachers conduct an informal mid-semester evaluation for their own benefit, it can be useful for a standard set of questions to be used periodically to help the program administrators develop workshops and support for instructors. Comparing responses to mid-semester surveys with those administered at the end of the course can contribute to an understanding of how the course developed across the semester.

Observations

Observations of classroom instruction are common in the summative evaluation of individual faculty, but they also serve as formative evaluation. By having a systematic approach to observing faculty, observations are also part of formative and summative program assessment. A systematic approach requires a protocol for the actual observation and subsequent report as well as a process for determining who will be observed, by whom, when, and how many times (e.g., Flanigan 1979; Flanagan 1994; Chase 1996; Strenski 1994; Minter 2002; and Chism 1999). In determining these procedures, the basic principles of writing assessment are helpful because local factors such as program structure, institutional context, and staffing need to be considered in adapting professional standards. Most of the literature recommends a standard protocol and form to ensure that the observations done across the program yield consistent kinds of information, which is especially important if multiple people are observers, as is the case in the peer review model. In writing programs, especially those staffed almost exclusively with contingent faculty, observations should be conducted by both instructors and program administrators. Appendix D contains a sample observation form that follows the process outlined below, which was modeled after Flanigan's (1979) recommendations.

In general, effective observations start with pre-observation discussion about the class to be observed, including goals for the class, materials, and other contextual information. The instructor being observed, depending on the local climate, may also indicate aspects of her teaching or class that she wants feedback on (e.g., the way students work in a small group or the length of wait time she uses when conducting a class discussion). During the observation, the observer should focus on recording information—that is, describing the student activities and behavior, the instructor's action, the material covered, the interaction among the students and between the students and the instructor, and the organization of the room. In general, the observer is not a participant in the class but a recorder of it.

After the observation, the instructor should jot down a self-assessment of the class, and then the observer and instructor should meet to review the class. During the meeting, the observer and instructor discuss the class events, the appropriateness of them, and other aspects of the class. After the meeting, the observer should write up an official report of the observation. The specific goal is to provide formative feedback, and yet it can contribute to an instructor's summative evaluation because after the observations and discussions, the observer does draw an evaluative conclusion. In most cases, multiple observations of an instructor, done across a semester or year, are preferred over one-time, isolated class visits.

Review of Course Materials

In evaluating faculty, review of course materials is essential. This can be handled in multiple ways. When observing faculty, evaluators should also be reviewing the course material as part of contextualizing the particular class being observed. Materials such as the syllabus, readings, handouts, assignments, and samples of student work may all be reviewed as part of the observation, depending on what activities are planned for the class. When included as part of an observation, course materials can be reviewed in context and discussed between the evaluator and the instructor, contributing to the formative aspect of the observation.

Faculty may also submit course materials in a more systematic way for review (Strenski 1994; Chism 1999). For example, all instructors may be required to submit their syllabus, including descriptions of major writing assignments, to the program administrator for review. The syllabi can be evaluated for basic information, depending on the program's structure and learning goals. Or, a program might require more complete course materials, such as a course portfolio (electronic or print) that includes all of the course materials generated by the instructor, along with student samples of the major writing assignments. Typically, the portfolio will include a self-reflection by the instructor, explaining the materials and identifying strengths, questions, or challenges. (See appendix G for sample directions for assembling a course portfolio.) The portfolio can be used as the basis of a course review for the instructor (as well as for program review, as we suggest in chapter 7). For example, a colleague with expertise in teaching the course could review the course portfolio, meet with the instructor to discuss it, and write an evaluation of the instructor's course for a yearly review. This approach provides opportunities for both formative and summative evaluation. (See the section below on teaching portfolios for more information.)

Guided Class Discussion

This type of evaluation is generally done by a colleague in consultation with the instructor but without the instructor present during the discussion (Strenski 1994). It is especially helpful as a formative assessment method, but it can also contribute to summative evaluation. If an instructor is trying to understand why he is struggling with a class, a guided discussion by a trusted peer can be very helpful. It can also be helpful for supplementing other evaluation methods, such as surveys and observations, because the guided discussion allows students to explain and elaborate on responses or behaviors. For example, in previously taught courses, a writing instructor may have noticed a particular pattern in the responses on the end-of-semester student ratings of instruction but may not understand how to respond to the results. A class discussion guided by a colleague, without the instructor present, can help to illuminate why students are responding in a certain way. Or, an instructor may want to get specific kinds of feedback about a particular pedagogical practice or a change made to a class, such as adding service learning or incorporating more multicultural materials than students expect. The guided discussion allows for more nuanced feedback from students than is accessible through a survey because the leader of the discussion can push students to elaborate through probing questions.

In general, this kind of guided discussion is similar to a focus group although the class size is usually much larger than recommended for a focus group. It is important that questions are planned ahead of time, that the interviewer explain the process to the class, and that notes are taken. After the discussion, the interviewer writes a summary, identifying general themes or patterns without referring to individual students. Again, the questions can be tailored to the individual instructor and class, or a program could have a set protocol used across sections. Specific procedures and content should be determined by the local context and the purpose of the evaluation.

Workshops

Workshops on pedagogy and course materials are common activities in most writing programs and are usually considered faculty development. However, faculty-development activities can also be part of a formative evaluation program, especially if the workshops provide hands-on opportunities to focus on teaching. For example, a workshop on crafting writing assignments would include information about basic principles of assignment design, with participants having the opportunity to work on assignments from one of their classes. This could be done in multiple ways, depending on the specific factors, such as the size of the group and facilities. Participants could have time to work with peers on getting feedback on the assignments and suggestions for improving them. Or, participants could do a self-critique of an assignment and then share with colleagues for additional suggestions. Follow-up from an initial workshop could include instructors revising assignments, using the revised assignments, and then drafting a self-evaluation report that addressed how the workshop influenced the re-designed assignments, how students responded to them, and the effectiveness of the revised assignments. This approach to faculty-development workshops could be used with almost any topic—from developing a syllabus to responding to student work to developing classroom discussion strategies to using new media. Additionally, if workshop leaders use materials from instructors in the program as samples and models in the presentation, then those instructors can get formative and/ or summative feedback, depending on how the materials are used.

The key to making a workshop contribute to a faculty-evaluation program is to have faculty participants reflecting on their own practices or materials and receiving feedback from others. If faculty participants are passively sitting through a presentation and not expected to use the workshop as an opportunity to actively engage in evaluation of their teaching, then the workshop not only may be less effective in improving practices but also will not be contributing to the evaluation of instruction. In this approach, simply attending the workshop is not enough; faculty need to be actively engaged in self-assessment.

Group Review of Student Work

Writing programs often hold group norming sessions, or calibration sessions, aimed at helping faculty develop shared evaluation criteria. These sessions are most often associated with holistic scoring of student writing, but they don't need to be linked to a formal assessment activity. In terms of individual faculty evaluation, these group sessions can function like workshops, providing opportunities for instructors to not just discuss principles and theories but to apply these principles to their own teaching. This can be especially useful for "problem" writing—an essay or portfolio that does not neatly fall into a particular grading category or falls in between scores on a rubric.

However, reviewing student work includes more than grading or scoring sessions. For example, a review meeting could include a round-robin structured reading of a student text that is more descriptive than evaluative (Anson 1994; Huot 1997). The purpose is different from that of a norming session; instead of trying to narrow our reading to achieve agreement, this type of reading aims at disrupting our tacit reading patterns to help us consider all of the possibilities in a text. A reading like this, with the focus on the nuances and possibilities in the text, can be structured in various ways, but the goal is to keep it from turning into a student (or teacher) bashing session.

Again, to move reflective reading beyond purely faculty development to faculty evaluation requires participants to use the reading experience to actively self-assess their own evaluation practices.

Teaching Portfolios

There is a rich literature on teaching portfolios, especially for writing teachers.[2] While there is no one-size-fits-all approach, since different purposes require different types of portfolios, teaching portfolios—whether electronic or not—typically require certain activities: collection, selection, reflection, and evaluation. The teaching portfolio can represent one course, several courses, or an instructor's career, but the contents usually include primary class materials, such as syllabus, assignments, and handouts for class activities, as well as secondary materials—that is, material about the primary documents. These secondary texts can be generated by the portfolio's author or by others (peers, observers, or students) and might include documents such as a self-reflective introduction or teaching narrative, an observation report, a review of an assignment sequence, and responses to a student survey. The portfolio should provide contextualizing information to help the reader of the portfolio more fully understand both the primary and secondary materials.

If a program requires teaching portfolios for either formative or summative assessment purposes, then it should provide guidelines and support for faculty to compile and maintain the portfolio, criteria for evaluation, and a process for reviewing them. For example, maybe all writing instructors exchange their teaching portfolio with a peer, each reviewing the portfolio and writing a one-page summary including strengths, weaknesses, and questions. The pairings may be done by choice or assigned. The process may include a meeting to discuss the portfolios in pairs, in small groups, or as a whole program, or it may simply be a written review that includes questions the reviewer responds to and a brief overall comment. (See appendix F for a sample teaching portfolio table of contents.)

While teaching portfolios are clearly linked to individual faculty evaluation, they can be used to assess program-wide instruction as we discussed in chapter 7.

---

2.   For more specific information on teaching portfolios, see the large body of literature on general teaching portfolios at the college level—most notably published by Peter Seldin (1990, 1997, 1999) and Edgerton, Hutchings, and Quinlan (1991). For teaching portfolios and composition, see, for example, Minter and Goodburn (2002); Yancey (1997); Weiser (1997); Anson (1994); and Paulson and Paulson (1997).

CHALLENGES

In spite of all of the potential positive outcomes associated with it, assessing faculty—even as part of a program review where the emphasis is not on the individual's performance per se but the aggregate performance of the program—can create anxiety, especially for contingent faculty who have little if any job security. Junior faculty may also feel apprehensive and vulnerable even when the emphasis is on formative assessment; and faculty who have tenure can feel exposed, depending on the departmental culture and history. Although a writing program should include formative assessment and faculty development, summative evaluation is also necessary, whether as part of annual reviews, rehiring decisions, or formal program review. Typically, there is some sort of faculty evaluation program in place, if only an institution's minimal system for yearly reviews or for extreme problems. The de facto system may not be consistent and coherent, it may not be inclusive of all faculty, or it may not be taken seriously by some or all faculty. The goal—or challenge—is to have a systematic, theoretically consistent system in place that is fair for all faculty and produces results that improve teaching and learning. If no system is in place for the writing program, then one needs to be developed. However, initiating change, even change aimed at improvement, can meet resistance, especially when the change could affect personnel decisions, curriculum, and responsibilities. Dealing with the resistance constructively is imperative, but specific decisions about how depend on the local culture and context.

While many factors contribute to resistance, the diversity of faculty found in many writing programs can make dealing with resistance and developing a strong evaluation program even more of a challenge. When writing program faculty are homogeneous in rank—such as all graduate assistants or all non-tenure lecturers—it can be easier to create a coherent, strong evaluation system because there is less variation and less job security. If non-tenure-track instructors don't participate, or even try to subvert the evaluation system, they can jeopardize their employment. If their positions are competitive—that is, there are more people who want to teach in the program than available slots—resistant instructors can be readily replaced (e.g., White 1994; Schwalm 1994). However, if there is a dearth of qualified instructors (whether graduate assistants or adjuncts), program administrators may have to tolerate more resistance.

The situation can be much more challenging when there is a mix of types of instructors teaching in a program because it may be difficult to create a consistent faculty evaluation program that includes everyone. For example, a program may have a formal, structured review process for graduate assistants but not for part-time lecturers. Or, junior faculty may be required to participate in a mentoring and observation program, but senior faculty may be exempt. Part-time lecturers or non-tenured faculty may feel compelled to attend faculty-development workshops or group reading sessions, but tenured faculty may be "too busy" or "not expected" to attend. For many writing faculty, especially contingent labor, there can be quite a bit of anxiety associated with assessment, whether formative or summative, because of the lack of job security or because yearly reviews may be non-existent or perfunctory at best. In some programs, the graduate teaching assistants may get little if any review after the initial training session unless there is a significant problem because their positions are funding their graduate studies, awarded by the graduate program, and the writing program may have little control over hiring and retention. If tenured faculty teach in the writing program, as is often the case in WAC programs and FYC programs at community colleges, liberal arts colleges, and comprehensive institutions, the evaluation of their teaching may be done by the department chair or a personnel committee. In some cases, the writing program administrator may have input in the faculty review, or she may have access to the faculty's evaluation materials. It is more likely, however, that evaluation of tenured faculty will be handled separately from the writing program administrator's purview; in some cases, the reviews will value scholarship over teaching with very minimal expectations in terms of faculty development or evaluation of instruction.

While successfully addressing these types of challenges is difficult, a program review can be an impetus for instituting a more thorough faculty review process that demands participation by all faculty across rank and status. Sometimes, it is useful to create situations where all faculty are reviewed the same way, and all participate in the same activities, such as group discussions of student papers. However, when faculty from across ranks participate in the same workshop or activity, the differences in status can affect how participants engage in the activity and how it is valued by others. Sometimes, it may be better to separate faculty into peer groups—graduate students, tenure-track faculty, and adjunct faculty—with notes or summaries of each group's discussion distributed to all. Sometimes, it can be more effective to let faculty group themselves, selecting workshops or discussion groups based on schedules, personalities, or topics. Deciding how to address faculty evaluation depends on your local culture—the program's and department's history, size, and climate, and institutional policies about faculty work and faculty development—as well as the purpose of the evaluation activities and the resources available (as discussed in chapter 7 on program assessment). Regardless of these factors, in a program review the administrator can diffuse some of the tensions and anxieties that accompany faculty evaluation by focusing on the learning goals and on instructional methods instead of on individual instructors.

This focus on learning goals de-emphasizes the instructor's personality and personal traits and can accommodate a wider range of acceptable classroom practices. For example, a student survey could ask questions based on course goals, such as "Does the instructor provide opportunities for students to write in multiple genres?" or "Does the instructor provide opportunities for students to receive feedback on drafts and revise before final grading of essays?", instead of those based on the instructor, such as "Is the instructor organized?" or "Is the instructor enthusiastic?" or "Does the instructor show concern for students?" Not only do the questions that are tied directly to the learning goals of the course contribute to understanding the extent to which students perceive that they are being given opportunities to accomplish the stated program outcomes, but they can also provide teachers and administrators with information that is helpful in revising and improving practice, especially if open-ended comments are tied to the questions. (See the student survey section above for more information.) In classroom observations of instruction, focusing on learning goals encourages faculty to think more specifically about how an activity or class contributes to the overall goals of the course and can help the observer determine if the instructor understands the goals of the course and how to effectively achieve them.

The focus on the learning goals during evaluation of instruction and instructors can also de-emphasize the belief that the instructor should be the center of the class and allow for more student-centered methods that are supported by current composition pedagogy. For example, if one of the course goals states that students will learn to "critique their own and others' work," then a class devoted to peer-response activities is appropriate for an observation even if the instructor is more of the facilitator than the main attraction. The observer would consider how the groups functioned, how the activity contributes to the attainment of the goal, and other issues that are related to the opportunities for learning the instructor provides. If an instructor is more comfortable with a teacher-centered classroom, she or he can still have students do peer response, but maybe it is organized differently. For example, students conduct the response activity via an electronic bulletin board outside of class. The instructor might lead a class discussion about the response activity during the observation with the electronic responses used as discussion prompts. In this example, the instructor is meeting the learning goals but in a different way than the instructor that has students doing small-group workshops in the classroom. (For more information on observations, see the section above.)

The focus on achieving the learning goals also provides information that is more readily aggregated to determine a view of instruction and teaching and learning across the program instead of information more relevant to the popularity of individual instructors. By compiling the results of a student survey focused on the learning goals, a program might determine that some goals are not being addressed across the board or that the program is consistently succeeding in teaching to certain goals. For example, if one of the goals states that students will "use multiple drafts to create and complete a successful text," an administrator could examine the responses to that one question, looking for patterns and consistency. Then, given the results on the survey, that goal could be targeted when evaluating course portfolios, with the portfolio readers identifying more specifically evidence that students used—or did not use—multiple drafts to successfully complete a text. After collating results from across the portfolios, the WPA could create a list of best practices for using multiple drafting to complete successful texts. Or, in scheduling classroom observations, teachers may be asked to identify classes for observation that directly contribute to this particular outcome. Based on the results of the survey, observations, and student work, the writing program administrator may decide to offer workshops (formative assessment) on helping faculty develop teaching strategies that address multiple drafts so student texts are more successful because of the drafting process. Or, the workshop could focus on exploring what is meant by "successful text" in the program, which would help establish or clarify criteria for evaluating student work. The workshops would provide the feedback loop that is the hallmark of effective program assessments. All of these activities, which can be considered part of evaluation, focus more on teaching and learning and less on identifying weak instructors or popular ones.

Once faculty realize that the program is not interested in making all instructors conform to a uniform teaching persona, nor in punishing or embarrassing instructors, but that it is concerned with ensuring all students have the opportunity to achieve the course goals, then the anxiety associated with evaluation can be reduced if not eliminated all together. When the tension surrounding evaluation subsides, the program can emphasize the formative parts of the assessment process—that is, supporting faculty so they can enhance their teaching and students' learning—without the faculty perceiving it as a threat.

In addition to the challenge posed by faculty resistance to evaluation, programs also must consider the resources—including money, time, personnel, and space—available for implementing a comprehensive, ongoing faculty evaluation system. Most of the evaluation methods we discuss above may not cost much in terms of materials, but they do require the time and energy of program faculty and administrators. Time and energy are precious resources for all levels of faculty: tenured faculty who typically must publish, serve on several committees, teach in multiple programs, and attend to all the other details of institutional life; part-time faculty who may be teaching at multiple campuses, programs, or institutions with very limited time available when on campus; graduate teaching assistants, who might be inexperienced teachers and are juggling their own coursework and research agendas with their teaching obligations; and program administrators, who usually have to fulfill regular faculty obligations as well as the administrative ones. In other words, everyone seems too busy to take on the "extra" burden of faculty evaluation, which is why it is critical to approach it thoughtfully.

Program administrators can help build a culture that is open to assessment by making sure they follow the basic principles of sound assessment as they develop a system over time. They need to be realistic about the resources and the time needed to do effective assessment activities. Planning activities so that they can be both formative and summative helps use limited resources wisely and dispel some of the anxiety. Administrators need to be sure that faculty feel that the evaluation system is meaningful to them as well as to those outside the program who require it. In focusing on improving effective teaching and learning, programs need to use the results of assessments in a feedback loop and to help instructors learn how to do this without feeling afraid to admit a weakness or "challenge."

APPENDIX A
Timeline: Contextualizing Key Events in Writing Assessment

Harvard requires English Composition Exam as part of the battery of admission exams for the first time. (1874)

College Entrance Examination Board establishes uniform college entrance requirements. (1900)

Charles Spearman publishes "The Proof and Measurement of Association between Two Things" and " 'General Intelligence.' Objectively Determined and Measured." The quantification of relational information was concurrently invented to establish G, or general intelligence. (1904)

Hillegas's "Scale for the Measurement of Quality in English Composition by Young People" is published. (1912)

Starch and Elliot publish essay on reliability of grading student essays. (1912)

US Army Alpha and Army Beta tests used to sort literate and illiterate recruits according to mental abilities. (1917)

Scholastic Aptitude Test (SAT) is first administered by Carl Cambell Brigham, a psychological researcher who had worked on the Army Alpha and Beta tests. (1926)

1874	
1900	
1902	
1904	
1906	
1908	
1910	
1912	
1914	
1916	
1918	
1920	
1922	
1924	
1926	
1928	
1930	

Expansion of the Morrill Act of 1862 that established land grant universities and colleges. Combined, the Acts lead to the establishment of seventy institutions. (1890)

National Council of Teachers of English is established. (1911)

American Association of University Professors forms and establishes the concept of "academic freedom." (1915)

John Dewey's Democracy and Education is published. (1916)

US enters World War I. (1917)

Every state requires compulsory education for all children (although the specific requirements vary from state to state). (1918)

Congress adopts a series of immigration acts establishing quotas based on nation of origin as well as other criteria such as ability to pass a literacy test. (1917-1924)

The ratio of college students to 18- to 24-year-olds rises from 2 per 100 in 1900 to 7 per 100 in 1930. Concomitantly, the average size of colleges rises from 243 students to 781. (1900-1930)

	1932
	1934
SAT is a regular option for CEEB and used by scholarship students who need to apply in the spring and early summer before the exams could be given and scored. (1937)	1936
	1938
CEEB suspends essay testing as an option in order to more efficiently process college students who are part of the military effort through the use of limited response tests. (1941)	1940
CEEB institutes English Composition Test (ECT) in response to English teachers' voiced objections to eliminating essay writing for college admission. (1943)	1942

US enters World War II. (1942)

1944

Congress passes GI Bill, which provides funding for college or vocational education to WWII veterans. (1944)

Educational Testing Service (ETS) is established. (1947) — 1946

Paul Diederich publishes a study in which raters from a particular institution agree on essay scores at a high rate. Study illustrates principles central to W. L. Smith's work on expert readers almost four decades later. (1950) — 1948, 1950

Conference on College Composition and Communication forms. (1949)

College Board starts the Advanced Placement Program, with scoring reliability of answers examined by Frances Swineford. (1954) — 1952

A joint committee of the American Psychological Association (APA), the American Educational Research Association (AERA) and the National Council on Measurement in Education (NCME) publishes "Technical Recommendations for Psychological Tests and Diagnostic Techniques," the first standards for testing. (1954) — 1954, 1956, 1958

Brown v. Board of Education decision overturns legal basis for segregated public education. (1954)

Successful launch of Sputnik, a USSR satellite. (1957)

National Defense Education Act passes, which provides economic aid for public and private education. (1958) — 1960

1962

Diederich, French & Carleton publish study that uses factor analysis to analyze readers' responses. (1966) — 1964

Ellis Page develops first program for automated scoring (PEG). (1966)

Congress passes the Civil Rights Act, which outlaws segregation in schools and public places as well as in employment. (1964)

Godschalk, Swineford & Coffman publishes study that establishes possibility that readers could achieve acceptable rates of inter-reader reliability on essay exams. (1966) — 1966

1968

Left events	Year	Right events
	1970	
First administration of the California State University Freshman Equivalency Exam, a faculty designed test that included both multiple choice and essay portions. (1973)	1972	The first class of students admitted through Opens Admissions starts at the City University of New York. (1970)
Richard Lloyd-Jones and others working on National Assessment of Educational Progress (NAEP) develop Primary Trait Scoring. (1974)	1974	CCCC approves "The Students' Rights to Their Own Language." (1974)
Paul Diederich publishes *Measuring Growth in English* with the National Council of Teachers of English. (1976)	1976	Bay Area Writing Project, which eventually gives rise to the National Writing Project, starts at the University of California Berkeley Graduate School of Education. (1974)
Charles Cooper and Lee Odell edit *Evaluating Writing: Describing, Measuring, Judging* for NCTE. (1977)	1978	
The Test of Standard Written English (TSWE), a multiple choice test widely used to measure writing ability, becomes a part of the College Board's repertoire of tests. (1977)		Mina Shaughnessy publishes Errors and Expectations: A Guide for the Teacher of Basic Writing. (1977)
Miles Myers publishes *A Procedure for Writing Assessment and Holistic Scoring* for NCTE. (1980)	1980	
ETS starts a pilot writing portfolio study to develop scale and scoring protocol. (1982)	1982	
First National Testing Network in Writing (NTNW) Conference. (1983)		
Edward M. White publishes 1st edition of *Teaching and Assessing Writing*. (1984)	1984	President Reagan's Commission on Excellence in Education releases A Nation at Risk: The Imperative For Educational Reform, *which contributes to the sense that schools are failing and initiates local, state, and federal educational reform efforts. (1983)*
Peter Elbow & Pat Belanoff publish work on replacing timed composition exit examinations with portfolio assessment programs. (1986)	1986	
	1988	
William L. Smith reports on research findings at CCCC that lead to the expert reader system (later publishes results in two chapters in Hayes and Williamson & Huot). (1989)		
Last NTNW Conference. (1990)	1990	
	1992	Release of first Internet browser, WorldWideWeb. (1991)
First issue of *Assessing Writing* is published (first journal devoted to writing assessment). (1994)		
Ellis Page releases new version of PEG for automated scoring. (1994)	1994	
College Board drops the TSWE from its repertoire of tests. (1994)		
CCCC adopts first position statement on Writing Assessment. (1995)	1996	
	1998	

AERA, APA & NCME publish edition of *Standards for Educational and Psychological Testing.* (1999)

2000

Council of Writing Program Administrators publishes "Outcomes for First Year Writing." (2000)

2002

Congress enacts No Child Left Behind legislation. (2002)

2004

Writing Section (limited response and timed essay) added to SAT Reasoning Test as part of a major revision of the test. (2005)

CCCC publishes revised "Writing Assessment: A Position Statement." (2006)

2006

The US Secretary of Education's Commission on the Future of Higher Education releases report A Test of Leadership: Charting the Future of U.S. Higher Education. *(2006)*

CCCC adopts "Principles and Practices in Electronic Portfolios." (2007)

2008

2010

APPENDIX B
Writing Assessment: A Position Statement

Conference on College Composition and Communication
Committee on Assessment, November 2006

INTRODUCTION

Writing assessment can be used for a variety of appropriate purposes, both inside the classroom and outside: providing assistance to students, awarding a grade, placing students in appropriate courses, allowing them to exit a course or sequence of courses, and certifying proficiency; and evaluating programs—to name some of the more obvious. Given the high stakes nature of many of these assessment purposes, it is crucial that assessment practices be guided by sound principles to insure that they are valid, fair, and appropriate to the context and purposes for which they are designed. This position statement aims to provide that guidance.

In spite of the diverse uses to which writing assessment is put, the general principles undergirding it are similar:

Assessments of written literacy should be designed and evaluated by well-informed current or future teachers of the students being assessed, for purposes clearly understood by all the participants; should elicit from student writers a variety of pieces, preferably over a substantial period of time; should encourage and reinforce good teaching practices; and should be solidly grounded in the latest research on language learning as well as accepted best assessment practices.

GUIDING PRINCIPLES FOR ASSESSMENT

1. Writing assessment is useful primarily as a means of improving teaching and learning. The primary purpose of any assessment should govern its design, its implementation, and the generation and dissemination of its results. As a result . . .

   a. *Best assessment practice is informed by pedagogical and curricular goals, which are in turn formatively affected by the assessment.* Teachers or administrators designing assessments should ground the assessment in the classroom, program, or departmental context. The goals or outcomes assessed should lead to assessment data, which is fed back to those involved with the regular activities assessed so that assessment results may be used to make changes in practice.

b. *Best assessment practice is undertaken in response to local goals, not external pressures.* Even when the external forces require assessment, the local community must assert control of the assessment process, including selection of the assessment instrument and criteria.

2. Writing is by definition social. Learning to write entails learning to accomplish a range of purposes for a range of audiences in a range of settings. As a result . . .

a. *Best assessment practice engages students in contextualized, meaningful writing.* The assessment of writing must strive to set up writing tasks and situations that identify purposes appropriate to and appealing to the particular students being tested. Additionally, assessment must be contextualized in terms of why, where, and for what purpose it is being undertaken; this context must also be clear to the students being assessed and to all stakeholders.

b. *Best assessment practice supports and harmonizes with what practice and research have demonstrated to be effective ways of teaching writing.* What is easiest to measure—often by means of a multiple-choice test—may correspond least to good writing; choosing a correct response from a set of possible answers is not composing. As important, just asking students to write does not make the assessment instrument a good one. Essay tests that ask students to form and articulate opinions about some important issue—for instance, without time to reflect, talk to others, read on the subject, revise, and have a human audience—promote distorted notions of what writing is. They also encourage poor teaching and little learning. Even teachers who recognize and employ the methods used by real writers in working with students can find their best efforts undercut by assessments such as these.

c. *Best assessment practice is direct assessment by human readers.* Assessment that isolates students and forbids discussion and feedback from others conflicts with what we know about language use and the benefits of social interaction during the writing process; it also is out of step with much classroom practice. Direct assessment in the classroom should provide response that serves formative purposes, helping writers develop and shape ideas, as well as organize, craft sentences, and edit. As stated by the CCCC *Position Statement on Teaching, Learning, and Assessing Writing in Digital Environments,* "we oppose the use of machine-scored writing in the assessment of writing." Automated assessment programs do not respond as human readers. While they may promise consistency, they distort the very nature of writing as a complex and context-rich interaction between people. They simplify writing in ways that can mislead writers to focus more on structure and grammar than on what they are saying by using a given structure and style.

3. Any individual's writing ability is a sum of a variety of skills employed in a diversity of contexts, and individual ability fluctuates unevenly among these varieties. As a result . . .

   a. *Best assessment practice uses multiple measures.* One piece of writing—even if it is generated under the most desirable conditions—can never serve as an indicator of overall writing ability, particularly for high-stakes decisions. Ideally, writing ability must be assessed by more than one piece of writing, in more than one genre, written on different occasions for different audiences, and responded to and evaluated by multiple readers as part of a substantial and sustained writing process.

   b. *Best assessment practice respects language variety and diversity and assesses writing on the basis of effectiveness for readers, acknowledging that, as purposes vary, criteria will as well.* Standardized tests that rely more on identifying grammatical and stylistic errors than authentic rhetorical choices disadvantage students whose home dialect is not the dominant dialect. Assessing authentic acts of writing simultaneously raises performance standards and provides multiple avenues to success. Thus, students are not arbitrarily punished for linguistic differences that in some contexts make them more, not less, effective communicators. Furthermore, assessments that are keyed closely to an American cultural context may disadvantage second-language writers. The CCCC *Statement on Second-Language Writing and Writers* calls on us "to recognize the regular presence of second-language writers in writing classes, to understand their characteristics, and to develop instructional and administrative practices that are sensitive to their linguistic and cultural needs." Best assessment practice responds to this call by creating assessments that are sensitive to the language varieties in use among the local population and sensitive to the context-specific outcomes being assessed.

c. *Best assessment practice includes assessment by peers, instructors, and the student writer himself or herself.* Valid assessment requires combining multiple perspectives on a performance and generating an overall assessment out of the combined descriptions of those multiple perspectives. As a result, assessments should include formative and summative assessments from all these kinds of readers. Reflection by the writer on her or his own writing processes and performances holds particular promise as a way of generating knowledge about writing and increasing the ability to write successfully.

4. Perceptions of writing are shaped by the methods and criteria used to assess writing. As a result . . .

a. *The methods and criteria that readers use to assess writing should be locally developed, deriving from the particular context and purposes for the writing being assessed.* The individual writing program, institution, or consortium should be recognized as a community of interpreters whose knowledge of context and purpose is integral to the assessment. There is no test which can be used in all environments for all purposes, and the best assessment for any group of students must be locally determined and may well be locally designed.

b. *Best assessment practice clearly communicates what is valued and expected, and does not distort the nature of writing or writing practices.* If ability to compose for various audiences is valued, then an assessment will assess this capability. For other contexts and purposes, other writing abilities might be valued, for instance, to develop a position on the basis of reading multiple sources or to compose a multi-media piece, using text and images. Values and purposes should drive assessment, not the reverse. A corollary to this statement is that assessment practices and criteria should change as conceptions of texts and values change.

c. *Best assessment practice enables students to demonstrate what they do well in writing.* Standardized tests tend to focus on readily accessed features of the language (grammatical correctness, stylistic choices) and on error rather than on the appropriateness of the rhetorical choices that have been made. Consequently, the outcome of such assessments is negative: students are said to demonstrate what they do wrong with language rather than what they do well. Quality assessments will provide the opportunity for students to demonstrate the ways they can write, displaying the strategies or skills taught in the relevant environment.

5. Assessment programs should be solidly grounded in the latest research on learning, writing, and assessment. As a result . . .

   a. *Best assessment practice results from careful consideration of the costs and benefits of the range of available approaches.* It may be tempting to choose an inexpensive, quick assessment, but decision-makers should consider the impact of assessment methods on students, faculty, and programs. The return on investment from the direct assessment of writing by instructor-evaluators includes student learning, professional development of faculty, and program development. These benefits far outweigh the presumed benefits of cost, speed, and simplicity that machine scoring might seem to promise.

   b. *Best assessment practice is continually under review and subject to change by well-informed faculty, administrators, and legislators.* Anyone charged with the responsibility of designing an assessment program must be cognizant of the relevant research and must stay abreast of developments in the field. The theory and practice of writing assessment is continually informed by significant publications in professional journals and by presentations at regional and national conferences. The easy availability of this research to practitioners makes ignorance of its content reprehensible.

APPLICATIONS TO ASSESSMENT SETTINGS

The guiding principles apply to assessment conducted in any setting. In addition, we offer the following guidelines for situations that may be encountered in specific settings.

Assessment in the Classroom

In a course context, writing assessment should be part of the highly social activity within the community of faculty and students in the class. This social activity includes:

- a period of ungraded work (prior to the completion of graded work) that receives response from multiple readers, including peer reviewers,

- assessment of texts—from initial through to final drafts—by human readers, and

- more than one opportunity to demonstrate outcomes.

Self-assessment should also be encouraged. Assessment practices and criteria should match the particular kind of text being created and its purpose. These criteria should be clearly communicated to students in advance so that the students can be guided by the criteria while writing.

ASSESSMENT FOR PLACEMENT

Placement criteria in the most responsible programs will be clearly connected to any differences in the available courses. Experienced instructor-evaluators can most effectively make a judgment regarding which course would best serve each student's needs and assign each student to the appropriate course. If scoring systems are used, scores should derive from criteria that grow out of the work of the courses into which students are being placed.

Decision-makers should carefully weigh the educational costs and benefits of timed tests, portfolios, directed self-placement, etc. In the minds of those assessed, each of these methods implicitly establishes its value over that of others, so the first cost is likely to be what students come to believe about writing. For example, timed writing may suggest to students that writing always cramps one for time and that real writing is always a test. Portfolio assessment may honor the processes by which writers develop their ideas and re-negotiate how their communications are heard within a language community. And machine-scored tests may focus students on error-correction rather than on effective communication.

Students should have the right to weigh in on their assessment. Self-placement without direction, sometimes touted as a student right, may become merely a right to fail, whereas directed self-placement, either alone or in combination with other methods, provides not only useful information but also involves and invests the student in making effective life decisions.

If, for financial or even programmatic reasons, the initial method of placement is somewhat reductive, instructors of record should create an opportunity early in the semester to review and change students' placement assignments, and uniform procedures should be established to facilitate the easy re-placement of improperly placed students. Even when the placement process entails direct assessment of writing, the system should accommodate the possibility of improper placement. If assessment employs machine scoring, whether of actual writing or of items designed to elicit error, it is particularly essential that every effort be made through statistical verification to see that students, individually and collectively, are placed in courses that can appropriately address their skills and abilities.

Placement processes should be continually assessed and revised in accord with course content and overall program goals. This is especially important when machine-scored assessments are used. Using methods that are employed uniformly, teachers of record should verify that students are appropriately placed. If students are placed according to scores on such tests, the ranges of placement must be revisited regularly to accommodate changes in curricula and shifts in the abilities of the student population.

ASSESSMENT OF PROFICIENCY

Proficiency or exit assessment involves high stakes for students. In this context, assessments that make use of substantial and sustained writing processes are especially important.

Judgments of proficiency must also be made on the basis of performances in multiple and varied writing situations (for example, a variety of topics, audiences, purposes, genres).

The assessment criteria should be clearly connected to desired outcomes. When proficiency is being determined, the assessment should be informed by such things as the core abilities adopted by the institution, the course outcomes established for a program, and/or the stated outcomes of a single course or class. Assessments that do not address such outcomes lack validity in determining proficiency.

The higher the stakes, the more important it is that assessment be direct rather than indirect, based on actual writing rather than on answers on multiple-choice tests, and evaluated by people involved in the instruction of the student rather than via machine scoring. To evaluate the proficiency of a writer on other criteria than multiple writing tasks and situations is essentially disrespectful of the writer.

ASSESSMENT OF PROGRAMS

Program assessment refers to evaluations of performance in a large group, such as students in a multi-section course or majors graduating from a department. Because assessment offers information about student performance and the factors which affect that performance, it is an important way for programs or departments to monitor and develop their practice.

Programs and departments should see themselves as communities of professionals whose assessment activities reveal common values, provide opportunities for inquiry and debate about unsettled issues, and communicate measures of effectiveness to those inside and outside the program. Members of the community are in the best position to guide decisions about what assessments will best inform that community. It is important to bear in mind that random sampling of students can often provide large-scale information and that regular assessment should affect practice.

APPENDIX C
Sample Scoring Rubrics

These samples are intended to give readers a sense of different ways of constructing scoring guides. They are not meant to serve as models.

RUBRIC 1: SAMPLE HOLISTIC SCORING RUBRIC FOR A BUSINESS SCHOOL[1]

Score of 4 Exemplary Performance	Particularly effective or sophisticated development and presentation of ideas, control of language, or appeal.
Score of 3 Expected Performance	Demonstrates ability to generate appropriate and detailed content, organize effectively, and utilize language and formatting conforming to professional and academic standards.
Score of 2 Passable Performance	Unbalanced or undeveloped with moderate awareness of acceptable business writing practices. Core writing assignments should enable the writer to develop competent business communication skills.
Score of 1 Unacceptable Performance	Needs remediation in regard to business writing conventions. Ineffective development and presentation.

---

1.   Developed by Karen Lentz Madison, University of Arkansas, for the Sellinger School of Business, Loyola College in Maryland. Used with permission.

RUBRIC 2: SAMPLE ANALYTIC SCORING GUIDE FOR GENERAL BUSINESS WRITING ASSESSMENT[2]

Characteristics	Score Point 4	Score Point 3	Score Point 2	Score Point 1
Evidence and Analysis	Provides concise and engaging details for and persuasive development of the decision document evaluated, including integrated data and visuals. Use of evidence illustrates significant facility with copyright obligations.	Provides concise details for and persuasive development of the decision document evaluated, including integrated data and visuals. Use of evidence illustrates facility with copyright obligations. Expansion of evidence and analysis needed.	Provides detail and development of decision document evaluated, including the use of data and visuals. Use of evidence satisfies copyright obligations. Expansion and integration of evidence needed.	Details to support claims are missing. Inability to tell the audience what is meant. Most points remain abstract or general. Some evidence used is unnecessary or distracting.
Focus	Focuses on a complex, specific, and particular message. Clearly maps reasons or points that contribute to the focus.	Focused on a specific and particular message. Several supporting points but needs more development.	Focused on a specific message. Document might stray from this focus once. Several areas may need improvement.	No clear focus or purpose. Focus may be divided or confusing.
Complexity	Engaging and careful word choice, sentence structure. Sophisticated choices of topic, organization, evidence, and style.	Generally successful, using concrete word choice to convey message. Distinct voice in most of the document. Takes some creative risk. Level of sophistication could be elevated or improved.	Uses some concrete words to establish tone. Lacking creativity or details that would enhance the message. Vague, general wording or topic.	Vague wording ("thing") or simplistic repetitive vocabulary. More telling than showing. Generic topic, approach, organization. Lack of engagement with the audience.
Coherence (Sense of organization and unity)	Each paragraph is focused and effectively developed around an individual point. Overall paragraph organization is strong. Transitions establish complex relationships between points.	Well organized. Individual paragraphs are well organized and developed. Some areas (paragraph breaks, effective transitions, etc.) of the document need improvement.	Ideas logically related, but document needs transitions or paragraph breaks. Some sections need to be moved. Confusing sentence level organization.	Paragraphs are nonexistent or breaks are nonsensical. Organization of points or paragraphs is confusing or random.
Audience Awareness	Adopts a professional tone, avoiding colloquial usage, for technical or nontechnical document requirements. States purpose directly. Develops document of appropriate length and sufficient interest to prove significance of message. Exemplary use of business writing conventions for decision documents, such as executive summaries.	Adopts a professional tone, avoiding colloquial usage, for technical or nontechnical document requirements. States purpose directly. Develops document with evidence meaningful to audience. Good use of business writing conventions.	Shows moderate ability to use examples and/or evidence meaningful to audience.	Grammar error patterns and inappropriate word choice. Little or no evidence of audience awareness or business writing conventions.

2.   Developed by Karen Lentz Madison, University of Arkansas, for the Sellinger School of Business, Loyola College in Maryland. Used with permission.

4 Portfolio

A grade of "4" indicates that the portfolio exceeds the basic requirements and is outstanding in quality. It will demonstrate that the writer
understands and has achieved the course goals. This portfolio will create a portrait of a writer who is able to communicate effectively to an educated audience. The polished work will be thoughtful and interesting to
read. The portfolio will illustrate the writer's process from initial drafting
through revising and polishing. The writer will demonstrate an ability to
respond to readers and incorporate suggestions to make more effective
final drafts. The writing in the portfolio will consistently demonstrate effectiveness in organization, content, sentence structure, and grammar, usage,
and mechanics. The "4" portfolio will also show an attention to detail:
titles are thoughtful and provocative; work is organized and neat; appropriate fonts and typeface are used. The "4" portfolio will also be complete
in terms of contents (see handout).

3 Portfolio

A grade of "3" also indicates above-average performance. The "3" portfolio will contain many of the same characteristics of the "4" portfolio but
not as consistently or at a lesser degree. For example, the "3" portfolio may
contain one polished piece that is not as smooth or effective as the others.
Or, it might not demonstrate as clearly the writer's ability to communicate
effectively to an educated, academic audience. It might have one piece that
illustrates effective revision but another piece that has not been revised as
much or as well. Like with "4" portfolios, a "3" portfolio must be complete
in terms of the required contents and attentive to details.

2 Portfolio

A "2" portfolio demonstrates that the writer understands the course
goals and has made substantial progress toward achieving them. The "2"
portfolio should, however, demonstrate through the writing that the writer
understands concepts such as purpose, audience, revision, and editing as
well as how to locate, evaluate, and incorporate appropriate sources. There
will likely be unevenness in the attainment of goals with clear strengths and
weaknesses. The polished work will not be as smooth—there will be some
sentences that are difficult to follow—and there may be some flaws in terms
of textual expectations. A "2" portfolio must also be complete.

1 Portfolio

A "1" portfolio fails to meet the minimum criteria for a "2." The work in these portfolios shows that the writer did not meet the course goals. The writing shows a lack of control over global concerns such as organization and development and/or serious concerns with editing and proofreading. In addition, portfolios may be scored a "1" because they are incomplete (e.g., missing the minimum number of revised, polished pages; the reflective essay; and/or the necessary process work).

RUBRIC 4: PRIMARY TRAIT SCORING GUIDE EXAMPLE — LITERARY ANALYSIS RUBRIC FOR UPPER DIVISION AND MASTERS LITERATURE CLASSES[3]

	Outstanding (A range)	Above Average (B range)	Competent (C range)	Insufficient (D to F range)
Writer's Approach	The analysis presents fresh and defensible insights into the work being analyzed. The writer's ethos is one of confidence and competence.	The analysis presents defensible insights into the work being analyzed but may not go much further than the obvious. The writer's ethos is one of competence.	The analysis limits itself to obvious perspectives and insights—it plays it safe. Writer seems to be relying on status quo instead of establishing her/his own ethos.	The analysis lacks insight, offers only commonplaces, or regurgitates class notes. There is no sense of the writer taking responsibility for the interpretation.
Application of Critical Technique and Perspective	Essay reflects mastery of the literary perspective applied. The writer is fluent in the language and theory behind the perspective.	Essay reflects a solid understanding of the literary perspective applied. The writer is using much of the language and theory behind the perspective.	Essay reflects some understanding of the literary perspective applied. The writer struggles to use the language and theory behind the perspective.	Essay reflects little to no understanding of the literary perspective applied. The writer barely uses the language and theory behind the perspective.
Use of Secondary Scholarship (if called for)	The analysis engages in dialogue with secondary scholarship on the work in a way that presents new insights to the reader. Powerfully chosen textual proof supports each point. The textual proof is thoroughly examined, explained, and clearly relevant to the thesis.	The analysis may engage in dialogue with secondary scholarship on the work but does not challenge or reinterpret what has already been said. Well-chosen textual proof supports each point. The textual proof is adequately examined, explained, and relevant to the thesis.	The analysis includes excerpts from secondary scholarship on the work but does not engage in dialogue with them; they are more "plunked in." Acceptably chosen textual proof supports most points. Sources are the obvious suspects—"An Intro to X" or the *Twayne's Authors Series* level, for instance. The textual proof may be inconsistently examined, explained, or relevant to the thesis.	The analysis may include some excerpts from secondary scholarship, but these may be uninterpreted or misinterpreted; use of these sources substitutes, sometimes unsuccessfully, for the writer's own analysis. Questionably chosen textual proof supports a few points. Much of it sounds like *CliffsNotes* or *Wikipedia*. The textual proof is usually insufficiently examined, explained, or relevant to the thesis.

3.   Some of the material in these rubrics was taken from a rubric published by Prentice-Hall and available on the TeacherVision Web site at http://www.teachervision.fen.com/tv/printables/07AAAM34.pdf; other material was taken from a rubric at the English Odyssey Web site, http://www.maitespace.com/englishodyssey/ScoringGuides/writingaboutlitrubric.htm. Developed by Dr. Jo Koster, Winthrop University. Used with permission.

Use of Summary	The analysis summarizes the work to the extent needed to clarify main points but does not retell the work.	The analysis may not consistently summarize the work to the extent needed to clarify main points, or it may unnecessarily retell the work.	The analysis may summarize instead of analyze or fail to summarize as needed to explain points.	Summary may be substituted for analysis.
Organization	The analysis begins with a clear thesis statement that identifies the work by title, author, and genre and succinctly states the point of the overall analysis or some part of it. The body expertly explains and develops the thesis and provides supporting examples from the work itself or from related works that back up the thesis. The conclusion leaves the reader with a question, a quotation, a fresh insight, or another memorable impression.	The analysis begins with a thesis statement that identifies the work by title and author and states the meaning of the overall analysis or some part of it. The body explains and develops the thesis and provides supporting examples from the work. The conclusion brings the analysis to a satisfactory close.	The analysis begins with a thesis statement that identifies the work by title and author, but it may not address the meaning of the overall analysis or some part of it. The body only partially explains or develops the thesis; few supporting examples from the work are given. The conclusion may be weak, repetitive, or missing.	The analysis does not begin with a thesis statement, and the writer fails to identify the work by title, author, and genre. No organizational plan is evident.
Writer's Language	Word choice is consistently precise, vivid, or powerful.	Word choice is generally precise.	Word choice is generally imprecise and may be misleading.	Word choice is incorrect or confusing.
Use of Borrowed Information	All borrowed material is incorporated smoothly without error, and citations are complete and correct.	Borrowed material may be inserted clumsily, but its incorporation is without error; citations are complete and correct.	Borrowed material may be inserted clumsily, and/or its incorporation may have a few minor errors in the format of citations.	Borrowed material is incorrectly inserted or not clearly identified as borrowed material, or not correctly or completely documented.
Execution	Essay is flawlessly written with a flair for academic style. There are few or no errors in mechanics, usage, grammar, or spelling. This is ready to be submitted as a conference paper or article now.	Essay is well written with a solid academic style. There may be a few errors in mechanics, usage, grammar, or spelling. With revision, this can be submitted as a conference paper or article.	Essay is acceptably written with some academic style. There are several errors in mechanics, usage, grammar, or spelling—enough to distract a reader. This is not yet ready to present to a professional audience.	Essay is poorly written with little academic style. There are serious errors in mechanics, usage, grammar, and spelling. This is not up to the level we expect for academic writing in advanced courses.

APPENDIX D
Sample Classroom Observation Form

CLASSROOM OBSERVATION PROCESS

Instructions for the observer

A. Pre-observation

What are the instructor's goals for this particular class?

How do these fit with the course as a whole?

B. Observation

Describe in detail the activities of the class. Be sure to note the actions and interactions of the instructor and the students. At this point, you should be recording and reporting what occurs in the class, not evaluating it and not participating in the class activities. Be sure to attach any hand-outs, photocopies of parts of texts (i.e., readings), or printouts of Internet/ Blackboard materials used during the class.

C. Post-Observation

After the class, write a paragraph or more evaluating the class using the attached form. Consider the following questions: Were the instructor's goals for the class appropriate? Did the classroom instruction, materials, etc. work to help achieve these goals? How did the instructor and students interact? Were students on-task? Did the students and instructor seem to be able to communicate effectively with each other?

Discuss the observation with the instructor. Set up an appointment, or send the copies of the observation notes and post-observation write-up to the instructor being observed and talk about it on the phone.

Send the original *Classroom Observation Form* to the chair and a copy to the instructor.

Instructions for the instructor being observed

A. Pre-observation

At least two days prior to the scheduled observation, provide the observer with necessary materials (handouts, readings, brief plan/goals for the class, background on the class, etc.). Be sure the students know that some-one will be in the class to observe.

B. Observation

During the class visitation, you can introduce the observer to the class, but you don't need to do anything else. The observer is not a participant, so you shouldn't assume the observer will lead a group, partake in the discussion, etc.

C. Post-observation

As soon as possible after the observation, you should write a brief reflection on the class. What happened during the class? How did you feel about it? Were there any unusual or mitigating circumstances that may have influenced the class?

Discuss the observation with the instructor who did the observation. Be sure to read and review the written report. Submit a written self-reflection of the class/observation to the chair.

CLASSROOM OBSERVATION FORM

Instructor Observed _____

Course (Title, Section, Time) _____

Observer (Name and Rank) _____

Date of Observation _____

Complete the following and attach classroom notes. Be sure to sign and date below. Send the original to the department chair and a copy to the instructor observed.

Goals of the Class

Summary of Class Activities

Evaluation

Signed _____ Date Submitted_____

APPENDIX E
Sample Outcomes-Based Student Survey

END-OF-COURSE STUDENT EVALUATION[4]

Thank you in advance for conscientiously completing the questionnaire. Your responses will help us as we work to provide effective writing instruction.

Directions: Circle the number that best represents your thoughts and experience in this course. Explain your rating in the open-ended comment section immediately following the scale.

1. Evaluate the success of this course in providing opportunities for you to "use writing and reading for inquiry, learning, thinking, and communicating."

    Not Successful ← 0 1 2 3 4 5 6 7 8 9 10 → Very Successful

Explanatory Comment:

2. Evaluate the success of this course in helping you explore how genre (a particular type of text) shapes reading and writing as you wrote contemporary American essays (e.g., literary, scholarly, and/or narrative essays).

    Not Successful ← 0 1 2 3 4 5 6 7 8 9 10 → Very Successful

Explanatory Comment:

3. Evaluate the success of this course in helping you learn to identify and respond to different rhetorical situations by adopting appropriate voice, tone, and level of formality in your writing.

    Not Successful ← 0 1 2 3 4 5 6 7 8 9 10 → Very Successful

Explanatory Comment:

---

4.   This survey was developed by the Writing Department at Loyola College based on the course learning aims for WR100 Effective Writing. Peggy O'Neill was the primary author of the survey with contributions and feedback from the department's faculty and Director of Institutional Research Terra Schrer.

4. Evaluate the success of this course in helping you learn how to formulate an original thesis, focus, or controlling idea and support it.

Not Successful ← 0 1 2 3 4 5 6 7 8 9 10 → Very Successful

Explanatory Comment:

5. Evaluate the success of this course in helping you learn how to appropriately integrate ideas and information from others in your writing.

Not Successful ← 0 1 2 3 4 5 6 7 8 9 10 → Very Successful

Explanatory Comment:

6. Evaluate the success of this course in helping you learn how to critique your own and others' work.

Not Successful ← 0 1 2 3 4 5 6 7 8 9 10 → Very Successful

Explanatory Comment:

7. Evaluate the success of this course in helping you learn how to create successful texts through multiple drafts that encourage re-thinking and revising.

Not Successful ← 0 1 2 3 4 5 6 7 8 9 10 → Very Successful

Explanatory Comment:

8. Evaluate the success of this course in helping you learn how to participate in a community of writers.

Not Successful ← 0 1 2 3 4 5 6 7 8 9 10 → Very Successful

Explanatory Comment:

9. Evaluate the success of this course in helping you appreciate peers and/or cultures that are different from you or your home culture.

     Not Successful ← 0 1 2 3 4 5 6 7 8 9 10 → Very Successful

Explanatory Comment:

10. Evaluate the availability of individual attention—through activities such as meetings outside of class, written responses, e-mails, or phone conversations—from your instructor.

     Not Successful ← 0 1 2 3 4 5 6 7 8 9 10 → Very Successful

Explanatory Comment:

11. What parts of the course contributed the most to your development as a writer?

APPENDIX F
Sample Teaching Portfolio Table of Contents

APPENDIX G
Sample Course Portfolio Directions

OVERVIEW

Each instructor will create a course portfolio for his/her fall FYC course. These portfolios will be assembled by the instructor and submitted in early January. Materials and portfolios will be anonymous, identified by the section numbers only. The purpose is not to evaluate an individual instructor but rather to get a sense of what is happening in the program. The focus is on the big picture not on a close-up of one instructor or one classroom. Results will be reported for the group, not for individuals.

Readings and evaluations of the portfolios will be done by instructors of the course in small groups.

In general, instructors will assemble one portfolio even if they have two or more sections of FYC in the fall. In unusual circumstances (such as an instructor using different texts or different major assignments), instructors should compile a portfolio for each section of FYC (see the director of comp if you have questions).

The course portfolio will include:

- the syllabus (course policies and calendar);
- a copy of all handouts (or printouts from Blackboard course software) such as assignment sheets, classroom activities;
- reading materials (copy of textbook title page and table of contents, copy of a course pack, copies of supplemental readings);
- a high, middle, and low sample of student work for an essay assignment completed late in the semester;
- all process work, including drafts, responses, and in-class activities, for one of the three student samples; and
- a one-page introduction to the course portfolio written by the instructor.

STEP-BY-STEP DIRECTIONS

Collect your materials as you go through the semester. Simply keep the file folder distributed this semester readily available and drop in a copy of your course materials as you use them for class. Waiting until the end of the semester takes more time, makes for more aggravation, and usually results in omissions.

Delete your name or other identifying material from the handouts. This is important. Even if you don't mind being identified, it may influence readers. And, even though readers (who are your peers) may be able to identify your course, the lack of names will help us avoid using specific references in discussion. Remember, this is a program review, not reviews of individuals.

Organize the materials chronologically, for the most part. Start with the syllabus and then move through the semester.

Include, at the end, three samples of student work (produced late in the semester) representing different levels of achievement. These essays should also be anonymous but labeled "high" (A/B+ work), "middle" (C range), and "low" (C-/D). These copies should also be devoid of grades or comments. If there are no examples of one of these ranges, please note that in your introduction. *For one of the samples,* include all the process work (invention, drafts, responses, etc.) that contributed to the final essay draft.

Write the introduction at the end of the semester. This text, which should be no more than one single-spaced, typed page, should provide readers with the context of the course(s) as well as any information that may be useful for readers in understanding your course. For example, if you make extensive use of Blackboard, you might discuss that because the materials might not make that evident. If you had two sections that were remarkably different, you should note that.

Please remember that the portfolio is not about evaluating you as an instructor but rather about evaluating the program. The portfolios will be used as a way of seeing into the program. While portfolios can function as a panopticon, exposing you and your practices, we hope to downplay this aspect by making the portfolios anonymous. You might also approach the assembling of the portfolio, especially after the course is over and you are writing the portfolio introduction, as an opportunity to reflect on your teaching.

FINISHED PORTFOLIO CHECKLIST

_____ Introduction (one page)

_____ Syllabus

_____ Copy of all handouts (or printouts from Blackboard) such as assignment sheets, classroom activities

_____ Reading materials (copy of textbook title page and table of contents, copy of a course pack, copies of supplemental readings)

_____ Sample of student work for a late essay assignment (high, middle and low work)

_____ Process work for one of the student samples (drafts, responses, in-class activities)

_____ Materials are anonymous, identifying material blacked out or deleted

_____ Materials are in chronological order

APPENDIX H
Sample Course Portfolio Reading Guidelines

Note: *The specifics of the reading process and questions outlined below were developed for a specific program and its curriculum. Other programs will need to develop specifics that are appropriate for their needs and context.*

PROCESS FOR EVALUATING THE COURSE PORTFOLIOS

1. Instructors will be divided into small groups of four or five to do the reading in January. Each group will have an assigned group leader. Groups will include tenure-track and non-tenure-line faculty. Groups will not be reading their own portfolios.

2. In small groups, individuals will read portfolios and complete an anonymous questionnaire for each. Every portfolio should be read by at least three people. Two hours is allotted for this portion. The completed questionnaires will be collected by the group leader at the end of the session. The group leader will participate as a reader if needed (depending on the number of group members and number of portfolios).

3. For the last hour of the session, the group leader will facilitate a discussion about each portfolio based on the questionnaire responses. During the discussion, the leader should take notes and prompt discussion among faculty but not dominate it.

4. After the discussion, the group leader will write a brief report that summarizes the discussion.

5. Share group reports with faculty.

6. Discuss with faculty the results of the readings in light of the Outcomes Statement.

PORTFOLIO READING QUESTIONNAIRE

Portfolio Number_____

General Approach

How many *formal writing assignments* do students do? What types? (Specify type of essay if possible.)

What kind of *informal writing* do students do?

What *audiences* do students address in their writing?

What do students read? (Specify type of essay if possible.) How is the reading connected to the writing?

Writing Process

What activities are evident in the course that encourage students to develop an effective writing process and to learn how to critique their own work and others'? Please be specific.

Student Writing Samples

Look at the student writing samples designated "high." Is there an original thesis, focus, or controlling idea for each sample? How is it supported? Or, what writing techniques does the writer use to support the thesis, focus, or controlling idea?

Do the writers integrate others' ideas appropriately in their writing? Do the students use academic documentation conventions (if appropriate)? If so, is it MLA form?

What do you think about the designation of "high," "middle," and "low" for the student samples? Are they appropriate?

Overall

What other opportunities for students to develop as writers are evident in this portfolio that have not already been addressed?

What do you see as the strengths of this course/portfolio?

What questions do you have for the instructor about his/her portfolio or course?

How does this course compare to your own approach to FYC?

APPENDIX I
Getting Started Guide for Program Assessment

WRITING PROGRAM ASSESSMENT: GETTING STARTED

Use the grid to help identify what you know and what questions you have as you begin planning your program assessment.

What constitutes my "program"?	
Why am I doing the assessment?	
What is the timeline?	

What do I want to know
  about/from students?
  about/from faculty?
  about/from administrators?	

How can I answer my questions? Or what methods should I use? (e.g, surveys, student writing samples, teachers' course portfolios, assignments, focus groups, observations, etc.)	
What information do we already have or can get relatively easily? (e.g., from Institutional Research NSSEE/ FSSEE info for school, annual reports, teaching evaluations, grades, retention rates, etc.)	
What are my resources? (e.g., personnel, money, time, professional resources such as WPA self-study guide, conference workshops, scholarly expertise)	
What are my constraints and limitations?	
How will the results be reported?	
How will the results be used and by whom?	
How will I ensure evaluation of materials is done reliably as appropriate?	

What are the potential consequences
  for teaching and learning?
  for teachers and students?	

QUESTIONS, METHODS, AND RESOURCES

After this initial brainstorming, you need to consider how everything fits together—questions, methods, and resources. In the end, a program assessment seems to be a negotiation among these issues. For example, how many people will be needed to read samples or participate in a focus group? What will the costs be for the reading? Will you need to make many copies of student papers? (This can cost a lot.) Will you need to pay focus-group leaders? for mailing? for audio taping or videotaping? for transcribing of tapes? Is digital archiving available? What are the costs and benefits of this? A grid such as the one below can help you brainstorm and articulate these types of issues.

Question	Method(s)	Personnel Involved	Costs	Benefits

APPENDIX J
Sample Program Assessment Surveys

SURVEY OF WRITING: FOR FACULTY ACROSS THE DISCIPLINES

The English Department Composition Committee is surveying teachers across the disciplines in an effort to understand how you and your students use writing in your classes and to open a university-wide dialogue about writing. We'd appreciate your detailed responses to the following questions.

Name (optional) _____ Department _____
Number of years of college-level teaching experience: _____
Names/numbers of the courses you usually teach: _____

_____

1. Which of the courses that you teach have a writing component?

2. Please describe this component (for example, the kinds of writing assignments, number, purpose, audience, etc.).

3. What criteria do you use to evaluate the writing students do in your courses? (for example, ability to follow assignment, focus, development, organization, mechanics, etc.)

4. Of the criteria you use to evaluate student writing, which are the most important to you and why?

5. Do the criteria you use to evaluate student writing and the importance assigned to certain criteria depend on the particular kind/level of course you're teaching? Please explain.

6. What is your overall assessment of students' writing strengths and weaknesses? Please be specific.

7. What kinds of writing assistance do your students get? (for example, assignment sheet, teacher and/or peer feedback, writing center consultations, etc.)

8. Other comments, questions, concerns:

Thank you for your time and attention. Survey results will be circulated.

SURVEY OF WRITING: FOR NON-COMPOSITION FACULTY IN THE ENGLISH DEPARTMENT

The Composition Committee is surveying teachers throughout the department in an effort to understand how you and your students use writing in your classes and to open a department-wide dialogue about writing instruction. We'd appreciate your detailed responses to the following questions.

Name (optional): _____

Number of years of college-level teaching experience: _____

Names/numbers of the courses you usually teach: _____

1. Which of the courses that you teach have a writing component?

2. Please describe this component (i.e., the kind of writing assignments, number, purpose, audience, etc.).

3. What criteria do you use to evaluate the writing students do in your courses? (for example, ability to follow assignment, focus, development, organization, mechanics, etc.)

4. Of the criteria you use to evaluate student writing, which are the most important to you and why?

5. Do the criteria you use to evaluate student writing and the importance assigned to certain criteria depend on the particular kind/level of course you're teaching? Please explain.

6. What is your overall assessment of students' writing strengths and weaknesses? Please be specific.

7. What kinds of writing assistance (i.e., assignment sheet, teacher and/or peer feedback, writing center consultations) do your students get?

8. What do you think students should learn in a one-semester 100-level writing course?

9. What do you think students should learn in a 200-level writing course, such as our _____ course? Our _____ course?

10. To what extent do our 100- and 200-level writing courses address the kinds of things you think students should be learning? (*Please see attached course descriptions.*)

11. Other comments, questions, concerns:

Thank you for your time and attention. Survey results will be circulated.

SURVEY OF WRITING: FOR COMPOSITION FACULTY

The Composition Committee is surveying teachers throughout the department in an effort to better understand how you and your students use writing in your classes and to open a department-wide dialogue about writing instruction. We'd appreciate your detailed responses to the following questions.

Name (optional): _____

Number of years of college-level teaching experience: _____

1. What writing course(s) do you usually teach?

2. What is your overall assessment of students' writing strengths and weaknesses?

3. Of the criteria you use to evaluate student writing, which are the most important to you and why?

4. What kinds of writing assistance (i.e., assignment sheet, teacher and/or peer feedback, writing center consultations, etc.) do your students get?

5. What do you think students should learn in a one-semester 100-level writing course such as _____, _____, or _____?

6. What do you think students should learn in a 200-level writing course, such as our _____ course?

7. What are students NOT learning to do in 100-level courses that you think they should be learning to do?

8. What are students NOT learning to do in 200-level courses that you think they should be learning to do?

9. What suggestions do you have for making our 100-level writing courses better meet the needs of our students? (When responding to this question, please consider course goals, recommended approaches, and textbook lists.) Do they need to be revised? modified? Why or why not?)

10. What suggestions do you have for making our 200-level course better meet the needs of our students? (When responding to this question, please consider course goals, recommended approaches, and textbook lists. Do they need to be revised? modified? Why or why not?)

11. Other comments, questions, concerns:

Thank you for your time and attention. Survey results will be circulated.

APPENDIX K
Sample Student Focus Group Outline[1]

Introduction

Hello everyone and thank you for coming tonight. My name is _____ and I'm going to be leading our discussion. We're here tonight to talk about your first-year writing course. From here on, we'll simply refer to these courses as Effective Writing, but whichever you took, we're interested in hearing your opinions about your experience in this class. We want to know how you honestly felt about the course while you were taking it, and what you think now. There are absolutely no right or wrong answers to any of our questions. Even if your opinion is completely different than the rest of the group's, we still want to hear it, so please don't hesitate to speak your mind. Although your teachers probably played a large part in your experience, please focus on the course and not the teacher, and do not use the names of your teachers from this point on.

And now to begin, why don't we have everyone introduce themselves and give their major.

Warm-up

What was your favorite class during your first year of college?

How do you feel about taking the required core courses here at Loyola?

When you realized you would have to take the Effective Writing class, what did you think or feel? Did you think it would be similar to something you had taken already in high school?

What were your expectations for this course? In other words, what kinds of assignments and class activities did you expect?

Adjective Exercise

Now that you have taken Effective Writing, what three adjectives would you use to describe the course?

Specifics About the Effective Writing Course

Explain how the course, the assignments you did, and the things you talked about in class differed from your expectations prior to the class.

---

1. This outline is based on one developed by students in a communication research class for Peggy O'Neill, director of composition at Loyola College, who were their "client." After working with Professor O'Neill to develop the outline, the students conducted the focus groups for the composition program. Since then, the outline has been revised.

What were students required to do in your course?

What were typical assignments? Did you read books, articles, watch movies . . . . PROBE

What kind of essays did you write? PROBE

Did they require you to visit the library or do outside research?

What do you think the intended purpose or goals of taking Effective Writing were?

Do you think your teacher reached these goals? If yes, how? If no, then why not?

Effective Writing Techniques

What techniques and strategies did you learn in Effective Writing?

Which of these techniques, if any, do you still use? How do you use them and for what?

What was the difference between the techniques and strategies you learned in Effective Writing and those you learned in high school? Which do you find you use more today? Why do you think that is?

Effective Writing Objectives

I'm passing out a list of objectives that the Writing Department has defined as the goals and purpose of Effective Writing. Please take a moment to read through them.

Are all or some of these objectives familiar to you?

Which of these objectives do you feel were best accomplished in your course? Can you give specific examples of how they were accomplished?

Are there objectives on the list that were not fulfilled adequately? If so, what do you think could have been done to accomplish these goals?

Closing Questions

If you could change something about the Effective Writing course (such as objectives, assignments, etc.), what would it be, and why?

Do you think Effective Writing is an important core course? Why or why not?

Do you have anything else to add?

Thank participants for coming.

APPENDIX L
Selective Annotated Bibliography of Additional Readings

The following annotated bibliography is a list of essential texts for readers who want to learn more about college writing assessment but are not sure where to begin. This list is just a starting place and is not meant to be comprehensive. The entries privilege large-scale assessment—that is, assessment done beyond the classroom—although several texts address both areas. We have not included texts that address educational measurement more generally or those on topics such as sociolinguistics or literacy theory, which are significant in understanding theoretical assumptions that inform writing assessment. We have only included books, not individual articles or chapters, because many of the books are collections. We have also included the two peer-reviewed journals that are strictly devoted to writing assessment although there are many important articles in more general journals such as *Research in the Teaching of English* and *Educational Measurement: Issues and Practice.*

JOURNALS

Assessing Writing. This refereed journal, founded in 1994 by co-editors Brian Huot and Kathleen Blake Yancey, was the first journal devoted exclusively to writing assessment. Its aim was to bridge the K–16 and composition constituency to the educational measurement community. Currently, it is edited by Liz Hamp-Lyons and published by Elsevier, and it includes an international focus.

Journal of Writing Assessment. First published in 2003, and founded by Kathleen Blake Yancey and Brian Huot, *JWA* is a refereed journal published by Hampton Press. It was founded to continue the goals that inspired Yancey and Huot to start *AW*. Currently, it is edited by Huot. It gives a biennial award to the best book published in writing assessment. Most issues also include annotated bibliographies on specific topics in writing assessment such as validity, automated scoring, and diversity.

BOOKS

Black, Laurel, Donald A. Daiker, Jeffrey Sommers, and Gail Stygall, eds. 1994. *New Directions in Portfolio Assessment: Reflective Practice, Critical Theory, and Large-scale Scoring.* Portsmouth, NH: Boynton/Cook Heinemann.

One of the early collections that focused exclusively on writing portfolios, the book addresses both classroom-based and large-scale uses of portfolios. The twenty-six chapters are organized into three sections that address theory, classroom practices, and large-scale uses. Across the sections, multiple perspectives are offered. For example, one section focuses on students' voices while another represents teachers' voices. On the topic of using portfolios with graduate teaching assistants, one essay advocates for it and one cautions against it. Noteworthy about the collection is that it is one of the first volumes that included critical discussions of writing portfolios to balance the enthusiastic praise emphasized in the earlier portfolio literature.

Broad, Bob. 2003. *What We Really Value: Beyond Rubrics in Teaching and Assessing Writing* Logan: Utah State University Press.

This book-length study reports on a qualitative research project Broad conducted that investigated a first-year composition exit portfolio system at a large urban university. Based on his research, Broad developed dynamic criteria mapping as a way for programs to determine and articulate their values. He argues that DCM—as both a process and a product—provides more authentic and theoretically consistent means for writing assessment than traditional rubrics and rubric-based assessment. His edited collection, *Organic Writing Assessment: Dynamic Criteria Mapping in Action* (2009), reports on how DCM has been used by specific writing programs.

Ericsson, Patricia Freitag, and Richard Haswell, eds. 2006. *The Machine Scoring of Student Writing: Truth and Consequences.* Logan: Utah State University Press.

This volume includes sixteen essays, all written by compositionists, on different aspects of computer automated scoring of essays. Selections address uses of machine scoring in a variety of contexts as well as specific scoring programs, such as ACCUPLACER's WritePlacer and COMPASS's E-Write. Contributors represent a range of institutions from community colleges to research-oriented universities.

Hamp-Lyons, Liz, and William Condon. 2000. *Assessing the Portfolio: Principles for Practice, Theory and Research.* Cresskill, New Jersey: Hampton Press.

A comprehensive overview of the basics of writing portfolios. The five chapters provide an overview of trends and practices, portfolio use in college writing programs, large-scale and classroom practices, and a discussion of theory and research. The text is clear and easy to follow for those unfamiliar with writing assessment literature and a good starting point for those interested in portfolios. It also includes several helpful examples or heuristics, such as a protocol for developing portfolio criteria, to illustrate concepts and practices.

Haswell, Richard, ed. 2001. *Beyond Outcomes: Assessment and Instruction within a University Writing Program.* Greenwich, CT: Ablex.

This text is a comprehensive examination of the Washington State University writing assessment program, which includes both placement and mid-career assessments. The text includes fourteen essays divided into five sections with three appendices. It covers the history and development of the innovative two-tiered expert reader system developed at WSU under Haswell's leadership in the early 1990s. Contributors such as Haswell, Diane Kelly-Riley, Susan Wyche, Lisa Johnson-Shull, and Bill Condon, who have been associated with the WSU writing program at one time or another, address theory, practice, and validity. Many of the chapters have appeared elsewhere in various forms, but this book gives readers a sense of how the different parts work together.

Huot, Brian, and Peggy O'Neill, eds. 2009. *Assessing Writing: A Critical Sourcebook.* Boston: Bedford St. Martin's and National Council of Teachers of English.

This anthology offers reprints of twenty-four key articles in writing assessment by scholars such as White, Yancey, Haswell, Williamson, Huot, Moss, and Broad, among others. The book is organized in three sections: *Foundations,* which includes ten articles on theory and history; *Models,* which includes six essays on different types of assessments, such as placement, exit testing and writing-across-the-curriculum; and *Issues,* which includes eight essays on a range of issues such as cultural bias, second language assessment, and machine scoring. The text also includes an extensive bibliography of additional readings that covers writing assessment and other topics essential to understanding theory and practice. The introduction provides an historical overview of writing assessment.

Huot, Brian. 2002. *(Re)Articulating Writing Assessment for Teaching and Learning.* Logan: Utah State University Press.

A comprehensive study of writing assessment, both large-scale and classroom-based, that focuses on the role of writing assessment in both teaching and learning. In positing a theory of writing assessment, Huot discusses the history of writing assessment and its relationship to educational measurement as well as language and literacy theories. Although grounded in psychometric, education, and composition research and theory, the text is appropriate for those just beginning to study writing assessment as well as for those who are more experienced.

White, Edward M., William Lutz, and Sandra Samakiri, eds. 1996. *Assessment of Writing: Politics, Policies, Practices.* Research and Scholarship in Composition Series. New York: Modern Language Association.

This collection of essays addresses many of the key issues in writing assessment with contributors coming from a variety of perspectives and positions. Topics covered include legal issues, validity and reliability, portfolios, gender, race, and computer-assisted assessment, and address both classroom-based and large-scale concerns. The contents are divided into five sections, each of which concludes with a response essay written by a notable scholar.

Williamson, Michael M., and Brian A. Huot, eds. 1993. *Validating Holistic Scoring: Theoretical and Empirical Foundations.* Cresskill, NJ. Hampton Press.

An influential collection of nine essays that focuses on timed impromptu essays and holistic scoring, which were the popular methods of assessing students' writing during the 1980s and 1990s and which are still popular today. Essays report on empirical research studies, theoretical discussions, and historical perspectives. This volume marked a turn in writing assessment scholarship from a focus on reliability—getting raters to agree at acceptable rates—to validity. Several of the chapters have made significant contributions to writing assessment scholarship, particularly William L. Smith's comprehensive essay on the expert reader method that he developed and Roberta Camp's essay "Changing the Model for the Direct Assessment of Writing."

Yancey, Kathleen Blake, and Brian Huot, eds. 1997. *Assessing Writing Across the Curriculum: Diverse Approaches and Practices.* Greenwich, CT: Ablex.

This is the first volume devoted exclusively to writing assessment and writing-across-the-curriculum. The fourteen essays primarily report on ways particular WAC programs conducted program assessments given their context, needs, and resources. Contributors include many familiar scholars such as Barbara Walvoord, Cynthia Selfe, Richard Haswell, Marty Townsend, Charles Moran, Anne Herrington, and Chris Thais and Terry Zawacki. While the focus is on the specific challenges and needs of WAC programs, many of the methods and approaches can be useful in any kind of writing program assessment.

GLOSSARY

We have defined the terms below in the context of college writing assessment. Definitions are by necessity brief and not meant to address all aspects of the terms. In some cases, we suggest references that offer more complete discussions. Readers should also consult the index.

accreditation review. This typically refers to institutional program reviews required for accreditation by one of the regional accrediting agencies such as Middle States Association of Colleges and Schools or a specialized accrediting review such as National Council of Accreditation for Teacher Education (NCATE). Writing programs are often involved in accrediting reviews because of their role in general education as well as in specialized programs, such as writing-across-the-curriculum, or in disciplines, such as engineering and business.

analytic scoring. A type of scoring used for writing samples that evaluates individual features of a text to determine the value of the text as a whole. Rubrics used for analytic scoring are generic and are not specific to the particular writing task or genre. For example, an analytic rubric might have readers evaluate the text on a scale of 1–4 in each of the following areas: thesis, organization, development, style, grammar/mechanics, and usage. The overall score would be determined by adding the score assigned for each feature. Analytic scores can be weighted differentially so that features like thesis, organization, and development receive more weight in the overall score than other features like grammar/mechanics and usage. See also *holistic scoring* and *primary trait scoring*. For more information, including samples, see Cooper and Odell (1977) and Wolcott and Legg (1998).

assessment. "Any systematic method of obtaining information from tests and other sources, used to draw inferences about characteristics of people, objects, or programs" (AERA, APA, and NCME 1999, 172). Although some scholars and practitioners distinguish among assessment, evaluation, and testing, we have not because all of these activities depend on the same basic technology. See chapter 3, footnote 2.

automated scoring (machine scoring). In writing assessment, this refers to computer programs that generate scores for essays. Automated scoring is sometimes incorrectly considered a form of holistic, analytic, or primary trait scoring. Computer scoring programs can be modified to provide scores that agree at a higher rate with scores generated solely by human readers. Automated scoring programs cannot read texts; rather, their score reliability is achieved through complex algorithms that correspond to textual features like length. See Ericcson and Haswell in appendix L, and Willamson (2003).

communal assessment. Refers to an approach to writing assessment in which instructors in a program work together to evaluate student writing. Broad (1997, 2000) uses the term to refer to the portfolio assessment system he studied in which the instructors worked first in large groups to negotiate and discuss student writing and standards for evaluation. Then, instructors gathered in groups of three at the midpoint and the end of the semester to evaluate each others' student portfolios. The specific details and procedures of communal assessment vary, but it is based on the notion that the instructors of a program participate as a community of instructors and readers in the articulation and application of standards.

competency assessment. Evaluates student performance against a specified set of criteria, standards, or competencies. See *criterion referenced assessment.*

construct. The ability, skill, or domain that the test or assessment seeks to evaluate. Construct underrepresentation occurs when the assessment fails to address important aspects of the construct (in writing assessment this can be any part of the process that simplifies or omits the act of writing). Construct-irrelevance occurs when results are influenced by factors or constructs irrelevant to the particular construct the test intends to evaluate.

correlation coefficient. A single number that describes the degree of relationship between two variables. It is presented as a number between -1 and 1. A perfect relationship is 1; 0 means there is no linear relationship between the two variables. In writing assessment, correlations are most often associated with holistic scoring and interrater reliability, which is the rate of agreement of two independent raters. If raters agreed on the scores of the texts every time, they would have a coefficient of 1. If they never agreed, the coefficient would be 0. There are specific statistical formulas for calculating correlation coefficients although there is no standard method used in writing assessment. For more information, see Hayes and Hatch (1999), Cherry and Meyer (1993) and the AERA, APA, and NCME's *Standards for Educational and Psychological Testing* (1999).

criterion-referenced assessment. This type of assessment measures students' performance against a certain set of criteria or standards. The performance of other test takers does not influence the scores in this type of assessment. Criterion-referenced writing assessments may also be referred to as proficiency or competency tests. Although criterion-referenced testing is often used to refer to standardized multiple-choice exams, it is not limited to one form of testing. For example, a writing program may have articulated learning outcomes for its composition program. These outcomes can be used as the assessment criteria to evaluate a sample of student portfolios as part of a program review.

direct measure. In the measurement literature on writing assessment, this means that students produce written text for the assessment, which is then evaluated. It is opposed to *indirect measures* such as performance on multiple-choice exams about writing processes, language conventions, and/ or editing exercises.

directed self-placement. Developed and popularized by Royer and Gilles (1998), DSP allows students to select their first-year composition course based on a self-evaluation of their writing experiences and expertise. DSP depends on a program that guides students in their selection process by providing clear information for students about the requisite competencies needed for various composition courses and accurately describing the course activities and learning goals. Several programs have adapted DSP for their needs. See Royer and Gilles (1998, 2003) for more information.

dynamic criteria mapping. A method of evaluation, developed by Broad (2003), that is offered as an alternative to traditional rubrics. DCM "is a streamlined form of qualitative inquiry that yields a detailed, complex, and useful portrait of any writing program's evaluative dynamics" (Broad 2003, 13). Broad advocates DCM as a workable method for discovering, negotiating, and publicizing the rhetorical values used in judging students' writing (14). See Broad's edited collection, *Organic Writing Assessment: Dynamic Criteria Mapping in Action* (2009) for more on how various programs have used DCM.

educational measurement. The field of study concerned with assessment theory and practice as related specifically to education, such as students' knowledge, abilities, and achievement. The term *measurement* implies quantification, using numerical expressions for reporting results. In writing assessment, and educational assessment in general, there is more acceptance of qualitative results that are not always expressed numerically. It deals with large-scale as well as classroom-based and individualized testing and does not depend upon a specific subject or ability. Writing assessment is a specific subfield.

exit testing. A barrier assessment administered at the end of a course or program. Typically, to successfully complete the course of study, the student must pass the exit exam. An exit test can be classroom-based, large-scale or a combination. It can be criterion-referenced or norm-referenced.

expert reader system. In this approach to evaluating writing samples, readers (raters give scores and readers make decisions) are prepared for the evaluation session through their teaching experience and preparation instead of through training and calibrating with rubrics and anchor papers as is done in holistic scoring. It was initially developed by William L. Smith (1992, 1993) at the University of Pittsburgh. Richard Haswell and his colleagues at Washington State University developed a two-tiered expert reader system (2001b).

formative assessment. Assessment received while a person is still able to improve his or her performance. The purpose of this type of evaluation is to generate feedback from the assessment to improve performance. It is generally considered low stakes—that is, there is no significant consequence attached to the results. See *summative assessment.*

holistic scoring. A method of scoring writing samples premised on the theory that the whole of the text is greater than a sum of its parts. Raters are trained to read quickly to get a general impression and then to identify the score from the rubric that most closely describes the text. The scoring rubric, usually a 4- or 6-point scale, provides general descriptions for each score point. Anchor papers operationalize the score point descriptions. In pure holistic scoring, the samples are ranked relative to the other papers being evaluated not against an absolute standard. See White (1994), Cooper and Odell (1977), and Wolcott and Legg (1998) for more information. See also *primary trait* and *analytic scoring.*

impromptu essay exam. A type of writing exam where students respond to a prompt on demand, usually within a fixed time limit. Administration of the test is usually standardized so that the conditions for all test takers are the same. Impromptus usually do not allow students any preparation time or access to the prompt or task ahead of time; however, some programs do allow students to access the task ahead of time or extend the writing process over multiple days. Examples include national standardized exams such as the SAT essay portion as well as many state-administered tests and locally designed placement exams.

indirect measure. This refers to tests or assessments that do not require students to produce actual texts. Examples include multiple-choice tests about writing processes, grammar, mechanics, and usage; fill-in-the-blank exams or sentence completions; and editing exercises or corrections. In our view, these types of exams are not actually writing assessments because they are not assessing writing per se but something else such as knowledge of language conventions or editing skills. See *direct measure.*

instrument reliability. The aspect of reliability that looks at the instrument—the test or assessment—and what would happen if "the same assessment were to be done again in the same way, with the same distribution of students, the same method of assessment, and the same general kinds of topics" (Cherry and Meyer 1993, 118). Instrument reliability, Cherry and Meyer (1993) pointed out, "makes claims about the validity of a test by correlating performance on a test with other measures of writing ability" (118). Variation across topics/prompts, however, can be a validity issue because the underlying construct being tapped is different if the writing tasks are different. See also *reliability* and *interrater reliability.*

interrater reliability. Typically this refers to the rate of agreement between two independent raters in scoring a particular exam. It is usually reported as a *correlation coefficient.* Various methods can be used to calculate the interrater reliability, and at present, there is not an agreed-upon standard (see Hayes and Hatch 1999; Cherry and Meyer 1993). Although we endorse reporting a straight percentage of agreement in most situations, Hayes and Hatch (1999) argue for using particular statistical formulas that take into account the influence of chance in the agreement rates. Besides the variability in ways of calculating the coefficient, there is variability in how to accommodate the *split resolvers.*

large-scale assessment. Evaluation that occurs primarily beyond an individual course, such as placement, proficiency testing, exit testing, or program assessment. It can be connected to classroom-based assessment, for example, with students producing work in a course but that work being evaluated beyond the scope of the course. It can involve assessing every student individually or sampling students, and it can be locally designed and administered or standardized and national.

norming. In composition programs, norming, also referred to as calibrating, refers to groups of writing instructors reading, discussing, and evaluating student writing to establish shared evaluation criteria. The sessions may be guided by a rubric and anchor papers, which are sample texts that exemplify the score points, or they may be less structured with participants discussing the strengths, weaknesses, and evaluative decisions without a rubric. It can also refer to the training sessions used in large-scale writing assessments.

norm-referenced testing. Scores are reported in percentiles, using a scoring scale which is determined by a norming group of students. An individual's score is relative to the scores and performance of other students or a group of students selected as the norming or reference group. It is opposite of *criterion-referenced testing*.

placement assessment. The procedure, whether a formal test, standardized test scores (e.g., SAT or ACT), a standardized multiple-choice exam (e.g., ACCUPLACER), directed self-placement, or some combination of methods, used to determine students' entry point into the composition curriculum. It assumes a differentiated curriculum—that is, multiple courses of first-year composition in which a student could enter.

population. Consists of a particular group that satisfies the conditions for analysis or evaluation from which a smaller sample might be selected. See *sample*.

portfolio assessment. Uses portfolios as the sampling method. The portfolio is created through the processes of collection, selection, and reflection (Yancey 1992). The specific contents of the portfolio are determined by the assessment's purpose. Writing programs have used student portfolios for placement, exemption, proficiency, and program assessments. Methods for evaluating or scoring the portfolios vary. Teacher portfolios or course portfolios can be used for program assessment and faculty evaluation.

primary trait scoring. It assumes that different types of writing (e.g., a technical report, personal narrative, and a literary analysis) differ in significant ways, and therefore, require different writing skills. It highlights the role of purpose, audience, and context in evaluating writing. According to Lloyd-Jones, it requires users to "define the universe of discourse, to devise exercises which sample that universe precisely . . . to devise workable scoring guides and to use the guides" (1977, 37). A scoring guide for a literary analysis might include categories such as Thesis, Organization, Support, Style, and then requirements for each category that are specific to a literary explication. Like analytic scoring, primary trait scoring involves the reporting of various scores that can be weighted, according to their importance, for an overall score. For more information, see Lloyd-Jones (1977) and Wolcott and Legg (1998).

proficiency testing. See *competency testing* and *criterion-referenced testing.*

psychometrics. The field of study that is concerned with the theory and practice of educational and psychological measurement. See *educational measurement.*

regression analysis. Demonstrates the statistical relationships between variables and can consider the various influences of different variables. Can also provide a p-value (a percentage of the probability that results are not due to chance). The 1999 edition of *Standards for Educational and Psychological Testing* is very clear about the preferred use of regression analysis over correlations: "Regression equations are more useful than correlation coefficients, which are generally insufficient to fully describe patterns of association between tests and other variables" (AERA, APA, and NMCE 21).

reliability. One of the basic concepts in psychometrics that usually is considered a significant component in a validity argument. It addresses consistency in results and scoring and the reporting of the results. According to the *Standards,* reliability is "the degree to which test scores for a group of test takers are consistent over repeated applications of a measurement procedure and hence are inferred to be repeatable for an individual test taker." It also includes the "degree to which scores are free of errors of measurement for a given group" (AERA, APA, and NMCE 1999, 180). Haertel (2006) explains that the "definition, quantification, and reporting of reliability must each begin with considerations of intended test uses and interpretations. . . . [Reliability] is concerned solely with how the scores resulting from a measurement procedure would be expected to vary across replications of that procedure" (65). Complex statistical methods are typically used in determining reliability. For more information specific to reliability in writing assessment, see Cherry and Meyer (1993).

rubric. A scoring guide for evaluating writing samples. It specifies the point scale and identifies the salient features of the text for each point. Rubrics vary in detail, ranging from a checklist to paragraph-length descriptions for each score point. See *holistic, analytic,* and *primary trait scoring.* Wolcott and Legg (1998) have several examples.

sample. A selection from a particular population. The sample can be determined in a variety of ways, depending on the assessment and its purpose. Random sample is drawn randomly from the specified population (e.g., writing from 20 percent of the students enrolled in a particular course may be randomly selected for evaluation as part of a program assessment). A stratified random sample is a set of random samples drawn from larger sets (e.g., writing samples may represent 10 percent of all students receiving As, 10 percent receiving Bs, etc). Other sampling techniques may be more purposeful, with specific criteria established for selecting the sample (e.g., students failing basic writing, or students who are exempt from the writing course).

split resolvers. In scoring writing samples, two independent raters are traditionally used to determine the score. Typically, if the scores assigned by the initial two raters disagree by more than one score point, a third rater scores the text. The third reader is the split resolver. Specific procedures for using a split resolver vary: in some cases, raters know they are functioning as the split resolver, while in other situations, the rater won't know. In writing assessment, there isn't a standard procedure for accommodating these decisions in calculating the reliability coefficient. See Cherry and Meyer (1993).

summative assessment. An evaluation that occurs at a fixed point beyond which the individual can no longer improve her work or performance. Its purpose is to determine, or summarize, learning, achievement, or performance that has occurred at a certain point. Examples of this type of evaluation include unit or final exams, a final course portfolios, course grades, and exit exams. See *formative assessment* and *proficiency.*

trios. In communal portfolio assessment, this term refers to the small groups consisting of three instructors that work together to operationalize the program standards and to grade each others' portfolios. Trios can function in different ways depending on the structure of the program. Sometimes, they grade student work; sometimes, they address the borderline students only; and sometimes, they decide the pass/fail distinction with instructors assigning the specific grades. See *communal assessment.*

validation. The process of determining the validity of an assessment's results. Often referred to as a validation argument. See also *validity* and *validity inquiry.*

validity. An essential concept in testing and assessment. Validity refers to the degree to which evidence supports the use and interpretation of an assessment's results. Validity does not reside in the test or assessment instrument but rather in the interpretation and use of the results. In other words, a test is not itself valid or invalid, but the results are valid or invalid for particular uses. For example, instead of asking if a test is valid or invalid, the question should be, "Are the results of this test valid for this particular use?" The validity argument should address both theoretical and empirical evidence. Although validity is an evolving concept, current consensus, as articulated in the *Standards* (1999) and *Educational Measurement* (2006), considers it a unitary concept. That is, there are not distinct types of validity but rather different types of evidence (e.g., construct, content, consequential) that need to be considered in constructing a validity argument. See Kane (2006), Messick (1989b) and AERA, APA, and NCME (1999).

validity inquiry. The process of investigating the validity of an assessment's results. See also *validity* and *validation.*

REFERENCES

Abrami, Philip C. 2001a. Improving Judgments about Teacher Effectiveness Using Teacher Rating Forms. Special Issue: Student Ratings Debate. *New Directions for Institutional Research* 109 (Spring): 59–88.

———. 2001b. Improving Judgments about Teacher Effectiveness: How to Lie Without Statistics. Special Issue: Student Ratings Debate. *New Directions for Institutional Research* 109 (Spring): 97–102.

———, Michael Theall, and Lisa A. Mets. 2001. Editors' Notes. Special Issue: Student Ratings Debate. *New Directions for Institutional Research* 109 (Spring): 1–6.

Adler-Kassner, Linda. 1999. Just Writing, Basically: Basic Writers on Basic Writing. *Journal of Basic Writing* 18.2 (1999): 69–90.

Agnew, Eleanor, and Margaret McLaughlin. 2001. Those Crazy Gates and How They Swing: Tracking the System that Tracks African-American Students. In *Mainstreaming Basic Writers Politics and Pedagogies of Access*, ed. Gerri McNenny and Sallyanne H. Fitzgerald, 85–100. Mahwah, NJ: Lawrence Erlbaum Associates.

Allen, Michael. 1995. Valuing Differences: Portnet's First Year. *Assessing Writing* 2:67–90.

American Educational Research Association, American Psychological Association, and National Council on Measurement in Education. 1999. *Standards for Educational and Psychological Testing*. Washington, DC: American Educational Research Association.

———. 1974. *Standards for Educational and Psychological Tests*. Washington, DC: American Psychological Association.

———. 1985. *Standards for Educational and Psychological Tests*. Washington, DC: American Psychological Association.

American Psychological Association. 1954. Technical Recommendations for Psychological Tests and Diagnostic Techniques. *Psychological Bulletin* 51:201–38.

———. 1966. *Standards for Educational and Psychological Tests and Manuals*. Washington, DC: American Psychological Association.

Angoff, William H. 1988. Validity: An Evolving Concept. *Test Validity*, ed. H. Wainer and H. I. Braun. Hillsdale NJ: Lawrence Erlbaum Associates.

Anson, Chris M. 1994. Portfolios for Teachers: Writing Our Way to Reflective Practice. In Black, Daiker, Sommers, and Stygall, 185–200.

——— and Deanna P. Dannels. 2002. The Medium and the Message: Developing Responsible Methods for Assessing Teaching Portfolios. In Minter and Goodburn, 89–100.

Applebee, Arthur. 1981. *Writing in the Secondary Schools: English and the Content Areas*. Urbana, IL: National Council of Teachers of English.

Argyris, Chris, and Donald Schön. 1981. *Theory and Practice: Increasing Professional Effectiveness*. San Francisco, CA: Jossey-Bass.

Aultman, Lori Price. 2006. An Unexpected Benefit of Formative Student Evaluations. *College Teaching* 54.3:251.

Bain, Ken. 2004. *What the Best College Teachers Do*. Cambridge, MA: Harvard University Press.

Baldwin, Tamara, and Nancy Blattner. 2003. Guarding against Potential Bias in Student Evaluations: What Every Faculty Member Needs to Know. *College Teaching* 51.1:27–32.

Ball, Arnetha F., and Pamela Ellis. 2008. Identity and the Writing of Culturally and Linguistically Diverse Students. In *Handbook of Research on Writing: History, Society, School, Individual, Text*, ed. Charles Bazerman. New York: Lawrence Earlbaum Associates, 499–514.

———. 1997. Expanding the Dialogue on Culture as a Critical Component When Assessing Writing. *Assessing Writing* 4:169–202.

Barr-Ebest, Sally. 1995. Gender Differences in Writing Program Administration. *WPA: Writing Program Administration* 18.3:53–73.

Basow, Susan, and Suzanne Montgomery. 2005. Student Ratings and Professor Self-Ratings of College Teaching: Effects of Gender and Divisional Status. *Journal of Personnel Evaluation in Education* 18.2:91–106.

Bean, John C. 1994. Evaluating Teachers in Writing-across-the-Curriculum Programs. In Hult, 147–66.

———, David Carrithers, and Theresa Earenfight. 2005. Transforming WAC through a Discourse-Based Approach to University Outcomes Assessment. *WAC Journal* 16:5–21.

Beason, Larry, and Laurel Darrow. 1997. Listening as Assessment: How Students and Teachers Evaluate WAC. In Yancey and Huot, 97–118.

Belanoff, Pat, and Marcia Dickson, eds. 1991. *Portfolios: Process and Product.* Portsmouth, NH: Boynton/Cook.

Black, Laurel, Donald A. Daiker, Jeffrey Sommers, and Gail Stygall, eds. 1994. *New Directions in Portfolio Assessment: Reflective Practice, Critical Theory, and Large-Scale Scoring.* Portsmouth, NH: Boynton/Cook Heinemann.

Blakesley, David. 2002. Directed Self-Placement in the University. *WPA: Writing Program Administration* 25:9–39.

Board of Regents of the University System of Georgia. 21 Dec 2006. Overview of the Regents' Writing and Reading Skills Requirement. http://www2.gsu.edu/~wwwrtp/overview.htm (accessed 28 Oct 2007).

Borrowman, Shane. 1999. The Trinity of Portfolio Placement: Validity, Reliability, and Curriculum Reform. *WPA: Writing Program Administration* 23.1/2, 7–28.

Brandt, Deborah. 1998. Sponsors of Literacy. *College Composition and Communication* 49:165–85.

Brereton, John C., ed. 1995. *The Origins of Composition Studies in the American College 1875–1925: A Documentary History.* Pittsburgh, PA: University of Pittsburgh Press.

Broad, Bob. 2000. Pulling Your Hair Out: Crises of Standardization in Communal Writing Assessment. *Research in the Teaching of English.* 35: 213-60.

———. 2003. *What We Really Value: Beyond Rubrics in Teaching and Assessing Writing.* Logan: Utah State University Press.

———, Linda Adler-Kassner, Barry Alford, et al. 2009. *Organic Writing Assessment: Dynamic Criteria Mapping in Action.* Logan, UT: Utah State University Press.

Broad, Robert L. 1994. 'Portfolio Scoring': A Contradiction in Terms. In Black et al., 263–77.

Camp, Roberta. 1993. Changing the Model for the Direct Assessment of Writing. In Williamson and Huot, 45–78.

Carleton College Writing Program. "The Sophomore Writing Portfolio." http://apps.carleton.edu/campus/writingprogram/carletonwritingprogram/portfolio (accessed 20 Dec 2007).

Carter, Michael. 2001. Ways of Knowing, Doing, and Writing in the Disciplines. *College Composition and Communication* 58:385–418.

Cazden, Courtney. 2001. *Classroom Discourse: The Language of Teaching and Learning.* 2nd ed. Portsmouth, NH: Heinemann.

Chase, Geoffrey. 1996. A Professional Development Program for Graduate Students: Fostering Collaboration in the Writing Program at Northern Arizona University. In Hutchings, 85–88.

Cherry, Roger, and Paul Meyer. 1993. Reliability Issues in Holistic Assessment. In Williamson and Huot, 109–41.

Chism, Nancy Van Note. 1999. *Peer Review of Teaching: A Sourcebook.* Bolton, MA: Anker.

Condon, William. 1997. Building Bridges, Closing Gaps. In Yancey and Weiser, 196–213.

Conference on College Composition and Communication. 1982. Position Statement on the Preparation and Professional Development of Teachers of Writing. http://www.ncte.org/cccc/resources/positions/123789.htm (accessed 9 Aug 2007).

———. 1989. *Statement on Principles and Standards for the Postsecondary Teaching of Writing.* http://www.ncte.org/cccc/resources/positions/123790.htm (accessed 9 Aug 2007).

———. 2004. CCCC Certificate of Excellence for Writing Programs. *College Composition and Communication* 55:793.

————. Nov. 2006. Writing Assessment: A Position Statement. Rev. ed. http://www.ncte.org/cccc/resources/positions/123784.htm (accessed 10 Nov 2007).

Conference on College Composition and Communication Committee on Teaching and Its Evaluation. 1982. Evaluating Instruction in Writing: Approaches and Instruments. *College Composition and Communication* 33:213–29.

Cook-Gumperz, Jenny. 2006. *The Social Construction of Literacy.* 2nd ed. Cambridge, UK: Cambridge University Press.

Cooper, Allene, Martha Sipe, Teresa Dewey, and Stephanie Hunt. 1999. What Happens When Discourse Communities Collide? Portfolio Assessment and Non-Tenure Track Faculty. In *Administrative Problem-Solving for Writing Programs and Writing Centers: Scenarios in Effective Program Management,* ed. Linda Myers-Breslin, 44–52. Urbana, IL: NCTE.

Cooper, Charles R. 1977. Holistic Evaluation of Writing. In *Evaluating Writing: Describing, Measuring and Judging,* ed. C. R. Cooper and L. Odell. Urbana, IL: National Council of Teachers of English.

———— and Lee Odell, eds. 1977. *Evaluating Writing: Describing, Measuring, Judging.* Urbana, IL: National Council of Teachers of English.

Cronbach, Lee J. 1988. Five Perspectives on Validity Argument. In *Test Validity,* ed. Howard Wainer and Henry Braun, 3–17. Hillsdale: Laurence Erlbaum.

————. 1989. Construct Validation after Thirty Years. In *Intelligence Measurement, Theory and Public Policy: Proceedings of a Symposium in Honor of L. G. Humphreys,* ed. R. L. Linn. Urbana and Chicago: University of Illinois Press.

d'Apollonia, Sylvia, and Philip C. Abrami. 1997. Navigating Student Ratings of Instruction. *American Psychologist* 52:1198–1208. http://web12.epnet.com (accessed 22 April 2003).

Daiker, Donald A., Jeff Sommers, and Gail Stygall. 1996. The Pedagogical Implications of a College Placement Portfolio. In White, Lutz, and Kamusikiri, 257–70.

Diederich, Paul B. 1950. *The 1950 College Board English Validity Study.* Princeton: Educational Testing Service. RB No. 50-58.

————. 1996. Turning Fords into Lincolns: Reminiscences on Teaching and Assessing Writing. *Research in the Teaching of English* 30:352–60.

————, John W. French, and Sydell T. Carlton. 1961. *Factors in Judgments of Writing Quality.* Princeton: Educational Testing Service. RB No. 61-15 ED 002 172.

Durst, Russel K. 2007. Crossing Over: The Move from Education to Composition. In O'Neill, 291–306.

Durst, Russel K., Marjorie Roemer, and Lucille Schultz. 1994. Portfolio Negotiations: Acts in Speech. In Black et al., 286–300.

Edgerton, Russell, Pat Hutchings, and Kathleen Quinlan. 1991. *The Teaching Portfolio: Capturing the Scholarship of Teaching.* Washington. DC: American Association for Higher Education.

Edgington, Anthony. 2005. What Are You Thinking: Understanding Teacher Reading and Response through a Protocol Analysis Study. *Journal of Writing Assessment* 2:125–48.

Elbow, Peter. 1994. Making Better Use of Student Evaluations of Teachers. In Hult, 97–107.

————. 1996. Writing Assessment: Do It Better, Do It Less. In White, Lutz, and Kamusikiri, 120–34.

———— and Pat Belanoff. 1986. Staffroom Interchange: Portfolios as a Substitute for Proficiency Examinations. *College Composition and Communication* 37:336–39.

Elliot, Norbert. 2005. *On a Scale: A Social History of Writing Assessment in America.* New York: Peter Lang.

England, James, Pat Hutchings, and Wilbert J. McKeachie. 1996. *The Professional Evaluation of Teaching.* American Council of Learned Societies. Occasional Paper No. 33. http://www.acls.org/op33.htm (accessed 25 Oct 2007).

Ericsson, Patricia Freitag, and Richard Haswell, eds. 2006. *The Machine Scoring of Student Writing: Truth and Consequences.* Logan, UT: Utah State University Press.

Faigley, Lester, Roger Cherry, David A. Jolliffe, and Anna M. Skinner. 1985. *Assessing Writers' Knowledge and Processes of Composing.* Norwood, NJ: Ablex.

Flanagan, Anne Marie. 1994. The Observer Observed: Retelling Tales In and Out of School. In Hult, 86.

Flanigan, Michael C. 1979. Observing Teaching: Discovering and Developing the Individual's Teaching Style. *Writing Program Administration* 3.2:17–24.

Fosen, Chris. 2006. 'University Courses, Not Department Courses': Composition and General Education. *Composition Studies* 34.1:11–33.

Fuess, Claude. 1967. *The College Board: Its First Fifty Years.* New York: College Entrance Examination Board.

Gale, Xin Liu. 1997. Judgment Deferred: Reconsidering Institutional Authority in the Portfolio Writing Classroom. In *Grading in the Post-Process Classroom: From Theory to Practice,* eds. Libby Allison, Lizabeth Bryant, and Maureen Hourigan, 75–93. Portsmouth, NH: Boynton/Cook Heineman.

Gee, James Paul. 1996. *Social Linguistics and Literacies: Ideology in Discourses.* 2nd ed. London: Taylor and Francis.

Gere, Anne Ruggles. 1980. Written Composition: Toward a Theory of Evaluation. *College English* 42:44–48, 53–58.

Gleason, Barbara. 2000. Evaluating Writing Programs in Real Time: The Politics of Remediation. *College Composition and Communication* 51:560–88.

Godshalk, Fred I., Frances Swineford, and William E. Coffman. 1966. *The Measurement of Writing Ability.* Princeton, NJ: Educational Testing Service. CEEB RM No. 6.

Goodburn, Amy. 2002. The Course Portfolio: Individual and Collective Possibilities. In Minter and Goodburn, 65–75.

Grand Valley State University Department of Writing. 2007. First-Year Writing. http://www. gvsu.edu/writing/index.cfm?id=3750FD1F-925D-CBE5-B1384DC3B3E70063 (accessed 20 Dec 2007).

Greenberg, Karen L. 1998. Grading, Evaluating, Assessing: Power and Politics in College Composition. *College Composition and Communication* 49:275–84.

Greenwald, Anthony G. 1997a. Validity Concerns and Usefulness of Student Ratings of Instruction. *American Psychologist* 52:1182–86. http://web12.epnet.com (accessed 22 April 2003).

———. 1997b. No Pain, No Gain?: The Importance of Measuring Course Workload in Student Ratings of Instruction. *Journal of Educational Psychology* 89:743–51. http://web12. epnet.com (accessed 22 April 2003).

Guilford, J. P. 1946. New Standards for Test Evaluation. *Educational and Psychological Measurement* 6:427–39.

Hamp-Lyons, Liz, and William Condon. 2000. *Assessing the Portfolio: Principles for Practice, Theory, and Research.* Cresskill, NJ: Hampton Press.

Harrington, Susanmarie. 1998. New Visions of Authority in Placement Test Rating. *WPA: Writing Program Administration* 22:53–84.

———. 1999. The Representation of Basic Writers in Basic Writing Scholarship, or Who is Quentin Pierce? *Journal of Basic Writing* 18.2:91–107.

———. 2005. Learning to Ride the Waves: Making Decisions about Placement Testing. *WPA: Writing Program Administration* 28:9–30.

———, Steve Fox, and Tere Molinder Hogue. 1998. Power, Partnership, and Negotiations: The Limits of Collaboration. *WPA: Writing Program Administration* 21. 2/3:52–64.

Harris, Joseph. 1997. *A Teaching Subject: Composition since 1966.* Upper Saddle River, NJ: Prentice Hall.

Harris, Muriel. 1999. Diverse Research Methodology at Work for Diverse Audiences: Shaping the Writing Center to the Institution. In Rose and Weiser, 1–17.

Haskell, Robert E. 1997. Academic Freedom, Tenure, and Student Evaluation of Faculty: Galloping Polls in the 21st Century. *Education Policy Analysis Archives* 5.6. http://epaa.asu/ epaa/v5n6.html (accessed 10 Oct 2003).

Haswell, Richard H. 1998. Multiple Inquiry into the Validation of Writing Tests. *Assessing Writing* 5:89–110.

———. ed. 2001a. *Beyond Outcomes: Assessment and Instruction within a University Writing Program.* Vol. 5, Perspectives on Writing Theory, Research and Practice. Westport, CT: Ablex.

———. 2001b. The Two-Tier Rating System: The Need for Change. In Haswell (2001a), 39–52.

———. 2001c. Validation: Part of the Circle. In Haswell (2001a), 125–39.

———, and Janis Tedesco Haswell. 1996. Gender Bias and Critique of Student Writing. *Assessing Writing* 3:31–84.

———, and Susan McLeod. 2001. Working with Administrators: A Dialogue on Dialogue. In Haswell (2001a), 169–85.

———, and Susan Wyche. 2001. Authoring an Exam: Adventuring into Large-Scale Writing Assessment. In Haswell (2001a), 13–24.

———, and Susan Wyche-Smith. 1994. Adventuring into Writing Assessment. *College Composition and Communication* 45:220–36.

Hayes, John R., and Jill A. Hatch. 1999. Issues in Measuring Reliability: Correlation versus Percentage of Agreement. *Written Communication* 16:354–67.

Heath, Shirley Brice. 1983. *Ways with Words: Language, Life, and Work in Communities and Classrooms.* Cambridge, UK: Cambridge University Press.

Hester, Vicki, Peggy O'Neill, Michael Neal, Anthony Edgington, and Brian Huot. 2007. Adding Portfolios to the Placement Process: A Longitudinal Perspective. In O'Neill (2007), 261–90.

Hillocks, George. 2002. *The Testing Trap: How State Writing Assessments Control Learning.* New York: Teachers College Press.

Hobson, Suzanne M., and Donna M. Talbot. 2001. Understanding Student Evaluations: What All Faculty Should Know. *College Teaching* 49.1:26–31.

Horner, Bruce, Kelly Latchaw, Joseph Lenz, Jody Swilky, and David Wolf. 2002. Excavating the Ruins of Undergraduate English. In *Beyond English, Inc.: Curricular Reform in a Global Economy,* ed. David B. Downing, Claude Mark Hurlbert, and Paula Mathieu, 75–92. Portsmouth, NH: Boynton/Cook Heinneman.

Hughes, Gail F. 1996. The Need for Clear Purposes and New Approaches to the Evaluation of Writing-across-the-Curriculum Programs. In White, Lutz, and Kamusikiri, 187–203.

Hull, Glynda, and Mike Rose. 1990. 'This Wooden Shack Place': The Logic of an Unconventional Reading. *College Composition and Communication* 41:287–98.

Hull, Glynda, Mike Rose, Kay Losey Fraser, and Marisa Castellano. 1991. Remediation as Social Construct: Perspectives from an Analysis of Classroom Discourse. *College Composition and Communication* 42:299–329.

Hult, Christine A., ed. 1994. *Evaluating Teachers of Writing.* Urbana, IL: National Council of Teachers of English.

Huot, Brian. 1990. The Literature of Direct Writing Assessment: Major Concerns and Prevailing Trends. *Review of Educational Research* 60:237–63.

———. 1993. The Influence of Holistic Scoring Procedures on Reading and Rating Student Essays. In Williamson and Huot, 206–36.

———. 1994. A Survey of College and University Writing Placement Practices. *WPA: Journal of Writing Program Administration* 17:49–65.

———. 1994. Introduction. *Assessing Writing* 1:1–9.

———. 1996. Toward a New Theory of Writing Assessment. *College Composition and Communication* 47:549–66.

———. 1997. Beyond Accountability: Reading with Faculty as Partners Across the Disciplines. In Yancey and Huot, 69–78.

———. 2002. *(Re)Articulating Writing Assessment for Teaching and Learning.* Logan: Utah State University Press.

———, and Ellen Schendel. 2001. Reflecting on Assessment: Validity Inquiry as Ethical Inquiry. *Journal of Teaching Writing* 17:37–55.

———, and Ellen Schendel. 2002. A Working Methodology of Assessment for Writing Program Administrators. In *The Allyn & Bacon Sourcebook for Writing Program Administrators,* ed. Irene Ward and William J. Carpenter, 207–27. New York: Longman.

———, and Michael Neal. 2006. Writing Assessment: A Techno-History. In *Handbook of Writing Research,* ed. C. A. MacArthur, S. Graham, and J. Fitzgerald. New York: Guilford Press.

Hutchings, Pat, ed. 1996. *Making Teaching Community Property: A Menu for Peer Collaboration and Peer Review.* Washington, DC: American Association for Higher Education.

Ittenbach, Richard F., Irvin G. Esters, and Howard Wainer. 1997. The History of Test Development. In *Contemporary Intellectual Assessment: Theories Tests and Issues*, ed. D. P. Flanagan, J. L. Genshaft, and P. L. Harrison. New York: Guilford.

Johnston, Peter. 1989. Constructive Evaluation and the Improvement of Teaching and Learning. *Teachers College Record* 90:509–28.

Jones, Jesse. 1994. Evaluating College Teaching: An Overview. In Hult, 30–45.

Kamphaus, Randy W., Anne Pierce Windor, Ellen W. Rowe and Sangwon Kim. 2005. A History of Intelligence Test Interpretation. In *Contemporary Intellectual Assessment: Theories, Tests, and Issues*, ed. Dawn P. Flanagan and Patti L. Harrison. New York: Guilford Press, 23-38.

Kane, Michael T. (2006). Validation. In R. L. Brennan (Ed). *Educational Measurement*, fourth edition. Westport, CT: ACE Praeger Series in Higher Education.

Kinkead, Joyce. 1997. Documenting Excellence in Teaching and Learning in WAC Programs. In Yancey and Huot, 37–50.

Kulik, James A. 2001. Student Ratings: Validity, Utility, and Controversy. Special Issue: Student Ratings Debate. *New Directions for Institutional Research* 109 (Spring): 9–25.

Lemann, Nicholas. 1999. *The Big Test: The Secret History of the American Meritocracy*. New York: Farrar, Straus and Giroux.

Leonhardy, Galen and William Condon. 2001. Exploring the Difficult Cases: In the Cracks of Writing Assessment. In Haswell (2001a), 65–79.

Lerner, Neal. 2003. Writing Center Assessment: Searching for the 'Proof' of Our Effectiveness. *The Center Will Hold*, ed. Michael Pemberton and Joyce Kinkead. Logan: Utah State University Press, 58–73.

Levernez, Carrie Shively. 2002. The Ethics of Required Teaching Portfolios. In Minter and Goodburn, 132–42.

Lloyd-Jones, Richard. 1977. Primary Trait Scoring. In *Evaluating Writing: Describing, Measuring and Judging*, ed. C. R. Cooper and L. Odell. Urbana, IL: National Council of Teachers of English, 33–68.

Lowe, Teresa J. and Brian Huot. 1997. Using KIRIS Writing Portfolios to Place Students in First-Year Composition at the University of Louisville. *Kentucky English Bulletin* 46.2:46–64.

Lynne, Patricia. 2004. *Coming to Terms: A Theory of Writing Assessment*. Logan: Utah State University Press.

MacNealy, Mary Sue. 1999. *Strategies for Empirical Research in Writing*. New York: Longman.

Madaus, George F. 1994. A Technical and Historical Consideration of Equity Issues Associated with Proposals to Change the Nation's Testing Policy. *Harvard Educational Review* 64:76–94.

McKeachie, Wilbert J. 1984. *Teaching Tips: Strategies, Research, and Theory for College and University Teachers*. 9th ed. Lexington, MA: Heath.

Mehan, Hugh. 1979. *Learning Lessons: Social Organization in the Classroom*. Cambridge: Harvard University Press.

Merriam, Sharan B. 1998. *Qualitative Research and Case Study Applications in Education*. San Francisco, CA: Jossey-Bass.

Messick, Samuel. 1989. Meaning and Value in Test Validation: The Science and Ethics of Assessment. *Educational Researcher* 18.2:5–11.

———. 1989a Validity. *Educational Measurement Third Edition*, ed. R. L. Linn. Washington, DC: American Council on Education and National Council on Measurement in Education.

Miller, Hildy. 1996. Postmasculinist Directions in Writing Program Administration. *WPA: Writing Program Administration* 20.1/2:49–61.

Minter, Deborah. 2002. Peer Observation as Collaborative Classroom Inquiry. In Minter and Goodburn, 54–64.

———, and Amy Goodburn, eds. 2002. *Composition Pedagogy & the Scholarship of Teaching*. Portsmouth, NH: Boynton/Cook Heinneman.

Mirtz, Ruth. WPAs as Historians: Discovering a First-Year Writing Program by Researching Its Past. In Rose and Weiser, 119–30.

Moran, Charles, and Anne Herrington. 1997. Program Review, Program Renewal. In Yancey and Huot, 123–40.

Morgan, Meg. 1997. Achieving WAC Program Assessment. In Yancey and Huot, 141–57.

———. 2002. The GTA Experience: Grounding, Practicing, Evaluating, and Reflecting. In *The Writing Program Administrator's Resource: A Guide to Reflective Institutional Practice*, ed. Stuart C. Brown, Theresa Enos, and Catherine Chaput, 393–410. Mahwah, NJ: Erlbaum.

Moss, Pamela A. 1992. Shifting Conceptions of Validity in Educational Measurement: Implications for Performance Assessment. *Review of Educational Research* 62.3:229–58.

———. 1994. Can There Be Validity Without Reliability? *Educational Researcher* 23.4:5–12.

———. 1996. Enlarging the Dialogue in Educational Measurement: Voices from Interpretive Research Traditions. *Educational Researcher* 25.1: 20-28.

———. 1998. Testing the Test of a Test: A Response to "Multiple Inquiry in the Validation of Writing Tests." *Assessing Writing* 5:111–22.

———. 2007. Joining the Dialogue on Validity Theory in Educational Research. In O'Neill (2007), 91–100.

Murphy, Sandra. 2003. That Was Then, This is Now: The Impact of Changing Assessment Policies on Teachers and the Teaching of Writing in California. *Journal of Writing Assessment* 1:23–45.

———. 2007. Culture and Consequences: The Canaries in the Coal Mine. *Research in the Teaching of English*, 42:228–44.

———, and Roberta Camp. 1996. Moving toward Systemic Coherence: A Discussion of Conflicting Perspectives on Portfolio Assessment. In *Writing Portfolios in the Classroom: Policy and Practice, Promise and Peril*, eds. Robert C. Calfee and Pamela Perfumo, 103–48. Mahwah, NJ: Lawrence Erlbaum.

———, Sybil Carlson, and Paul Rooney, with the CCCC Committee on Assessment. 1993. *Report to the CCCC Executive Committee: Survey of Postsecondary Writing Assessment Practices*. Unpublished manuscript.

———, and Kathleen Blake Yancey. 2007. Construct and Consequence: Validity and Writing Assessment. In *Handbook of Research on Writing: History, Society, School, Individual Text*, ed. Charles Bazerman, 365–85. New York: Lawrence Erlbaum.

Nelson, Alexis. 1999. Views from the Underside: Proficiency Portfolios in First-Year Composition. *TETYC* 26:243–53.

Nelson, Jennie, and Diane Kelly-Riley. 2001. Students as Stakeholders: Maintaining a Responsive Assessment. In Haswell (2001a), 143–60.

Newton, Camille, Tracy Singer, Amy D'Antonio, Laura Bush, and Duane Roen. 2002. Reconsidering and Reassessing Teaching Portfolios: Reflective and Rhetorical Functions. In Minter and Goodburn, 3–13.

O'Neill, Peggy, ed. 2007. *Blurring Boundaries: Developing Researchers, Writers, and Teachers*. Cresskill, NJ: Hampton Press.

———. 1998. *Writing Assessment and the Disciplinarity of Composition*. Dissertation. University of Louisville.

———. 2003. Moving Beyond Holistic Scoring through Validity Inquiry. *Journal of Writing Assessment* 1:47–65.

———. 2008. Reliability in College Writing Assessment. Under review at *Journal of Assessing Writing*.

———, Sandra Murphy, Brian Huot, and Michael Williamson. 2005. What Teachers Say about Different Types of State Mandated Writing Tests. *Journal of Writing Assessment* 2.2:81–108.

———, Ellen Schendel, and Brian Huot. 2002. Defining Assessment as Research: Moving from Obligations to Opportunities. *WPA: Writing Program Administration* 26.1/2:10–26.

Ory, John C., and Kathrine Ryan. 2001. How Do Student Ratings Measure Up to a New Validity Framework? Special Issue: Student Ratings Debate. *New Directions for Institutional Research* 109 (Spring): 27–44.

Page, Ellis. 1966. The Imminence of Grading Essays by Computer. *Phi Delta Kappan* 46: 238-243.

Palmer, Orville. 1960. Sixty Years of English Testing. *College Board* 42:8–14.

Parker, Palmer. 1998. *The Courage to Teach: Exploring the Inner Landscape of a Teacher's Life*. San Francisco, CA: Jossey-Bass.

Parkes, Jay. 2007. Reliability as Argument. *Educational Measurement: Issues and Practice* 26.4:2–10.

Paulson, Pearl R., and F. Leon Paulson. 1997. A Different Understanding. In Yancey and Weiser, 278–91.

Peele, Thomas. 2007. What Do We Mean When We Say 'Writing'? *Composition Studies* 35.1:95–96.

Peeples, Tim. 1999. 'Seeing' the WPA with/through Postmodern Mapping. In Rose and Weiser, 153–67.

Perlman, 2005. "The Beauty of Brevity." Editorial. Chicago *Tribune* May 6. http://www.chicagotribune.com/news/opinionchi_050506029/May06,17735619.story?ctrack=1=true.

Peters, Bradley. 1998. Enculturation, Not Alchemy: Professionalizing Novice Writing Program Administrators. *WPA: Writing Program Administration* 21.2/3:121–36.

Phelps, Louise Weatherbee. 1989. Images of Student Writing: The Deep Structure of Teacher Response. In *Writing and Response: Theory, Practice and Research*, ed. Chris M. Anson, 37–67. Urbana, IL: National Council of Teachers of English.

Pula, Judith J., and Brian A. Huot. 1993. A Model of Background Influences on Holistic Raters. In Williamson and Huot, 237–65.

Pytlik, Betty, and Sarah Liggett, eds. 2001. *Preparing College Teachers of Writing: Histories, Theories, Practices, and Programs.* New York: Oxford University Press.

Roemer, Marjorie, Lucille M. Schultz, and Russel K. Durst. 1991. Portfolios and the Process of Change. *College Composition and Communication* 42:445–69.

Roen, Duane. 1997. Writing Administration as Scholarship and Teaching. In *Academic Advancement in Composition Studies: Scholarship, Publication, Promotion, Tenure*, ed. Richard C. Gebhardt and Barbara Genelle Smith Gebhardt, 43–55. Mahwah, NJ: Lawrence Erlbaum.

Rogers, Rebecca. 2003. *A Critical Discourse Analysis of Family Literacy Practices: Power in and out of Print.* Mahwah, NJ: Lawrence Erlbaum.

Rose, Shirley K. 1999. Preserving Our Histories of Institutional Change: Enabling Research in the Writing Program Archives. In Rose and Weiser, 107–18.

———, and Irwin Weiser, eds. 1999. *The Writing Program Administrator as Researcher.* Portsmouth, NH: Boynton/Cook.

———, and Irwin Weiser, eds. 2002. Introduction. *The Writing Program Administrator as Theorist.* Portsmouth, NH: Boynton/Cook Heinemann, 1–6.

Royer, Daniel, and Roger Gilles. 1998. Directed Self-Placement: An Attitude of Orientation. *College Composition and Communication* 50:54–70.

———, eds. 2003. *Directed Self-Placement: Principles and Practices.* Cresskill, NJ: Hampton.

Ruth, Leo, and Sandra Murphy. 1988. *Designing Writing Tasks for the Assessment of Writing.* Norwood, NJ: Ablex.

Sacks, Peter. 1999. *Standardized Minds: The High Price of America's Testing Culture and What We Can Do to Change It.* Cambridge, MA: Perseus.

Schell, Eileen. 1998. Who's the Boss?: The Possibilities and Pitfalls of Collaborative Administration for Untenured WPAs. *WPA: Writing Program Administration* 21.2/3:65–80.

Schendel, Ellen, and Peggy O'Neill. 1999. Exploring the Theories and Consequences of Self-Assessment through Ethical Inquiry. *Assessing Writing* 6: 199-227.

Schön, Donald. 1983. *The Reflective Practitioner.* New York: Basic Books.

Schuster, Charles I. 1991. Theory and Practice. In *An Introduction to Composition Studies*, eds. Erika Lindemann and Gary Tate, 33–48. New York: Oxford University Press.

Schwalm, David A. 1994. Evaluating Adjunct Faculty. In Hult, 123–32.

Seldin, Peter, ed. 1990. *How Administrators Can Improve Teaching.* San Francisco, CA: Jossey-Bass.

———. 1997. *The Teaching Portfolio: A Practical Guide to Improved Performance and Promotion/Tenure Decisions.* 2nd ed. Bolton, MA: Anker.

Seldin, Peter, and Associates. 1999. *Changing Practices in Evaluating Teaching: A Practical Guide to Improved Faculty Performance and Promotion/Tenure Decisions.* Bolton, MA: Anker.

Shamoon, Linda, and Celest Martin. 2007. Which Part of the Elephant is This?: Questioning Creative Non-Fiction in the Writing Major. *Composition Studies* 35.1:53–54.

Shepard, Lorrie A. 1993. Evaluating Test Validity. *Review of Educational Research in Education* 19:405–50.

————. 2000. The Role of Assessment in a Learning Culture. *Educational Researcher* 29.7:4–14.

Shuy, Roger W. 1981. A Holistic View of Language. *Research in the Teaching of English* 15:110–12.

Smit, David W. 1994. A WPA's Nightmare: Reflections on Using Portfolios as a Course Exit Exam. In Black et al., 303–13.

Smith, William L. 1992. The Importance of Teacher Knowledge in College Composition Placement Testing. In *Reading Empirical Research Studies: The Rhetoric of Research*, ed. John R. Hayes, 289–316. Norwood, NJ: Ablex.

————. 1993. Assessing the Reliability and Adequacy of Using Holistic Scoring of Essays as a College Composition Placement Technique. In Williamson and Huot, 142–205.

Sojka, Jane, Ashok K. Gupta, and Dawn R. Deeter-Schmelz. 2002. Student and Faculty Perceptions of Student Evaluations of Teaching: A Study of Similarities and Differences. *College Teaching* 50.2:44–49.

Starch, Daniel, and Edward C. Elliott. 1912. Reliability of the Grading of High School Work in English. *School Review* 20:442–57.

Strenski, Ellen. 1994. Peer Review of Writing Faculty. In Hult, 55–72.

Stygall, Gail. 2000. At the Century's End: The Job Market in Rhetoric and Composition. *Rhetoric Review* 18.2:375–89.

Taylor, Rebecca. 2004. Preparing WPAs for the Small College Context. *Composition Studies* 32.2:53–73.

Thais, Christopher, and Terry Myers Zawacki. 1997. How Portfolios for Proficiency Help Shape a WAC Program. In Yancey and Huot, 79–96.

Theall, Michael. 2001. Can We Put Precision into Practice?: Commentary and Thoughts Engendered by Abrami's Improving Judgments about Teacher Effectiveness Using Teacher Rating Forms. Special Issue: Student Ratings Debate. *New Directions for Institutional Research* 109 (Spring): 89–96.

————, and Jennifer Franklin. 2001. Looking for Bias in All the Wrong Places: A Search for Truth or a Witch Hunt in Student Ratings of Instruction? Special Issue: Student Ratings Debate. *New Directions for Institutional Research* 109 (Spring): 45–58.

Thorndike, Robert M. 1997. The Early History of Intelligence Testing. *Contemporary Intellectual Assessment: Theories, Tests and Issues*, ed. D. P. Flanagan, J. Gershaft, and P. L. Harrison. New York: Guilford.

Townsend, Martha. 1997. Integrating WAC into General Education. In Yancey and Huot, 159–72.

Trachsel, Mary. 1992. *Institutionalizing Literacy: The Historical Role of College Entrance Exams in English.* Carbondale, IL: Southern Illinois University Press.

Veal, L. Ramon, and Sally Ann Hudson. 1983. Direct and Indirect Measures for Large-Scale Evaluation of Writing. *Research in the Teaching of English* 17:290–96.

Von Mayrhauser, Richard T. 2005. The Mental Testing Community and Validity: A Prehistory. In *Evolving Perspectives on the History of Psychology*, ed. W. E. Pickren and D. A. Dewsbury. Washington DC: American Psychological Association.

Wachtel, Howard K. 1998. Student Evaluation of College Teaching Effectiveness: A Brief Review. *Assessment & Evaluation in Higher Education* 23.2:191–211. http://ezp.dyndns.org/login?url=http://search.ebscohost.com/login.aspx?direct=true&db=eric&AN=EJ570426&site=ehostlive (accessed 24 Oct 2007).

Washington State University Writing Assessment Office. 2007. Junior Writing Portfolio. Writing Programs. http://writingportfolio.wsu.edu/ (accessed 20 Dec 2007).

Wasserman, John D., and David S. Tulsky. 2005. A History of Intellectual Assessment. *Contemporary Intellectual Assessment: Theories, Tests and Issues Second Edition*, ed. D. P. Flanagan and Patti L. Harrison. New York: Guilford.

Weiser, Irwin. 1994. Teaching Assistants as Collaborators in Their Preparation and Evaluation. In Hult, 133–46.

————. 1997. Revising Our Practices: How Portfolios Help Teachers Learn. In Yancey and Weiser, 293–301.

White, Edward M. 1989. *Developing Successful College Writing Programs*. San Francisco, CA: Jossey-Bass.

———. 1993. Holistic Scoring: Past Triumphs and Future Challenges. In Williamson and Huot, 79–108.

———. 1994. *Teaching and Assessing Writing*. 2nd ed, Portland, ME: Calendar Islands.

———. 1994. The Devil Is in the Details: A Cautionary Tale. In Hult, 49–54.

———. 1995. The Rhetorical Problem of Program Evaluation and the WPA. In *Resituating Writing: Constructing and Administering Writing Programs*, eds. Joseph Janangelo and Kristine Hansen, 132–50. Portsmouth, NH: Boynton/Cook.

———, William D. Lutz, and Sandra Kamusikiri, eds. 1996. *Assessment of Writing: Politics, Policies, Practices*. New York: MLA.

———. 1985. *Teaching and Assessing Writing*. San Francisco: Jossey-Bass.

Willard-Traub, Margaret K. 2002. Beyond Course Evaluations: Representing Student Voice and Experience. In Minter and Goodburn, 79–88.

———, Emily Decker, Rebecca Reed, and Jerome Johnston. 1999. The Development of Large-Scale Portfolio Placement at the University of Michigan 1992–1998. *Assessing Writing* 6: 41–84.

Williamson, Michael M. 1993. An Introduction to Holistic Scoring: The Social, Historical and Theoretical Context for Writing Assessment. In Williamson and Huot, 1–43.

———. 1994. The Worship of Efficiency: Untangling Theoretical and Practical Considerations in Writing Assessment. *Assessing Writing* 1:147–74.

———. 2003. Validity of Automated Scoring: Prologue for a Continuing Discussion of Machine Scoring Student Writing. *Journal of Writing Assessment* 1:85–104.

———, and Brian A. Huot, eds. 1993. *Validating Holistic Scoring: Theoretical and Empirical Foundations*. Cresskill, NJ: Hampton Press.

Witte, Stephen P., and Lester Faigley. 1983. *Evaluating College Writing Programs*. Carbondale, IL: University of Southern Illinois Press.

———, Lester Faigley and Roger Cherry. 1994. Think-aloud Protocols, Protocol Analysis, and Research Design: An Exploration of the Influence of Writing Tasks on the Writing Process. In *Speaking about Writing: Reflections on Research Methodologies*, ed. Peter Smagorinsky, 20–54. Thousand Oaks, CA: Sage.

Wolcott, Willa, with Sue M. Legg. 1998. *An Overview of Writing Assessment: Theory, Research and Practice*. Urbana, IL: National Council of Teachers of English.

Wolfe, Edward M. 1997. The Relationship between Reading Style and Scoring Proficiency in a Psychometric Scoring System. *Assessing Writing* 4:83–106.

Writing Study Group of the NCTE Executive Council. 2004. NCTE Beliefs about the Teaching of Writing. Urbana, IL: National Council of Teachers of English. http://www.ncte.org/about/over/positions/category/write/118876.htm (accessed 9 Aug 2007).

Yancey, Kathleen Blake. 1992. Portfolios in the Writing Classroom: A Final Reflection. In *Portfolios in the Writing Classroom: An Introduction*, ed. Kathleen Blake Yancey. Urbana, IL: NCTE.

———. 1997. Teacher Portfolios: Lessons in Resistance, Readiness, and Reflection. In Yancey and Weiser, 244–62.

———. 1999. Looking Back as We Look Forward: Historicizing Writing Assessment. *College Composition and Communication* 50:483–503.

———, and Brian Huot, eds. 1997. *Assessing Writing Across the Curriculum: Diverse Approaches and Practices. Perspectives on Writing: Theory, Research, Practice*. Greenwich, CT: Ablex.

———, and Irwin Weiser, eds. 1997. *Situating Portfolios: Four Perspectives*. Logan: Utah State University Press.

Zebroski, James Thomas. 1994. *Thinking through Theory: Vygotskian Perspectives on the Teaching of Writing*. Portsmouth, NH: Boynton/Cook Publishers.

———. 1997. Reciprocal Authorities in Communal Writing Assessment: Constructing Textual Value within a "New Politics of Inquiry." *Assessing Writing* 4: 133-67.

INDEX

ABOUT THE AUTHORS

PEGGY O'NEILL, associate professor of writing, directs the composition program and teaches writing in the Department of Writing at Loyola University, Maryland. Her scholarship focuses on writing assessment, pedagogy, and program administration and the disciplinarity of composition. Her work appears in journals such as the *Journal of Writing Assessment* and *College Composition and Communication,* as well as in several edited collections. She has edited or co-edited four books, most recently *Blurring Boundaries: Developing Writers, Researchers and Teachers* (Hampton Press 2007) and, with Brian Huot, *Assessing Writing: A Critical Sourcebook* (Bedford St. Martin's / NCTE 2009).

CINDY MOORE serves as associate professor and chair of the Department of Writing at Loyola University, Maryland. Over the past ten years, she has directed writing programs and taught a wide range of writing courses at universities in Indiana, Minnesota, and Kentucky. Her current scholarly interests include professional mentoring and program assessment. She has co-edited or co-authored several books, including *The Dissertation and the Discipline: Reinventing Composition Studies* (Boynton/Cook 2002), *Practice in Context: Situating the Work of Writing Teachers* (NCTE 2002), and *A Guide to Professional Development for Graduate Students in English* (NCTE 2006).

BRIAN HUOT has been working in writing assessment for two decades. His focus has been to integrate theories and principles from educational measurement with an understanding of the ways in which writing is theorized and researched. His work has appeared in several edited collections, and in journals including *College English, Review of Educational Research,* and *College Composition and Communication.* He co-edited *Validating Holistic Scoring for Writing Assessment, Assessing Writing Across the Curriculum* and *Assessing Writing: A Critical Sourcebook.* His monograph, *(Re)Articulating Writing Assessment for Teaching and Learning,* was also published by Utah State University Press (2002). Huot is professor of English and coordinator of the writing program at Kent State University.